St. George's Day

St. George's Day

A Cultural History of England's National Day

Hanael Bianchi

Caliber and Kempis

Owings Mills, Maryland

Publisher's Cataloging-in-Publication Data

Bianchi, Hanael.
    St. George's Day : a cultural history of England's national day / Hanael Bianchi.
        pages cm
    ISBN: 978-1409-7778-4 (pbk.)
    Includes bibliographical references and index.
    1. Holidays—England—History. 2. Nationalism—England—History. 3. England—Social life and customs.
    4. Secularism.   I. Title.
GT4843 .B35 2014
394.26942—dc23
                                                    2013912510

For Three Mothers:

My Mother, My Children's Mother, and the Mother of us All

Contents

Notable Dates

285-305	Reign of Diocletian
303	Martyrdom in Eusebius' *Historia Ecclesiastica*
361	Martyrdom of George, Arian bishop
494	*Decretum Gelasianum*
5th cent.	Vienna Palimpsest
515	Inscription at Ezra
7th cent.	Adamnan's *De Locis Sanctis*
8th cent.	Bede's *Martyrology*
9th cent.	*Old English Martyrology*
9/10th cent.	*Durham Collectar*
c. 1000	Aelfric's *Lives of Saints*
1060s	*Portiforium of Saint Wulstan*
1096–1099	First Crusade
11th cent.	*Missal of the New Minster*
1189–1192	Third Crusade
1189–1199	Reign of Richard I
1222	Synod of Oxford
1266	Jacobus de Voragine's *Legenda Aurea*
1277	First reference to the arms of St. George
1327-1377	Reign of Edward III
1337-1453	Hundred Years' War
c. 1348	Order of the Garter
1380s	John Mirk's *Festial*
1413-1422	Reign of Henry V
1415	Battle of Agincourt
1415	Elevated to double major in Province of Canterbury
1421	Elevated to double major in Province of York
1509–1547	Reign of Henry VIII
1547–1553	Reign of Edward VI
1549	*Book of Common Prayer*, no feast of St. George
1552	*Book of Common Prayer*, black letter day
1553–1558	Reign of Mary I
1558–1603	Reign of Elizabeth I
1559	*Book of Common Prayer*, red letter day
1561	*Book of Common Prayer*, black letter day

1568	Tridentine Calendar, semi-double
1590	Edmund Spenser's *The Faerie Queene*
1596/7	R. Johnson's *The Famous Historie of the Seven Champions*
1642–1651	English Civil War
1645	*Directory for the Public Worship of God*, feast eliminated
1662	*Book of Common Prayer*, black letter day
1707	Great Britain created
1733	St. George's Society in Charleston
1772	Sons of St. George in Philadelphia
1786	St. George's Society of New York
1801	United Kingdom created
1818	Order of St. Michael and St. George
1871	Order of the Sons of St. George in Pennsylvania
1874	Sons of England Benefit Society
1894	Royal Society of St. George
1918	Zeebrugge Raid
1969	Catholic Calendar, optional memorial
1996	Church of England, major festival
2000	Solemnity for Catholics in England

Introduction:
England's National Day

Every year, an increasing number of English celebrate St. George's Day as their national day. The day is meant to celebrate all things English, but amid the roast beef and Yorkshire pudding, St. George appears as an unusual English symbol, having no historical connection to England. He was not born in England, nor did he ever visit the island. Though his origins are ambiguous, he is most often said to have lived far from England in Turkey and Palestine. In addition, the feast of a Christian martyr of uncertain origins makes an improbable holiday for a secular Protestant nation, and for centuries, English Protestants and secularists have scrutinized the legends of St. George filled with miraculous apparitions and mythical encounters with dragons. The oddity of the marriage between St. George and England has caused many English revelers to wonder how April 23 became their national day.

Scholars have often looked to the medieval period to explain the rise of St. George's Day, arguing that the Crusades and the Hundred Years' War led to greater devotion to St. George and that the declarations of the Synod of Oxford (1222) and the Province of Canterbury (1415), which allegedly elevated the feast of St. George to a major holy day in England, initiated April 23 as England's national day. Historians have also exhaustively chronicled medieval festivities, including religious liturgies, popular ridings of St. George, and the great feast of the Order of the Garter, but they have neglected the period after the Reformation, ignoring several hundred years of history and failing to acknowledge that the medieval feast of St. George differs greatly from the modern, nationalistic celebration of St. George's Day.

This book argues that the medieval feast of St. George does not adequately explain the rise of St. George's Day as the national day of England and that the period after the Reformation was a time of great change in the meaning of April 23, setting the groundwork for the modern holiday. During the Middle Ages, St. George appeared in many guises as a martyr, knight, and dragon-slayer. He was seen by all, ultimately, as a saint, and his feast day was an occasion to venerate him in order to gain his intercession. As his cult grew at the end of the medieval period, St. George became the patron and protector of the country, and his feast was widely celebrated throughout England. It is, however, anachronistic to claim that April 23 became the national day of England during the medieval period, or that it celebrated the nation. The Reformation initiated the decline of St. George's Day, but St. George's image was altered in a way that enabled a modern revival of April 23. Unlike prior transformations of St. George which added new layers to the saint's image, religious reformers and Enlightenment scholars successfully attacked and removed the most essential element of St. George during the medieval period, his status as a saint and martyr. St. George retained his image as a knight and dragon-slayer, but free from his Middle-Eastern roots, he was viewed increasingly as a mythical figure native to England. In short, he began to represent England, and when English colonists in North America revived the celebration of St. George's Day in the eighteenth century, they celebrated the feast of the ideal Englishman, not a martyr. Undoubtedly, the medieval feast played a necessary role in the resurgence of St. George's Day in the early part of the twentieth century, but without the history of the last five hundred years, the modern celebration that focuses on English nationalism would be unintelligible.

Even though St. George's Day has experienced a resurgence of interest, the celebration is still marked by apathy and confusion over St. George's status as patron of England. A poll by *This England* in 2009 revealed that seven out of ten young people did not know the date of St. George's Day, and 40 percent of all those polled did not know why St. George is the patron of England.[1] The level of indifference surrounding the English national day is not found in American celebrations on July 4, or French on Bastille Day, or Irish on St. Patrick's Day. It begs the question: can St. George's Day be considered the national day of England? On the one hand, St. George's Day is not officially recognized as a holiday in England, and since the Reformation, the majority of English have had to work on April 23. On the other hand, no holiday serves as an alternative to St. George's Day. Bank holidays in England include important Christian feasts, international holidays like New Year's Day and May Day, and the ambiguous spring and summer holidays. Notable dates on the English calendar that are not bank holidays include the anniversary of the birth, accession, and coronation of the current monarch, but these anniversaries change with each ruler. Other important days in English history include Royal Oak Day, Guy Fawkes Day, and Remembrance Days, but none of these constitute a national celebration. In short, St. George's Day has been marked by indifference and has suffered periods of complete neglect, but it remains the most significant day to celebrate England.

The lack of knowledge surrounding St. George's life surprisingly aided the development of his cult. In one sense, he was a blank slate on which different groups could place their values. In England, it was helpful that his origins were unknown because his cult was not tied to one location, and therefore, the whole nation had an equal claim to

---

[1] Sofia Petkar, "George Who? England's Patron Saint Forgotten," *Sky News*, April 23, 2009, http://news.sky.com/skynews/Home/UK-News/St-Georges-Day-New-Survey-Reveals-Majority-Of-English-People-Have-Forgotten-Englands-Patron-Saint/Article/200904415267361?lpos=UK_News_Third_Home_Page_Article_Teaser_Region__2&lid=ARTICLE_15267361_St_Georges_Day%3A_New_Survey_Reveals_Majority_Of_English_People_Have_Forgotten_Englands_Patron_Saint (accessed 12-23-09).

his patronage. The uncertainty of his life also made it possible for him to appeal to different levels of society. Clerics, nobles, and common-ers could all relate to different aspects of his life as a martyr, knight, and hero. The mysterious nature of St. George made him an appeal-ing figure not only in England but throughout the world. It is difficult to find a saint with a more diverse following than St. George. He has been claimed by countries and regions such as Aragon, Armenia, Cat-alonia, Ethiopia, Georgia, Greece, Lithuania, Malta, Palestine, Portugal, and Russia. He is the protector of many cities, including Antioch, Barcelona, Beirut, Genoa, Milan, and Moscow. He is the patron of armorers, butchers, farmers, knights, scouts, and soldiers, and he is said to heal those suffering from leprosy, skin diseases, and syphilis. His cult has also been associated with pagan spring festivals, and he is venerated by Catholics, Anglicans, Muslims, and Orthodox believers. The widespread devotion can be attributed to the flexibility inherent to his legends. The values associated with St. George can change even within one particular tradition, and as this study demon-strates, the celebration of St. George's Day in England was not static.

The primary focus of this investigation is on St. George's Day and not St. George. The life of St. George and the origins of his cult re-main controversial topics, and it is difficult, nearly impossible, to uncover the "real" St. George. Modern scholarship has clarified some of the questions surrounding St. George, but there is a need for a thorough investigation of the early sources of the saint.[2] This study does not attempt to fill that void. The following pages contain a re-

---

[2] Ernest A. Wallis Budge, *George of Lydda, the Patron Saint of England: A Study of the Cultus of St. George in Ethiopia* (London: Luzac, 1930); Ernest A. Wallis Budge, *The Martyrdom and Miracles of St. George of Cappadocia* (London: D. Nutt, 1888); Karl Krumbacher, *Der heilige Georg in der griechischen uberlieferung* (Munchen: J. Roth, 1911); John E. Matzke, "Contributions to the History of the Legend of Saint George, with Special Reference to the Sources of the French, German, and Anglo-Saxon Metrical Versions," *Proceedings of the Modern Language Association* 17 (1902): 467-476; John E. Matzke, "Contributions to the History of the Legend of Saint George, with Special Reference to the Sources of the French, German, and Anglo-Saxon Metrical Versions," *Proceedings of the Modern Language Association* 18 (1903): 99-171; Christopher Walter, "The Origins of the Cult of St. George," *Revue des Études Byzantines* 53 (1995): 295-326.

view of the early evidence for St. George and scholars' analysis of those sources, but no new evidence or argument will be added to the ongoing investigation into the origins of St. George. Instead, the celebration of St. George's Day in England and how St. George was viewed during the periods under consideration form the heart of this study. In other words, the myriad of "invented" St. Georges—apocryphal martyr, crusader, dragon-slayer, scout, warrior, English ideal—are far more central to the story of St. George's Day in England than the "real" St. George.

The geographical scope of this book is limited to England and North America. St. George's Day is celebrated throughout the world, but not always on April 23. His feast is marked by the Orthodox, using the Julian calendar, on May 6, and his feast day in Russia is celebrated on December 9. Celebrations in many countries eclipse the festivities in England. *La Diada de Sant Jordi* in Barcelona, for example, is a major festival celebrated by the exchange of books and roses. Celebrations outside of England unfortunately fall outside the reach of this investigation. The single exception to this rule is the examination of St. George's Day in North America during the nineteenth century. The American festivities are included because those who orchestrated the celebrations viewed themselves as English, and they celebrated English values. Furthermore, the North American holiday played an integral part in the development of St. George's Day in England. In brief, English immigrants in North America were responsible for the modern revival of the holiday and the transfer of the holiday back to England during the nineteenth century. Celebrations in the British Empire—India, Africa—were an extension of the events in England and did not have a substantial impact on the course of St. George's Day in England; therefore, they are not examined in detail. This study also reviews the celebration of St. Patrick's Day, St. Andrew's Day and to a lesser degree, St. David's Day, insofar as the promoters of St. George's Day often compared April 23 to the national days of other ethnicities in the United Kingdom.

This investigation attempts to be exhaustive in terms of the time period, covering the celebration from its introduction into England in the Early Middle Ages to the present day. The long range of time is essential to the study. One premise of cultural history, as opposed to the study of events, is that change is not limited to the activities of monarchs, politicians, and wars. Cultural change is often located below the level of events, hidden from the view of the casual observer. Historians can best discern these changes by examining history over a long period of time, the *longue durée*.[3] The central argument of this study hinges on the distinction between the medieval and modern celebration of St. George's Day, and it is only possible to make this distinction with a thorough description of both. In an investigation encompassing such diverse periods, nuances may be missed, but the potential benefits of a long term study outweigh the lost detail that might be found in a more focused examination.

This work, therefore, is a cultural history of St. George's Day. In this sense, it builds on a historical tradition that has been developing for the last forty years.[4] Cultural historians are deeply indebted to the contributions of cultural anthropologists, and the starting point for many cultural historians is Clifford Geertz's definition of culture: "Believing, with Max Weber, that man is an animal suspended in webs of significance he himself has spun, I take culture to be those webs, and the analysis of it to be therefore not an experimental science in search of law but an interpretative one in search of meaning."[5] That is to say, societies create their own cultures, and these cultures are the locus of meaning for each society. My investigation seeks not only to recreate the events which occurred on St. George's Day, providing a thin description of the holiday, but inspired by Geertz's method, it also aims to go beyond the surface of the festivities and uncover the meaning of

---

[3] The *longue durée* was first developed by social historians of the Annales school; Fernand Braudel, "Histoire et sciences socials: La longue durée," *Annales ESC* 4 (1958): 725-753.

[4] Peter Burke, *What Is Cultural History?* (Cambridge: Polity Press, 2008).

[5] Clifford Geertz, *The Interpretation of Cultures* (New York: Basic Books, 1973), 5.

the celebrations through a thick description of the rituals. Thus, the changing *meaning* of the holiday, not the changing method of celebration, is the primary concern.

This book also forms part of the emerging field of holiday studies. A holiday can be loosely defined as a period of time when work is suspended and an event is celebrated. In addition to this simple definition, holidays share certain characteristics. They typically reinforce values of participants, rely on symbols and arbitrary elements, have dramatic performances which communicate a narrative to the participants, and reaffirm common beliefs of those involved in the celebrations. These qualities make holidays an important and useful tool of historical research, and since holidays are communal events, they enable historians to study a large group of individuals through a single event. Holidays are also important to historians because they reflect the values of a particular culture. In time, old holidays either cease to exist or must adapt to new values to survive, and new holidays are created to reflect contemporary sentiments.[6] The popularity of Columbus Day, for example, has drastically diminished because of a reexamination of historical evidence and a new respect for indigenous populations of the Americas. Conversely, Earth Day, recently created, has grown in popularity as a result of the rise of environmentalism. Even holidays that have remained in place for centuries, in particular religious days, are in a continuous state of flux, adapting to the values of the population. In short, holidays are constantly changing communal events that reflect the principles of a group. Calendars, as a collection of holidays, form a microcosm of the societies that create them, and they reflect the values and beliefs of those societies. St. George's Day was a particularly fluid holiday with over a millennium of history in England; therefore, it is a good barometer to judge the changing sentiments and values of the English.

Holidays have been neglected as a field of study by social scientists, and the number of scholarly works on holidays is slim. There are

---

[6] Amitai Etzioni and Jared Bloom, eds., *We Are What We Celebrate: Understanding Holidays and Rituals* (New York: New York University Press, 2004), 1-42.

numerous encyclopedic books on holidays in the tradition of Robert
Chambers's *The Book of Days* (1864) and *The American Book of Days*
(1937) by G.W. Douglas, progressing through the calendar with short
entries for each day that describe anniversaries of events and traditional forms of celebrations.[7] Some festivals, such as Halloween and
Christmas, have created substantial interest and several monographs
are dedicated to exploring these days.[8] The most comparable book to
this study is *Wearing of the Green: A History of St. Patrick's Day* (2002),
the only book-length investigation of St. Patrick's Day, and its authors
were puzzled that St. Patrick's Day "has received so little attention
from prominent writers and publishers."[9] Another recent work, *Remember, Remember: A Cultural History of Guy Fawkes Day* (2005), is based
on a similar set of premises as this study, and the opening line reads,
"This is a book about remembering, commemoration, how the meaning of past events changes when cultures change."[10] The history of
English holidays has generated several works, notably David Cressy's
*Bonfires and Bells: National Memory and the Protestant Calendar in Elizabe-
than and Stuart England* (1989) and Ronald Hutton's *Stations of the Sun:
A History of the Ritual Year in Britain* (1996). Though the historiography
of holidays remains limited, these few works show the potential that
this untapped field has to offer.

The current revival of interest in St. George has produced several
works on the saint in the English tradition. A few works meant for

---

[7] Robert Chambers, *Chambers's Book of Days* (Philadelphia: J.B. Lippincott, 1879); George
William Douglas and Hellen Douglas Compton, *The American Book of Days* (New York: Wilson, 1952).
[8] Jack Santino, *Halloween and Other Festivals of Death and Life* (Knoxville: University of Tennessee Press, 1994); David J. Skal, *Death Makes a Holiday: A Cultural History of Halloween* (New
York: Bloomsbury, 2002); Stephen Nissenbaum, *The Battle for Christmas* (New York: Vintage,
1997); Bruce David Forbes, *Christmas A Candid History* (Berkeley: University of California
Press, 2007); John Gibson, *The War on Christmas: How the Liberal Plot to Ban the Sacred Christian
Holiday Is Worse Than You Thought* (New York: Sentinel, 2005).
[9] Mike Cronin and Daryl Adair, *The Wearing of the Green: A History of St. Patrick's Day* (London:
Routledge, 2002), xvii.
[10] J. A. Sharpe, *Remember, Remember: A Cultural History of Guy Fawkes Day* (Cambridge: Harvard
University Press, 2005), 1.

the general public have appeared and provide a brief overview of the history of the cult of St. George in England.[11] By and large, these books rework information that appeared in a slew of volumes on St. George in the early part of the twentieth century. Though the content in recent works is more reliable than earlier accounts, little new information has been introduced, and these works' usefulness is also limited by a lack of documentation. They augmented knowledge of St. George in the general public, but they did not have a significant impact on the historiography of St. George. Samantha Riches' *St. George: Hero, Martyr, and Myth* (2000) conversely provided a major contribution to the study of the cult of St. George in England, especially in its exploration of pre-Reformation visual representations of the patron of England.[12] Jonathan Good's book, *The Cult of St. George in Medieval England* (2009), contains extensive documentation, and provides a detailed reevaluation of the churches, monasteries, and guilds dedicated to St. George and an examination of the connection between medieval monarchs of England and St. George.[13] The only study exclusively on St. George's Day is a single journal article by historian Muriel McClendon that covers the city of Norwich during the Reformation.[14] All of the recent studies on St. George focus on the medieval period, considering the era after the Reformation only as an afterthought. This study, therefore, is the first book-length investigation of St. George's Day, and the first work to focus on St. George in the modern period.

The study of St. George's Day is complicated by the overlapping of English and British identities. St. George, his flag, and his day are English symbols in competition with separate British symbols. The

---

[11] Anthony Cooney, *The Story of Saint George: The Life and Legend of England's Patron Saint* (Cheltenham: This England Books, 1999); David Scott Fox, *Saint George: The Saint with Three Faces* (Windsor Forest, Berks: Kensal Press, 1983); Giles Morgan, *St. George: Knight, Martyr, Patron Saint and Dragonslayer* (Harpenden: Pocket Essentials, 2006); Christopher Stace, *St. George: Patron Saint of England* (London: Triangle, 2002).

[12] Samantha Riches, *St. George: Hero, Martyr, and Myth* (Stroud: Sutton, 2000).

[13] Jonathan Good, *The Cult of St. George in Medieval England* (Woodbridge: Boydell Press, 2009).

[14] Muriel C. McClendon, "A Moveable Feast: Saint George's Day Celebrations and Religious Change in Early Modern England," *The Journal of British Studies* 38:1 (January, 1999): 1-27.

decline of St. George's Day started with the Reformation, and thus predated the creation of a separate British identity. Yet, the establishment of the Kingdom of Great Britain under the Act of Union 1707 solidified the decline of the cult of St. George. The Union Flag, Britannia, John Bull and other British symbols replaced the numerous representations of St. George. A separate English identity, however, started to reappear at the end of the nineteenth century, and demands for a separate English government were repeatedly voiced during the twentieth century. The modern revival of English nationalism has prompted a resurgence of interest in St. George's Day. The popularity of St. George's Day thus mirrors the rise and decline of English nationalism.

This book also seeks to correct the periodization associated with the celebration of St. George's Day. The popularization of the cult of St. George and the elevation of his feast day in England took place later than previously acknowledged, and most of the evidence for an early acceptance of St. George as patron of England is now contested by historians, including Bede's inclusion of St. George in his martyrology (eighth century), the elevation of St. George's feast at the Synod of Oxford (1222), and the devotion of Richard I (r. 1189–1199) to St. George. Scholars, but not the general public, now accept that the cult of St. George in England rose to prominence under Edward III during the Hundred Years' War, and not as a result of Richard I and the Crusades.[15] Moreover, his feast day was not elevated at the Synod of Oxford during the thirteenth century, but in a series of declarations in the fifteenth century. In short, St. George's Day was not a significant feast day in the Early and High Middle Ages, but rather was elevated during the Late Middle Ages and reached its peak in the years imme-

---

[15] Olivier De Laborderie, "Richard the Lionheart and the Birth of A National Cult of St. George in England: Origins and Development of a Legend," *Nottingham Medieval Studies* 39 (1995): 37-53.

diately prior to the Reformation.[16] The periodization supports revisionist theories of the Reformation in England, which claim traditional, Catholic religious practices, such as celebrating feast days, remained strong directly before the Reformation.[17] The later date, however, challenges the notion that St. George's Day celebrations were the product of pagan spring festivals observed in pre-Christian England. The gap of eight centuries from the Christianizing mission of St. Augustine of Canterbury to the popularization of the festivals on April 23 is too long to argue for continuity, and there is no evidence of a hybrid celebration to bridge this span of time. In conclusion, celebrations of the saint began much later than previously recognized and were a creation of the Late Middle Ages, with no direct connection to pre-Christian festivals.

The chronology of the modern celebration also needs to be adjusted. Whereas modifications in the periodization of the medieval celebration are based on the work of other scholars, the chronological development of the modern celebration is based on a reexamination of the sources and challenges the dates accepted by most scholars of St. George. This study argues that St. George's Day went into decline primarily as a result of the Reformation. It was then attacked by Enlightenment thinkers in the eighteenth century, and English symbols and festivals were also replaced by British ones due to the creation of Great Britain during the same time period. The holiday was not observed in England from the seventeenth century to the end of the nineteenth century, with a few exceptions such as the birthday of George IV, Order of the Garter ceremonies, and the Norwich riding. This study also maintains that the celebration of the feast of St. George was revived by English colonists in North America who organized English societies dedicated to St. George in response to a growing non-English population. First formed in the eighteenth cen-

---

[16] In this study, Early Middle Ages refers to 500-1000, High Middles Ages to 1000-1300, and Late Middle Ages to 1300-1500.

[17] Eamon Duffy, *The Stripping of the Altars: Traditional Religion in England, C. 1400-1580* (New Haven: Yale University Press, 1992); Christopher Haigh, *The English Reformation Revised* (Cambridge: Cambridge University Press, 1987).

tury, the societies of St. George grew in number throughout the course of the following century. Their primary goal was to help poor English immigrants, but they also contained a social element and celebrated St. George's Day with much spectacle. Celebrations on April 23 were revived in England starting in the last decade of the nineteenth century, a full century after English societies in North America regularly celebrated the day. Furthermore, the American festivities directly inspired the revival of the holiday in England. Scholars frequently assumed that the modern celebration of the feast started with the Victorians because of their interest in chivalry and the medieval period.[18] In a recent book on St. George, David Fox wrote, "Generally speaking, St. George meant a great deal to the Victorian English, for he was part of the pride and pageantry of empire… The Victorians had been brought up on their saint's story. Now, however, the old tale seemed to have a startling new relevance, and they mounted as it were on George's spiritual white charger to ride out on their own battle against the forces of evil."[19] The evidence, however, suggests that no celebrations occurred on April 23 for most of the Victorian period. The founding of the Royal Society of St. George in 1894 marks the first significant attempt to revive St. George's Day in modern England, and celebrations were not widespread until after the turn of the century. Many commentators also mistakenly assume that the cult of St. George declined after World War I. Turning again to Fox's work, "But the war shattered many illusions. There had been no place for knights in the mud and squalid carnage of the trenches. The cult of chivalry was soon to be discarded, and George, as its great symbol, inevitably suffered in the process."[20] In contrast, this work contends that the cult of St. George and the celebration of his day greatly increased as a result of World War I. The patron saint was attached to

---

[18] Mark Girouard, *The Return to Camelot: Chivalry and the English Gentleman* (New Haven: Yale University Press, 1981).
[19] Fox, *Saint George*, 90.
[20] Fox, *Saint George*, 91.

many battles in the war, Zeebrugge being the most noteworthy, and he was said to have appeared during battles to aid the English as they fought the Germans on the Western Front. The climax of the celebration of St. George's Day in the modern period occurred during the interwar years. World War II and the process of decolonization, not World War I, brought the celebrations to a halt. After several decades without any festivals, St. George's Day was revived again in the 1990s, and renewed interest in the celebration continues to the present day.[21]

The feast of St. George can be separated into two distinct celebrations. The medieval holiday was a local, religious festival that venerated St. George as a real person martyred for his faith. The holy day grew in popularity with the nobility because of his association with the military and among the peasants because of the dragon legend, but he was primarily viewed by all social classes in the medieval period as a martyr. The religious feast came to an end due to the Reformation. According to the chronology developed above, a two-hundred-year gap exists between medieval and modern celebrations; therefore, this study stresses the discontinuity of the two versions of the holiday. In many ways, the dismantling of the religious feast and the attack on St. George during the Reformation and the Enlightenment made the modern, secular feast possible. Its modern iteration, in North America and the two revivals in England, celebrated the nation with St. George symbolizing England or the ideal Englishman.

In the historiography on St. George, the majority of scholars have argued that the symbol of St. George helped construct a primitive form of English nationalism in the medieval period. Jonathon Bengtson formulated this argument in his article, "St. George and the Formation of English Nationalism."[22] Jonathan Good further developed the argument in his work, *The Cult of Saint George in Medieval England.* The standard view of nationalism is that identity in the medieval period was local, and nationalism was a product of the modern

---

[21] In contrast to Good, *The Cult of St. George,* 122.
[22] Jonathan Bengtson, "Saint George and the formation of English nationalism," *Journal of Medieval and Early Modern Studies* 27 (1997): 317-40.

period. In the post-industrial era, the rise of transportation, universal education, class consciousness, and mass print culture gave rise to nationalism.[23] Several medievalists have questioned this assertion, arguing that nationalism was present in the medieval period.[24] In the history of England, some medievalists have argued that the existence of an English church, English political structure, and English litera-ture is evidence for an English nation.[25] Bengtson and Good fall in the revisionist camp, maintaining that St. George was an important symbol of early English nationalism. Contrary to the thesis of this work, Good argued that St. George survived the Reformation since he was a national symbol. He wrote, "If anything served to diminish his status, therefore, it was not religious, but political."[26] In Good's view, the Union of 1707 and creation of Britain marked the end of the cult of St. George. This study argues against the revisionist view and maintains that medieval celebrations of the saint were not nation-alist. The distinction between the medieval feast and the modern holiday is evident when the two celebrations are compared in detail, which prior to this work has not been done. The pattern of argumen-tation here mirrors James MacGregor's study on St. George in medieval England. MacGregor argued the majority of works on St. George "have concerned themselves so thoroughly with documenting the development of the saint as the symbol of the nation that they have forgotten or ignored the fact that medieval people venerated Saint George as a martyr."[27]

---

[23] Benedict R. Anderson, *Imagined Communities: Reflections on the Origin and Spread of Nationalism.* (London: Verso, 1991); Ernest Gellner, *Nations and Nationalism* (Ithaca: Cornell University Press, 1983); Eric J. Hobsbawm, *Nations and Nationalism since 1780: Programme, Myth, Reality.* (Cambridge: Cambridge University Press, 1990).

[24] Adrian Hastings, *The Construction of Nationhood: Ethnicity, Religion, and Nationalism* (Cam-bridge: Cambridge University Press, 1997).

[25] John Gillingham, *The English in the Twelfth Century: Imperialism, National Identity, and Political Values.* (Woodbridge, Suffolk: Boydell Press, 2000); Thorlac Turville-Petre, *England the Nation: Language, Literature, and National Identity, 1290-1340* (Oxford: Clarendon Press, 1996).

[26] Good, *The Cult of St. George*, xiii.

[27] MacGregor, "Salue Martir Spes Anglorum," vii.

Examination of the feast of St. George over the long term reveals that it transformed from a religious holy day to a national, secular holiday. The progress of the secularization of St. George's Day was not linear, simple, or complete, and though the distinction between the medieval and modern feast can be summarized in absolute terms, the reality of it is more complex. The medieval feast, while primarily religious in meaning, had significant political ramifications. Likewise, church services formed an important aspect of the modern, secular celebrations. A thin description might not capture the underlying meaning of unfolding events. The following chapters attempt a deeper investigation, aiming to illuminate the process of secularization in modern England. Studies on secularization typically cite statistical evidence to demonstrate the number of individuals who attend church or believe in God. Statistics, however, do not tell the whole story; measuring religion is more than determining who attends church and who does not. Callum Brown, in *The Death of Christian Britain: Understanding Secularisation, 1800-2000* (2001), called the statistical method flawed and reductionistic because "whole realms of religiosity… cannot be counted." [28] He advocated the use of cultural history to better understand secularization in Britain. Building on Brown's premise, this work investigates secularization on a cultural level through holidays. Using a cultural approach, we can see that while the majority of people may go to religious services or believe in God, they still live in a secular age because the "webs of significance" in which they are enmeshed are composed of non-religious values. Therefore, a modern holiday centered on a saint, celebrated with church services, and promoted by church officials can still be secular in nature. In other words, the surface level activities of St. George's Day do not determine its meaning.

Secularization has been defined in a variety of ways by social scientists. The general theory is that religion will decline or even disappear because it is not compatible with modernity. One explana-

---

[28] Callum G. Brown, *The Death of Christian Britain: Understanding Secularisation, 1800-2000* (London: Routledge, 2001), 12.

tion for secularization is the process of rationalization. The rationalist argument is deeply indebted to Max Weber's work from the early twentieth century. Proponents of this theory argue that the rise of science and rational thinking in the modern period has undermined religion as a system of beliefs. The process of secularization began during the Renaissance and Reformation and progressed with the Age of Reason, the Enlightenment, and the introduction of evolutionary biology.[29] A second explanation of secularization, based on the thought of Émile Durkheim, is known as the functionalist argument.[30] Sociologists influenced by Durkheim have argued that religion comprised more than a system of beliefs. In the medieval world, religious institutions directed healthcare, education, welfare, and political control, but as a result of industrialization, specialized institutions replaced religious entities in these capacities. The role of religion in the public sphere, therefore, dramatically declined, becoming a private affair. Social scientists of the 1960s and 1970s built on the work of Weber and Durkheim, and many leading scholars of the era, including Bryan Wilson, Peter Berger, David Martin, and Thomas Luckmann, accepted secularization theory as dogma.[31]

Secularization theory has fallen from favor in the past few decades. Jeffrey Hadden's presidential address to the Southern Sociological Society in 1986 fired a significant salvo at the thesis. He criticized the theory on four fronts: (1) the lack of a general theory; (2) statistical evidence demonstrating religious stability; (3) the emergence of dynamic new religious movements; and (4) the vitality of

---

[29] Max Weber, *The Protestant Ethic and the Spirit of Capitalism* (New York: Scribner, 1930); Max Weber, *Economy and Society: An Outline of Interpretive Sociology* (New York: Bedminster Press, 1968).
[30] Durkheim, *The Elementary Forms of the Religious Life.*
[31] Bryan R. Wilson, *Religion in Secular Society: A Sociological Comment* (London: Watts, 1966); Peter L. Berger, *The Sacred Canopy: Elements of a Sociological Theory of Religion* (Garden City, N.Y.: Doubleday, 1967); David Martin, *A General Theory of Secularization* (Oxford: Blackwell, 1978); Thomas Luckmann, *The Invisible Religion: The Problem of Religion in Modern Society* (New York: Macmillan, 1967).

religion in politics.[32] Even the leading supporters of secularization in the 1960s and 1970s have been forced to reevaluate the theory. Peter Berger, an adherent of secularization in the 1960s, stated in 1999 that the world "is as furiously religious as it ever was, and in some places more so than ever. This means that a whole body of literature by historians and social scientists loosely labeled 'secularization theory' is essentially mistaken."[33] Berger, however, sees Western Europe as one area that has remained secular as religion has grown worldwide.

The examination of holidays adds another dimension to the secularization debate. Undeniably, religion faces increased competition in the modern world. Science and rationalism challenge religion as a belief system, and the welfare state, educational institutions, hospitals, and countless other secular entities threaten the public and functional role of religion, forcing it into the private sphere. The impact of increased competition varies by location and is unpredictable. A single model of secularization does not exist, and it is hardly a linear process. While the secular alternative to the cognitive and functional role of religion has been well documented, modern challenges to the ritualistic dimension of religion have been neglected. Intellectual arguments can attack religious beliefs, secular institutions might diminish the role of religion, but a secular cultural system with intricate rituals and symbols can replace religion. Nationalism is a fitting replacement for religion with flags, holidays, anthems, heroes, and rituals dedicated to the nation. Sports, a more contemporary example, is another surrogate religion, with players replacing saints, stadiums replacing churches, schedules of games and tournaments replacing the liturgical year, and so forth. The creation of cultural systems that replace religion constitute a necessary and final element to the process of secularization. Is it too radical to assert that the popularization of sports has had a greater secularizing force than the publication of

---

[32] Jeffrey K. Hadden, "Toward Desacralizing Secularization Theory," *Social Forces* 65:3 (1987): 587-611.

[33] Peter L. Berger, *The Desecularization of the World: Resurgent Religion and World Politics* (Washington, D.C.: Ethics and Public Policy Center, 1999), 2.

Darwin's *On the Origin of Species?* Nationalism, sports, mass media, and consumerism are powerful secular cultural systems, but they have retained many elements of religious culture. St. George and his day has been adopted by nationalists, and St. George's Cross has become the most visible symbol of English sports fans. Newspapers have been behind the most recent revival of St. George's Day, and breweries and pubs stand to profit immensely from the promotion of the national day of England. The incorporation of old religious symbols, but with a new meaning, provide legitimacy and familiarity to secular culture.

Central to affirming values and creating sentiments, holidays play an important role in the process of cultural transformation. The ability to control the calendar and create or discontinue festivals provides great power. The main force behind the promotion of St. George's Day was not political. Monarchs and later elected officials had great power to terminate or suspend holidays, but they did not play a creative role in popularizing St. George's Day. Instead, over several centuries, small associations such as monastic communities, medieval guilds, ethnic societies, breweries, and internet sites promoted April 23 and helped shape St. George's Day as a national day. More studies of holidays will have to be undertaken to see if this pattern is universal, but the study of St. George's Day shows that a small number of people can have a substantial cultural impact by creating a new festival or promoting a holiday already in existence.

In conclusion, this book seeks to correct the periodization of St. George's Day, and it maintains that two distinct traditions exist with substantial differences. Celebrations in the medieval period were religious in nature, while modern celebrations are nationalistic. This study also challenges the argument that the cult of St. George in the medieval period provides evidence for nationalism. Instead, historians concerned with English nationalism should examine the revival of St. George's Day in North America, early twentieth-century England, and contemporary England to better understand the topic. In the highly controversial field of secularization, St. George's Day is evidence for a ritual's transformation from the religious to the secular. The reemergence of the traditionally religious symbol of St. George does not undermine the theory of secularization. Alterations in the celebration of St. George's Day, however, are not predetermined. The modern, nationalistic celebration is in the process of being supplanted by a holiday driven by consumerism. In the distant future, St. George's Day may fall into permanent decline, or St. George's Day could be revived as a thoroughly religious holiday. This investigation of St. George's Day does not establish a universal pattern for secularization, if there is a determined path. It attempts to illuminate the process of secularization by thoroughly examining one example of cultural history.

The organization of the book reflects the central argument. It is divided into two sections with the first examining the religious feast of St. George and the second probing the secular holiday of St. George's Day. The first section explores the development of the St. George's Day as a religious, royal, and popular feast, and the decline of the day during the Reformation. The second section investigates the revival of the feast in North America and modern England. A short epilogue chronicling the current resurgence of the holiday in England completes this investigation of St. George's Day.

Chapter One
A Religious Celebration:
St. George as Martyr

ost individuals know of St. George through stories of his heroic battle with the dragon and rescue of the princess, the most recognizable chivalrous legend. This popular tale, however, appeared nearly eight centuries after the alleged date of his death. Early documents on St. George did not focus on dragons and princesses, but on his persecution and death. Hagiographers label these sources "Passions," as opposed to "Lives," because the texts focus exclusively on the martyrdom of the saint. The *Codex Gallicanus*, a ninth-century manuscript, provides an exemplary version of the death of St. George, full of grotesque tortures and fantastic miracles. The Passion starts with the Emperor Datianus, ruler of Persia, threatening the Christian population with torture. St. George of Cappadocia, a military leader, enters the story by giving his money to the poor and proclaiming his adherence to Christianity. The emperor commands St. George to worship Apollo, but he refuses to worship a pagan god and instead blasphemes him. Placed on a rack, he is torn to pieces, has salt placed in his wounds, is thrown in a box filled with nails and hooks, is immersed in a cauldron of boiling water, and has his head beaten with a hammer causing his brain to ooze out of his nose; but miraculously, he survives unharmed. A divine vision then reveals to St. George that his enemies will torture him for seven years and kill him three times, but after the fourth death, he will go to heaven. The story continues with near endless list of unimaginable agonies, conversions, and miracles, and it ends with St. George's de-capitation, his fourth and final death.[1] This Passion of St. George, which focuses exclusively on his tortures and death, contrasts greatly with the romantic tale of the dragon and princess, but it was under the guise of a martyr that St. George's cult developed and spread in the medieval period.

Documents from the Early Middle Ages reveal a holiday with a very different meaning than the modern festival. Early sources related to the cult of St. George, including missals and breviaries, focus ex-clusively on the martyrdom of the saint and his intercessory role, and thus, the primary purpose of the holiday was to ask for the interces-sion of St. George. People honored St. George as an undeniably real individual who was heroically martyred for his faith, and as a result of his great sanctity, he had a great potential to dispense with supernatu-ral aid. Since it was a religious holiday, St. George's Day was directed by church authorities who determined the relative rank of feast days, and ecclesiastical declarations eventually elevated April 23 to a day of feasting and mandatory church attendance. Initially, the feast day was celebrated in monasteries, and only after it became widespread in the monastic world did it slowly spread into the secular world. St. George's Day was first organized on a local, not a national, level. With no universal religious calendar or liturgical books, celebration of the feast varied greatly from monastery to monastery and church to church, making the notion of a national day impossible.

Historians attempting to uncover the history of St. George face a difficult task.[2] The road of the researcher is paved with countless questions to which there are few reliable answers. The lack of accu-rate information presents the initial and most pressing problem.

---

[1] Published in Wilhelm Arndt, "Passio Santi Georgi," *Berichte über die Verhandlungen der Kö-niglich Sächsischen Gesellschaften der Wissenschaften zu Leipzig. Philologisch-Historische* 26 (1874): 43-70; also see Matzke, "Contributions to the History of the Legend of Saint George," 467-476.

[2] Christopher Walter quipped, "I realized that in George's case this would be beyond the scope of a single person; it would require the collaboration of a team." in Christopher Walter, *The Warrior Saints in Byzantine Art and Tradition* (Aldershot: Ashgate, 2003), 109.

There is no shortage of documents on St. George, but he has been associated with everything from fighting dragons to surviving multiple executions. How does one separate fact from fiction? Moreover, religious, political, and national biases slant many older studies on St. George, and therefore, past works serve more as a barrier than an aid to reaching the truth behind St. George. Sufficient evidence exists to say with some confidence that there was a "real" St. George, but it is nearly impossible to say anything more with any degree of certainty. The origins of St. George desperately need a comprehensive study, which this chapter does not provide. The intention of the following paragraphs is to wade through the myths and misinformation, review some of the works that laid a foundation for the study of the early cult of St. George and the early celebration of his feast, and draw a few, limited conclusions about the actual St. George.[3]

Some of the oldest evidence for St. George comes from records of early churches dedicated to him in the Near East. Inscriptions mentioning St. George have been dated from the fourth to the early sixth centuries, with modern scholarship supporting the later dates. A monastery dedicated in 515 at Ezra (Zorava) bears the following dedication: "A certain Christ-loving man, the town-councilor John, son of Diomedes, offered a gift to God from his own property, a beautiful building, after installing within it the worthy body of the martyr George, who appeared to this John not in a dream, but manifestly."[4] Researchers discovered another inscription at a church in Horvath Hesheq in northern Israel dedicated to the martyr in 519: "O Lord God of the holy and glorious martyr Georgius, remember for good Thy servant Demetrius the deacon who built this holy building, and Georgius (his) son and all their household. For the salvation of De-

---

[3] Budge, *George of Lydda;* Budge, *The Martyrdom and Miracles*; Walter, "The Origins of the Cult of St. George," 467-476; Matzke, "Contributions to the History of the Legend of Saint George," 99-171; Krumbacher, *Der heilige Georg*; Delehaye, *Les légendes grecques des saints militaries.*

[4] Frank R. Trombley, *Hellenic Religion and Christianization c.370-529* (Leiden: E.J. Brill, 1995), 2:363.

metrius the deacon and of Georgius (his) son and of all of their household, the whole work was completed in the month of April of the year 582."[5] A church at Shakka in Syria contains another inscription recording its dedication to St. George by bishop Tibernius in 535: "A church of the holy victorious martyrs George, and of the holy [men] with him, was built from the foundation with the offerings of Tiberinus."[6] Abundant evidence exists for other sixth-century churches dedicated to St. George, including a monastery in Jerusalem, a church in Bizani built by Justinian, several churches in Constantinople, a monastery in Jericho, a church in Edessa, a monastery in Dorylleon, and a church in Cairo.[7] Pilgrims to the Holy Land also recorded sites dedicated to St. George. Theodosius, writing in the early sixth century, referred to the burial site of St. George in Lydda where many miracles took place.[8] Cyril of Scythopolis in 515 mentioned a chapel of St. George in a hospice on the outskirts of Jerusalem.[9] The material evidence demonstrates that the cult of St. George was widespread by the sixth century, but with his death either in the third or early fourth century, a two-hundred-year gap exists between the death of the saint and evidence for holy sites dedicated to him.

The Passions of St. George provide further evidence for his existence. The first possible reference to the martyrdom of St. George is contained in Eusebius of Caesarea's *Historia Ecclesiastica*, a fourth-century work on the history of the church. In the eighth book, Eusebius recorded the story of a man who tore the imperial edict of Diocletian into pieces. "When the edict against the churches was published at Nicomedia and posted in a public place, a distinguished man

---

[5] Leah di Segni, "Horvath Hesheq: The Inscription," in *Christian Archaeology in the Holy Land New Discoveries: Essays in Honour of Virgilio C. Corbo, OFM*, Collectio maior, no. 36, ed. G.C. Bottini (Jerusalem: Franciscan Print Press, 1990), 379-87.

[6] John Hogg, "Supplemental Notes on St. George the Martyr, and on George the Arian Bishop," *Transactions of the Royal Society of Literature of the United Kingdom* 2:7 (1863): 116.

[7] Good, *The Cult of St. George*, 21-22.

[8] John Wilkinson, *Jerusalem Pilgrims Before the Crusades* (Warminster: Aris & Phillips, 1977), 65.

[9] Cyril, *Lives of the Monks of Palestine*, trans. R. M. Price (Kalamazoo: Cistercian Publications, 1991), 223.

was so moved by his burning faith that he seized it and tore it to pieces—this despite the presence in the same city of two emperors. But
he was only the first of those who so distinguished themselves at that
time, suffering the consequences of such a daring act with a cheerful
confidence to his very last breath."[10] The unnamed martyr has often
been mistaken for St. George, and many works on St. George claim
that Eusebius placed the martyrdom on April 23, 303, the reputed
date of St. George's martyrdom. Eusebius, however, did not use the
date of April 23; furthermore, the edict was issued on February 24.
The likely martyr is St. Euethius, who was martyred on February 24,
303, at Nicomedia.

The first known reference to St. George in the West further adds
to the uncertainty surrounding the origins of his cult. In 494, Pope
Gelasius held a synod at Rome with seventy-two bishops to discern
which religious works were canonical and which were apocryphal.
The resulting document, *Decretum Gelasianum*, contained a list of writings thought to be compiled by heretics or schismatic, and these the
Roman Church instructed the faithful to avoid. Among the works
deemed apocryphal was "Passio Georgii." The papal declaration contains the following passage related to St. George: "According to old
custom by the greatest caution they are not read in the holy Roman
church, because the names of those who wrote are not properly
known and [the deeds] through the agency of unbelievers and unedu-
cated are thought to be superfluous or less appropriate than the order
of the event was; like the *passio* Cyricus and Julitta, like Georgius and
the *passiones* of others which appear to have been composed by heretics. Because of this, as it was said, so that no occasion for trivial
mockery can arise, they are not read in the holy Roman church."[11]
The authenticity of *Decretum Gelasianum* has been challenged by a few

---

[10] Eusebius, *The Church History: A New Translation with Commentary*, trans. Paul L. Maier (Grand
Rapids: Kregel, 1999), 293.
[11] Kate Cooper and Julia Hillner, *Religion, Dynasty, and Patronage in Early Christian Rome, 300-
900* (Cambridge: Cambridge University Press, 2007), 255.

scholars, adding another concern to the matter.[12] To this day, a constant shadow surrounds the cult of St. George because of his inclu-inclusion in this condemnation, and it confirms the untrustworthiness of some of the early documents on St. George.

The condemnation in *Decretum Gelasianum* was based on a family of texts considered apocryphal, and these are the oldest sources documenting the death of St. George. First composed in Greek, the oldest known text is a fifth-century manuscript preserved in the Kunsthistorisches Museum in Vienna, of which only fragments survive.[13] The Greek Passion served as the basis of Syriac versions, and the oldest Syriac manuscript, written around 600, is at the British Library. Early translations of the apocryphal version also exist in Latin, Arabic, and Coptic.[14] The narrative of St. George's death in the apocryphal tradition follows the pattern outlined in the *Codex Gallicanus* at the beginning of the chapter. After the condemnation by Gelasius, a more plausible version of the story appeared, but the apocryphal version remained significant, most notably in the Western tradition. The canonical version started circulating in the sixth century, and it reduced the amount of torture inflicted on the saint as well as the number of miracles he performed. The oldest known canonical version is in the encomium composed by Andrea, Archbishop of Crete, from the seventh century.[15] The canonical version takes place during the persecution of Diocletian. According to this account, St. George lived in Palestine, but was born of Cappadocian parents. At court, the saint sees the harm done to Christians, and he is moved to give his possessions away and proclaim his faith in God. He then faces numerous forms of torture such as being placed on a wheel with knives, kept in a kiln for three days, and forced to wear heated iron boots, but

---

[12] F. C. Burkitt, "The Decretum Gelasianum," *Journal of Theological Studies* 14 (1913): 469-471.

[13] Palimpsest (*Cod. Vindob. lat.* 954) in Karl Krumbacher, *Der heilige Georg*, 1-3.

[14] The division of texts is covered in Matzke, "Contributions to the History of the Legend of Saint George," 467-476.

[15] Matzke, "Contributions to the History of the Legend of Saint George," 481; Godefroid Henschen and Daniel Van Papenbroeck, *Acta Sanctorum Aprilis. III: 22-30* (Bruxelles: Culture et civilisation, 1968), 119-124.

he is not harmed. The guards and empress are converted by his miraculous resistance to punishment. St. George battles with the magician Athanasius, and the saint drinks poison provided by the magician without harm. He also raises a dead man back to life. Athanasius converts to Christianity, and he and the resurrected man are executed. On St. George's last night on earth, he receives a vision foretelling his death, and he performs numerous miracles for those who visit him. On his last day, Diocletian tries to persuade St. George to renounce Christianity and offers him half of his kingdom. St. George surprisingly declares he is ready to worship the Roman gods. When he enters the temple and makes the sign of the cross, the idols proclaim that St. George worships the true God, and the statues fall to the ground, breaking into pieces. The empress then proclaims her secret faith in Christ and is executed. Finally, St. George is beheaded, which marks the end of the Passion. The canonical version shares many similarities with the apocryphal version, but some of the fantastical elements are deleted. The number of tortures is reduced dramatically, and the length of the tortures is shortened from seven years to seven days. St. George is only killed once, as opposed to four times, and he is not resurrected from the dead. The martyrdom also happens under the known persecution of Diocletian. The new version was more appealing to church leaders than the apocryphal version as it presented to the clergy a potentially plausible account of the saint's life.

Based on the evidence, a real individual certainly inspired the early cult of St. George. The churches, pilgrimage sites, and accounts of the martyrdom are too numerous and widespread to be completely invented. The "real" St. George, however, might be tainted with elements from other saints. St. Euethius, the inspiration for the unnamed martyr in Eusebius' account, could be the source of the challenge to the imperial edict. St. Helpidius, whose feast is also on April 23, might be another source for St. George. Some of the actions of George of Cappadocia, an Arian bishop of Alexandria, could have been incorporated into the life of St. George. In sum, with his numerous martyrdoms, St. George could also have been a conglomera-conglomeration of several martyrs.[16]

It is impossible to say anything certain about St. George beyond the fact of his existence. This study is not particularly interested in the accuracy of early accounts or the characteristics of the "real" St. George, but rather with how the image of St. George changed over time. Early texts share a few points in common, and by analyzing these similarities, one can determine the main features of the saint's depiction during the Early Middle Ages. From this early St. George, future changes to his image can be ascertained. Most importantly, St. George in the early medieval period was remembered as a martyr, and the primary focus of the documents was on the tortures he underwent and his subsequent martyrdom. The location of his birth and death varies with each account, but they all place them in the area of Asia Minor, Palestine, and North Africa. Cappadocia is the city most often cited as his birthplace; Lydda in Palestine is the traditional site of his martyrdom and burial. Notable variations are Eusebius' account, in which Nicomedia is the place of his martyrdom, and manuscripts discovered in Q'asr Ibrim during the construction of the Aswan Dam that claim that St. George was of Cappadocian descent but lived in northern Nubia before his persecution and death.[17] The time of his death is also contested, but is placed typically in the late third or early fourth century. Canonical works claim the martyrdom occurred during the persecution of Diocletian, and the traditional date of his martyrdom is in 303. Those who believe that St. George was actually George, the Arian bishop of Alexandria, place his death during the reign of Julian the Apostate in 361. Ernest A. Wallis Budge, eminent scholar of St. George, argued that the saint's death took place during

---

[16] Fox, *Saint George*, 18-19.
[17] W. H. C. Frend, "A Fragment of the *Acta Sancti Georgii* from Q'asr Ibrim (Egyptian Nubia)," *Analecta Bollandiana* 100 (1982): 79-86; W. H. C. Frend, "Fragments of a Version of the *Acta Georgii* from Q'asr Ibrim," *Jahrbuch für Antike und Christentum* 32 (1989): 89-104; Gerald M. Browne, *The Old Nubian martyrdom of Saint George* (Lovanii: Peeters, 1998).

the reign of Decius in the middle of the third century.[18] Lastly, all the
early accounts, from Eusebius to the apocryphal version to the canonical, present St. George as a military figure of various ranks, and even
the Arian George had ties to the military as a supplier of bacon to the
Roman Legions.

Early documents also contain references to the day of his martyrdom and cite special veneration reserved for his feast. The inscription
on the church in Horvath Hesheq stated that "the whole work was
completed in the month of April of the year 582."[19] The month of the
dedication leads one to believe that the church was dedicated near the
feast day of the martyr. The Vienna Palimpsest dates the martyrdom
to the eighth kalends of May, which is April 23.[20] The Coptic version
of the martyrdom starts with "the Martyrdom of Saint George, the
valiant martyr of our Lord Jesus Christ, who completed his strife on
the 23rd of the month Pharmuthi, in the peace of God," and later in
the text, "Saint George consummated his martyrdom on the twenty-
third day of the month Pharmuthi, on the Lord's day, at the ninth
hour of the day."[21] Pharmuthi, the eighth month in the Coptic calendar, corresponds to April in the Gregorian calendar. Another Coptic
text, the Encomium of Saint Theodosius, also relates devotion to St.
George on his feast day. In a miracle story, a wealthy Christian promises, if he is cured, on the "twenty-third day of Pharmuthi, which is
his great day, I will walk upon my legs to his shrine and will give one
hundred pounds of gold to it."[22] The sources thus identify April 23 as
the feast of St. George, and the miracle story and church dedication
mark the feast as a special day for veneration.

---

[18] Budge, *George of Lydda.*
[19] Segni, "Horvath Hesheq: The Inscription," 379-87.
[20] Krumbacher, *Der heilige Georg,* 1-3.
[21] Budge, *The Martyrdom and Miracles,* 203, 235.
[22] Budge, *The Martyrdom and Miracles,* 256.

On the outskirts of Uffington in Oxfordshire, grass reportedly does not grow on the summit of a hill. Local legend states that St. George fought the dragon on that hill, and the blood of the dragon prevents anything from growing.[23] Farther to the north in Coventry, one can visit the ruins of Caludon Castle, which some claim was the birthplace of the patron of England, and after the fatal fight with the dragon, also his resting place.[24] Traveling west to the coast, one arrives at St. George's Channel, which separates Ireland and Wales. The channel received its name from the legend that St. George visited England by sailing into the Irish Sea via St. George's Channel.[25] The origins of the connection between St. George and England are shrouded in mystery, and these physical landmarks are reminders of the "ancient" roots of the cult of St. George in England. Most of the legends, however, attempt to establish an earlier date than historically plausible for St. George's introduction to the island. The boldest claim is that St. George was born in England. Richard Johnson popularized this idea in his work, *The Seven Champions of Christendom* (1596). The first chapter of the work starts with the "wonderfull and straunge birth of Saint George of England." Among other claims, Johnson related that "the famous Cittie of Coventrie was the place wherein the first Christian Champion of England was bourne."[26] Johnson's work proved to be very popular and formed the basis of many chapbooks and plays. Thus, the completely fictional birth of St. George in England entered the public imagination. Speculation that St. George visited England is also rooted in legends. Early accounts present St. George as a soldier in the Roman army, and during his lifetime, the Roman Empire extended to England. Some speculate that St. George was stationed in England as part of his service in the Roman army. According to one

---

[23] Other places such as Dunsmore Heath, Warwickshire; Brinsop, Herefordshire; and the hamlet of Saint George in Derbyshire claim to be the place of the encounter.
[24] Richard Johnson, *The Seven Champions of Christendom (1596/7)*, ed. Jennifer Fellows (Aldershot: Ashgate, 2003), 264.
[25] Edward Clapton, *The Life of St. George* (London: Swan Sonnenschein & Co. Ltd, 1903), 14.
[26] Johnson, *The Seven Champions of Christendom*, 5.

theory, he began his service at Porta Sisuntiorum[27] in modern Lancaster, visited the court of Constantius Chlorus at York, and became acquainted with Constantine. He was then stationed at Caelwon-on-Usk, headquarters of the Second Roman Legion, before returning to the Near East.[28] Lastly, some claim St. Augustine of Canterbury brought knowledge of St. George to England when St. Gregory the Great sent him on a mission to convert England in 596. No evidence exists to support that St. George was born in England, ever visited England, or that he was known in England before the seventh century. Though elements of these three claims form part of the national cult of St. George, they are based solely on myths or circumstantial evidence.

It is established, however, that before the cult of St. George reached England, his popularity grew on the continent. After the condemnation of *Decretum Gelasianum,* St. George received papal approval of his cult when St. Gregory the Great ordered that a church under his patronage be repaired and furthermore when Pope Leo II built a church dedicated to him in Rome. In the same period, his cult expanded to the Franks. St. Gregory of Tours included St. George in his sixth-century martyrology, and Clotilde, the wife of Clovis, built a church dedicated to St. George.[29]

Late seventh-century writings of Adamnan, Abbot of Iona, are the first records in the British Isles to acknowledge St. George. Adamnan learned of St. George from Arculf, a bishop from Gaul, who shipwrecked on the coast of Iona, when returning from a pilgrimage to the Holy Land. Adamnan gave shelter to Arculf, and while a guest, Arculf recounted his experiences in the Holy Land. Adamnan collected the stories in his work, *De Locis Sanctis,* and two of the sto-

---

[27] Elder is unclear about the exact location, and she could mean Portus Setantiorum.
[28] Isabel Hill Elder, *George of Lydda: Soldier, Saint and Martyr* (London: Covenant, 1949), 18-20.
[29] Good, *The Cult of St. George,* 28-29.

ries were miracles attributed to St. George.[30] Adamnan's work contains no account of St. George's life or martyrdom. A unique element of this version is that Adamnan characterized St. George as a confessor and not a martyr.[31] This classification demonstrates that the story of St. George is anything but static. Adamnan's work circulated throughout the British Isles, and from this point forward, the cult of St. George started to spread.

The English began to celebrate the feast day of St. George soon after knowledge of the saint arrived in England. The feast of martyrs, as with St. George, is the day of their martyrdom, yet unlike most events associated with death, it is not a day of mourning. Rather, the day of their death is celebrated as the day of their birth in the next life (*dies natalis*) because the church teaches that individuals who die for their faith are assured of eternal life. In the first three centuries of the Christian church, many martyrs died for their beliefs because of the Roman authorities' hostility towards Christianity. Veneration of these martyrs and celebration of the anniversary of their death became an important part of the emerging practices of Christianity.

Celebration of martyrs' feast days can best be understood by examining the history of the Christian calendar, which places the development of the feast of St. George into a wider framework. The Christian calendar has its roots in two older calendars. The first is the Hebrew calendar, a lunisolar calendar of twelve months of twenty-nine days, with a thirteenth month periodically added to keep the months in line with the solar year of 365 days. This calendar contains the important Jewish feasts of Passover, Festival of Weeks, and Tabernacles. Jesus and his disciples used the Hebrew calendar, thus tying early Christian feasts to the Hebrew calendar. As Christians became increasingly intertwined with the Roman Empire, they began to adopt the Roman calendar. The Romans used the Julian calendar, based on

---

[30] Adamnan, *De locis sanctis*, ed. Denis Meehan (Dublin: Dublin Institute for Advanced Studies: 1958), 111-17.

[31] A confessor suffers for the faith, but unlike a martyr, he is not killed for his faith.

the reforms of Julius Caesar, who introduced a solar calendar inspired by an Egyptian model with twelve months. The months were the same length as those used today in the Gregorian calendar, and Caesar also introduced an extra day every four years to create the leap year. The use of the Julian calendar persisted in the West until the reforms of Gregory XIII in the sixteenth century, and in some places use of the Julian calendar lasted even longer. Gregory's reforms created a more accurate calendar by slightly adjusting the use of the leap year and removing ten calendar days.[32]

The most important Christian feast is Easter, the day commemorating the resurrection of Jesus. Easter significantly impacted the development of the Christian calendar when Sunday, the day of the resurrection, superseded Saturday, the Jewish Sabbath, as the day of rest. Additionally, the majority of important Christian feasts are tied to Easter. They include a penitential time before Easter called Lent, a commemoration of the passion of Jesus called Passiontide, the Ascension forty days after Easter, Pentecost fifty days after Easter, and many other movable feasts. The date of Easter was originally reckoned on the basis of the Hebrew calendar as the Sunday after the feast of Passover. As the Christian community expanded and adopted the use of the Roman calendar, the problem arose of how to synchronize the lunar cycle of Jewish feasts to the solar Julian calendar. The issue of the Easter controversy is a rich and complex topic and has been covered in some detail, but the debate is not central to this study.[33] Suffice it to say, the tenacity of the debate over the calculation of Easter demonstrates the importance of the calendar to the early church. In short, Easter was the heart of the Christian calendar because every Sunday was a celebration of Easter, and the majority of

---

[32] In 1582, October 4 was followed by October 15 in order to synchronize the seasons with the calendar as they were during the Council of Nicaea.
[33] Alden A. Mosshammer, *The Easter Computus and the Origins of the Christian Era* (Oxford: Oxford University Press, 2008); in the British Isles see Caitlin Corning, *The Celtic and Roman Traditions: Conflict and Consensus in the Early Medieval Church* (New York: Palgrave Macmillan, 2006).

important feasts and seasons rotated around it based on lunar calculations.[34]

In addition to movable feasts based on Easter, the Christian calendar celebrates fixed feast days, some of which are associated with
the life of Jesus. His birth is celebrated on December 25, and his conception, the Annunciation, is celebrated nine months before, on
March 25. The events of his adult life are mainly movable feasts. The
most important fixed feasts are occurrences in the life of Jesus, but
the vast majority of the fixed feasts are saint's days. Many of the early
saints commemorated by the church on special days were martyrs,
and the cult of martyrs formed an essential part of Christianity from
the beginning of the faith. The story of the first martyr, Stephen, recorded in the Acts of the Apostles, dates to around 35.[35] Local
churches collected the remains of the martyrs as relics and preserved
them in designated resting places, and the community also remembered the anniversary of saints' deaths with special liturgies. As the
number of martyrs increased, church authorities composed lists containing the names of martyrs and dates of their deaths to help
facilitate the memory of the saints. The writings of St. Cyprian of
Carthage contain one of the first acknowledgements of a list of martyrs. Writing in the middle of the third century, he instructed his
priests to bury martyrs and to note the day of their death.[36] The first
list of martyrs from the Roman church is the Chronography of 354,
also known as the Philocalian Calendar. It contains a list of Roman
martyrs and is organized chronologically along the lines of a calendar.
The list also includes the location of the body of the martyrs, which
was a way to aid those who wished to visit the saints on the anniversary of their death.[37]

Early martyrologies originating from these lists of martyrs, such as
the Philocalian Calendar, were tied to a local church and limited in

---

[34] Easter is the first Sunday after the first full moon after the vernal equinox.
[35] Acts 7: 54-60.
[36] Noele M. Denis-Boulet, *The Christian Calendar* (New York: Hawthorn Books, 1960), 54.
[37] Denis-Boulet, *The Christian Calendar*, 53-54.

scope. Like these early calendars, martyrologies catalogued saints by months and days. Originally, church leaders only listed martyrs, but later they included saints of all types. Later martyrologies were more complex than earlier documents as they mentioned not only local saints but also saints from all over the church. The growing number of holy individuals even resulted in multiple saints being commemorated on one day. Furthermore, martyrologies included topographical information relating to the location of the body of the martyr and biographical information about the saint.[38]

The oldest universal martyrology is the *Hieronymian Martyrology*, a compilation of literary sources and martyrologies from the Near East, Italy, and North Africa. Scholars believe it was compiled in Italy late in the fifth century and revised in Gaul around the year 600. The *Hieronymian* served as the basis for most medieval martyrologies. The historical martyrologies were the next step in the commemoration of saints. The eighth and ninth centuries were the classical age of historical martyrologies, and during this period, the number of saints included in the works greatly expanded and even more biographical information was provided. The classical age started with the work of Bede in the eighth century, followed by the continental authors Florus of Lyon, Ado of Vienne, and Usuard in the ninth century.

Calendars are human inventions, but based on astronomical movements. The rotation of the earth is the source of the day, the revolution of the moon around the earth constitutes the basis of the month, and the revolution of the earth around the sun is the root of the year. These three measurements form the basis of time in every society, yet every culture determines how they are organized. The organization of the calendar structures all commercial, agricultural, governmental, and religious undertakings. In the Early Middle Ages, the reckoning of time was, perhaps, the most important area of scien-

---

[38] Hippolyte Delehaye, "Martyrology," in *The Catholic Encyclopedia* (New York: Robert Appleton Company, 1910).

tific research. Over 9000 Latin manuscripts dealing with the calculation of time survive from the Middle Ages. One historian noted these
documents are the "best and thus far least known evidence for studies
in early medieval schools."[39] This substantial effort in the discipline of
reckoning, done primarily by monks, demonstrates that the medieval
period was an era of active learning, and that scholars of that period
considered the study of time a serious endeavor. The profound significance of the calendar to medieval scholars stemmed from its purpose
as a way to sanctify time. Early Christian calendars and martyrologies
were not commercial, political, or administrative; rather, they focused
on religious events. Each day was holy because it commemorated an
event in the life of Jesus or the feast of a saint. Calendars provided an
organizational tool to give honor and glory to God on a regular basis
and to connect the world and heaven through time.[40]

The seminal martyrology in the British Isles came from the hand
of Bede in the early eighth century. He was aware of St. George from
the writings of Adamnan, and many believe Bede's *Martyrology* contains the first reference to the feast of St. George in Britain. Historian
Joyce Hill, however, argues that St. George was not originally included in Bede's *Martyrology*. The examination of surviving manuscripts
reveals that they can be broken into two families based on shared
characteristics.[41] The older of the two families has fewer saints and
leaves April 23 blank. Hill speculates that Bede was either skeptical of
the stories recorded by Adamnan about St. George, or he was aware
of the condemnation in *Decretum Gelasianum*. While the reason for
Bede's omission may never be known, it is likely that later revisers
filled in the blanks in Bede's *Martyrology*, and the additions were attributed to the original author. The exclusion of St. George by Bede

[39] Wesley M. Stevens, *Cycles of Time and Scientific Learning in Medieval Europe* (Aldershot: Variorum, 1995), 1:46.
[40] E. G. Richards, *Mapping Time: The Calendar and Its History* (New York: Oxford University
Press, 1999); Charles Williams Jones and Wesley M. Stevens, *Bede, the Schools, and the Computus*
(Aldershot: Variorum, 1994).
[41] She bases her work on Henri Quentin, *Les Martyrologes Historiques Du Moyen Age: Etude Sur
La Formation Du Martyrologe Romain* (Paris: Librairie Victor Lecoffre, 1908).

...es the cult of St. George developed later than previously
...nt.[42]

The *Old English Martyrology*, another significant English martyrology, dates from the ninth century, and contains the first vernacular account of St. George written in Europe. The *Old English Martyrology's* entry begins with a brief account of the martyrdom of the saint and states that he was tortured for seven years and then beheaded.[43] The central aspect of the text is a prayer by St. George to God, in which he asks, whoever keeps "my commemoration on earth, Thou remove all sickness from the house of this man; no enemy may hurt him, nor hunger nor pestilence; and if a man mentions my name in danger either on sea or on a journey, then Thy mercy may attend upon him."[44] The entry emphasizes the intercessory power of the saint, and his capacity to help those who venerate him on his feast day. The document reveals that, in the two centuries after Adamnan, knowledge of the saint's feast day continued to grow and spread in the monastic world, and the use of the vernacular in the martyrology meant that veneration of the saint was open to a wider audience.

Monastic communities initiated the commemoration of St. George's feast day throughout England. Central to English civilization in the Early Middle Ages, monasteries provided small islands of order in a chaotic world by preserving learning and providing education for the masses. English monasticism has roots in the Irish and Benedictine traditions. Irish monasticism started with the conversion of the Irish by St. Patrick and the subsequent growth of Christian communities throughout the country. Numerous small, primitive monasteries were founded across the island and soon spread to Scotland. These monas-

---

[42] Joyce Hill, "Saint George before the Conquest," Society of the Friends of St. George's and the Descendants of the Knights of the Garter 6 (1986): 286-87; MacGregor, "Salue Martir Spes Anglorum," 47-48.

[43] MacGregor, "Salue Martir Spes Anglorum," 48.

[44] *An Old English Martyrology*, ed. George Herzfeld (London: English Early Text Society, 1900), 61.

teries survived the Germanic invasions that plagued the rest of Europe in the fourth and fifth centuries, and they were the one outpost of Western Civilization that remained intact during the fall of the Roman Empire.[45] In the south, the mission of St. Augustine of Canterbury brought the Benedictine tradition to England in the late sixth century. The fusion of Irish and Benedictine traditions, a frequently contentious process, created English monasticism.

The increasing number of monasteries dedicated to St. George in the medieval period suggests a growing connection between English monastic communities and the saint. The first Benedictine monastery dedicated to St. George was in Thetford by Uvius and occurred in the reign of King Cnut in the middle of the eleventh century.[46] Many monasteries followed: Benedictine priory in Dunster, Somerset (1090), monastery in Modbury, Devonshire (1140), monastery of Ogbourne in Wiltshire (late twelfth century), Augustinian canons in Gresley (twelfth century), priory of Cogges in Oxfordshire, and secular canons in Oxford castle.[47] Lastly, St. George's Chapel in Windsor was established with secular canons around 1348.[48] If St. George was the patron saint of a community, his feast would be kept with great solemnity and his cult would be spread to the surrounding areas.

Monastic life centered on prayers offered by monks for their own souls, those of their earthly benefactors, and for all of humanity. Monks' daily schedule consisted of a regulated cycle of prayers and liturgies that included the Mass and Divine Office. The Divine Office required monks to gather in the church several times a day—Matins, Lauds, Prime, Terce, Sext, None, Vespers, and Compline—to chant psalms, sing hymns and antiphons, listen to scripture readings, and

---

[45] Thomas Cahill, *How the Irish Saved Civilization* (New York: Nan A. Talese, Doubleday, 1995).

[46] Alison Binns, *Dedications of Monastic Houses in England and Wales, 1066-1216* (Woodbridge: Boydell Press, 1989), 87.

[47] Binns, *Dedications of Monastic Houses,* 96, 101-3, 129; Riches, *St. George,* 19.

[48] Also see David Knowles and R. Neville Hadcock, *Medieval Religious Houses: England and Wales* (London: Longmans, Green, 1953), 78, 87, 90, 154, 266-67, 434, 444.

recite prayers.[49] During the course of the Middle Ages, monks wrote down and compiled prayers for Mass and the canonical hours into liturgical books. The majority of prayers were fixed, repeated prayers, designated as "commons." Other prayers, called "propers," fluctuated based on the calendar. Unique propers were designated for each feast of the Christian calendar, and thus, prayers corresponded to a particular holy day. The propers for the feast of St. George in early liturgical books provide insight into how St. George was remembered during the period.

Only three manuscripts for the Divine Office survive from before the Norman invasion, and of the three, the *Durham Collectar* is the oldest, dating from the late ninth to early tenth century.[50] It contains a Collect for the feast of St. George, read at the night office of April 22, to announce the coming of the feast, and again at the end of the seven canonical hours on April 23: "The Feast of Saint George Martyr. O God who doth gladden us by the merits and intercession of blessed George thy martyr, mercifully grant that we who seek his aid, may, by the giving of thy grace, obtain it."[51] This prayer simply remembers St. George as a martyr and asks for his intercession.

Breviaries, collections of readings for the Divine Office, also provide evidence for the feast of St. George. The *Portiforium of Saint Wulstan* is an early English breviary composed in the 1060s at Worcester or Winchester.[52] St. George is listed in its calendar, and the book contains an abbreviated version of the Collect in the *Durham Collectar*.

---

[49] Sarah Foot, *Monastic Life in Anglo-Saxon England, C. 600-900* (Cambridge: Cambridge University Press, 2006), 191-205.

[50] Foot, *Monastic Life in Anglo-Saxon England,* 192.

[51] MacGregor, "Salue Martir Spes Anglorum," 137; translated from: "NATALIS SANCTI GEORGII MARTYRIS. Deus qui nos beati Georgii martyris tui meritis et intercessione laetificas, consede propitious ut qui eius beneficia poscimus donatione gratie consequamur" in *The Durham Collectar,* ed. Alicia Correa (Woodbridge: Boydell, 1992), 176.

[52] Julia Barrow and Nicholas Brooks eds., *St. Wulfstan and His World* (Aldershot: Ashgate, 2005), 14.

"O God who...us...of blessed George thy martyr."[53] In addition, it includes two prayers seeking the intercession of St. George.[54]

Like the canonical hours, some prayers of the Mass were determined by the day. Early English missals contain prayers for particular times during the Mass said only on the feast of St. George. One of the best preserved Mass books is the *Missal of the New Minster,* composed at Winchester in the eleventh century.[55] Prayers said on April 23 emphasize St. George as a martyr, mention the "diverse torments" that he suffered, and ask for his intercession several times. Numerous liturgical works appeared in England after the *Missal of the New Minster, Portiforium of Saint Wulstan,* and *Durham Collectar,* but these works laid the foundation for future compositions. With regards to St. George's Day, the central theme remained petitioning the martyred saint for his intercession.

The daily routine of a monastic community was marked by regularity as every day had a strict schedule of activities. The cycle of feasts and holy days, however, broke the monotonous cycle. The feast of St.

---

[53] Translated from "Deus qui nos beati georgii martyris tui" in *The Portiforium of Saint Wulstan,* Anselm Hughes, ed. (London: Henry Bradshaw Society, 1958), 1:122.

[54] *The Portiforium of Saint Wulstan,* ed. Hughes, 2:11.

[55] The Ninth Day Before the Kalends of May, the Feast of St. George, Martyr. O God thou hast protected me from the gathering of wicked men, alleluia; from the multitude of evil doers, alleluia, alleluia. Psalm "Hear O God" *The Collect of the Mass.* O God who doth gladden us by the merits and intercession of blessed George thy martyr, mercifully grant that we who seek his aid, may obtain the gifts of thy grace. Through... *A lesson from the Epistle of blessed Paul the apostle to the Corinthians.* (2 Corinthians 5: 1-11) Brethren: For we know, if our earthly... we are manifest; Through Jesus Christ our Lord, Alleluia. With glory and honor thou hast crowned him O Lord.
Gospel. (beginning of Mt. 16:24) If anyone shall come after me, let him deny... *Offertory.* (from Psalm 88:6) The heavens shall confess thy wonders, O Lord: and thy truth in the church of the saints. *Secret.* Sanctify, O Lord the gifts offered. And by the intercession of blessed George thy martyr, cleanse us by these offerings from the stains of sins, alleluia, alleluia. *Preface.* Through Christ, for whose name, the confession of which must be revered, the blessed martyr George bore diverse torments, and overcoming them, greatly merited the crown of perpetuity.
Communion. The just shall rejoice in the Lord, and shall hope in him: and all the upright in heart shall be praised, alleluia, alleluia. *Postcommunion.* Humbly we beseech thee almighty God, that to those who have been refreshed by thy sacraments, thou might also grant, by the intercession of blessed George, thy martyr, to serve thee with worthily with pleasing behavior. Through...
Translated from Latin in *The Missal of the New Minster,* ed. D. H. Turner, (London: Henry Bradshaw Society, 1962), 87-88.

George was one of many celebrations that altered the standard routine with special antiphons, readings, and prayers. Monastic calendars catalogued all the feasts and provide another source to inform our understanding of St. George's Day. Francis Wormald collected twenty monastic calendars in his work, *English Kalendars before A.D. 1100*. The calendars come primarily from Benedictine monasteries throughout England and range in time from the ninth to the end of the eleventh century. Upon examination, all of the calendars contain the feast of St. George, but the entries in the calendars mention only that he was a martyr. The inclusion of St. George in all the calendars from establishments across England proves that his feast day was a fixture in monastic life before 1100. Some of the calendars contain notations that point to the significance of the feast day. A calendar from Canterbury, dated between 1012 and 1023, contains the captions "in cappis" after the entry for St. George's feast.[56] This term, translated as "in copes," refers to the vestments worn during liturgies; wearing these long, elaborate vestments added to the solemnity of the day. Another calendar from Croyland in Lincoln, dated to the middle of the eleventh century, has an entry for St. George's Day in capital letters.[57] The increased size of the letters most likely signifies that the feast had greater importance than entries written in lowercase. Evidence from these calendars demonstrates that April 23 was a day celebrated throughout the monastic world; yet with the exception of Croyland and Canterbury, it was observed on the same level as other saint days celebrated by the church. The feast of St. George, however, increased in rank after the Crusades, as a direct result of the growing devotion to St. George in the military class and monarchy. Francis Wormald also collected eighteen calendars composed after 1100 in *English Benedictine Kalendars After A.D. 1100*; twelve of the calendars ranked April 23 as the highest possible feast for a saint's day. Thus, only after the Cru-

---

[56] Francis Wormald, ed., *English Kalendars Before A.D. 1100* (Woodbridge, Suffolk: Boydell Press for the Henry Bradshaw Society, 1988), 173.
[57] Wormald, ed., *English Kalendars Before A.D. 1100*, 257.

sades did St. George's Day begin to shift from a standard saint's day to one of the most revered days of the year.[58]

The calculation of when St. George's Day became a major feast in the English church, however, remains difficult to resolve. Most commentators claim that the Synod of Oxford in 1222 provided the first ecclesiastical endorsement of St. George's Day. The date corresponds to the era after the Third Crusade (1189–1192) and is central to the argument that the reign of Richard I, the Lionheart (r. 1189–1199) marked the genesis of the cult of St. George on a national level. The declaration of the Synod of Oxford is said to contain a list of feast days that were elevated to the status of a "minor feast," and the feast of St. George was included in the list.[59] Some historians have challenged the authenticity of this list of feast days, and subsequently, the elevation of St. George's feast. As early as the eighteenth century, Samuel Pegge remarked that he did not find a list of feast days in an authoritative edition of the Synod of Oxford and wondered about the omission.[60] The strongest argument against the authenticity of the list of feast days comes from historian C. R. Cheney's analysis of the document. He discovered that none of the seven manuscripts of the council dating from before the thirteenth century contain the list of feast days. The first manuscript that contains the list appeared in a printed edition from 1551. Another concern for historians is that the list, allegedly composed in 1222, contains the feast of St. Edmund the Confessor, canonized in 1247, which is a historical impossibility.[61] Based on this analysis, the Synod of Oxford was not the decisive event in the promotion of St. George's Day to a national feast.

Local ecclesiastical declarations, which have not received substantial attention, began the elevation of April 23 to a special status.

---

[58] Francis Wormald, ed., *English Benedictine Kalendars After A.D. 1100* (London: Harrison and Sons, 1939); MacGregor, "Salue Martir Spes Anglorum," 154.

[59] Laborderie, "Richard the Lionheart and the Birth of A National Cult of St. George," 41.

[60] Samuel Pegge, "Observation on the History of St. George, the patron of England," *Archaeologia* V (1779): 27.

[61] F. M. Powicke and C. R. Cheney, eds., *Councils and Synods and other Documents relating to the English Church Vol. II, Part 1, 1205-1265* (Oxford: Clarendon Press, 1964), 101, 104.

Around 1240, the Diocese of Norwich prohibited all work except plowing on the feast day.[62] The Diocese of London passed statutes between the years 1245-1259, prohibiting manual labor before Mass on St. George's Day, and the Abbey of Osney in Oxfordshire around 1300 prohibited labor on St. George's Day.[63]

In 1415, the most wide-reaching declaration occurred in the Province of Canterbury, which covered the southern half of England. The movement for the elevation of the feast started with a convocation of the province's clergy in 1399 under Archbishop Arundel, when the clergy petitioned that St. George's Day be raised to a major feast as a way to honor England's patron in an appropriate way.[64] The initial request was not fulfilled, but during the convocation of the Province of Canterbury in 1415, the feast was elevated to a double major (duplex majus) feast. The feast thus ranked equal to Christmas; the faithful were to abstain from all manual labor and church attendance was mandatory. Five years later in 1421, St. George's Day was elevated to a major feast in the Province of York, which oversaw the northern half of England.[65] The elevation of the feast in the early part of the fifteenth century marks the beginning of the promotion of the day throughout England, and occurred due to the growing association of St. George with the military and the monarchy during the Hundred Years' War, when St. George became increasingly regarded as the patron and protector of England. It is not coincidental that the elevation of the feast at Canterbury happened only months after the victory at Agincourt in 1415, a resounding success for the English cause in France and one of the greatest victories in the history of England.

In summary, the feast of St. George was first celebrated in England in monasteries across the country. Monastic martyrologies,

---

[62] Cheney, "Rule for the observance of Feast-Days," 139-40.
[63] Cheney, "Rule for the observance of Feast-Days," 138-39, 141-42.
[64] MacGregor, "Salue Martir Spes Anglorum," 179.
[65] MacGregor, "Salue Martir Spes Anglorum," 153.

calendars, and liturgical works included prayers and biographical information for recitation on his feast day. Monastic communities allowed for a reduced amount of labor and an increased level of feasting. Yet April 23 was no different from dozens of other feast days that occupied the liturgical calendar until the fifteenth century, when St. George's feast became a major holy day due to the royal and militaristic significance of the saint.

Monasteries were meant to separate their inhabitants from the world, but the practices and beliefs of monastic communities dramatically impacted the culture of the surrounding areas. The celebration of St. George's Day was no exception. Aelfric's *Lives of Saints* from the late tenth or early eleventh century is one example of how knowledge of St. George extended from monasteries to the outside world. His intention, as stated in the preface, was to spread devotion to saints who were known in the cloister, but not by the laity: "It has pleased me to set forth, in this book, the Passions as well as the Lives of those saints whom not the vulgar, but the monks, honour by special services."[66] Aelfric included a Passion of St. George, written in the vernacular, in his work. On the one hand, the selection of St. George suggests that he was not well-known outside the cloister; on the other hand, the fact that the saint was granted his own chapter demonstrates that he must have been especially revered among the saints celebrated in monastic settings. One purpose of the work was to provide material for sermons that clerics preached on the saint's feast day. Though not intended for the general public to read, it provided a means for commoners to be informed about St. George, for every April 23, those congregated at Mass could hear an account of St. George in the vernacular. Considering the size of the potential audience, it is easy to understand the role Aelfric's work played in spreading the celebration of St. George's Day from monasteries to the general population in the eleventh century.

---

[66] Aelfric, *Lives of Saints*, ed. Walter Skeat, (London: Early English Text Society, 1881), 3.

In addition to monasteries dedicated to St. George, numerous churches had St. George as their patron saint. Frances Arnold-Forster's classic *Studies in Church Dedications* (1899) lists 198 churches dedicated to St. George, of which 120 are pre-Reformation.[67] Jonathan Good examined Arnold-Forster's catalog of churches and found documentary evidence for twenty-seven pre-Reformation churches. He also discovered several churches dedicated to the saint not included by Arnold-Foster. Further investigations should lead to the verification of more churches mentioned by Arnold-Foster and even more churches not included in the classic text. Good speculated that Arnold-Foster's total is not "inflated; if anything it is too modest."[68] Of the documented churches, the oldest are from the tenth century, and churches were most frequently dedicated to St. George during the fourteenth and fifteenth centuries.[69] Returning to Arnold-Forster's data, St. George ranks as the nineteenth most popular patron of pre-Reformation churches in England, with only 1 percent of all churches dedicated to him.[70] One possible explanation of the low percentage is the relatively late development of his cult in England as most churches were dedicated to St. George in the Late Middle Ages. In relationship to the feast of St. George, churches dedicated to St. George would likely celebrate the feast of their patron saint with great pomp, and an increasing number of churches dedicated to St. George correlated to a rise in the prominence of his feast.

Pilgrimages to a holy site were another form of religious activity occurring regularly on the feast of St. George. No one epicenter of the cult of St. George existed as he never visited England and his body was not buried in England. No shortage of places, however, claimed to have a relic of the saint. The Augustinian priory at

---

[67] Frances Arnold-Forster, *Studies in Church Dedications; Or, England's Patron Saints* (London: Skeffington & Son, 1899).

[68] Good, *The Cult of St. George*, 98-99.

[69] Good, *The Cult of St. George*, 160.

[70] Good, *The Cult of St. George*, 162.

Haltemprice, visited frequently by pilgrims, allegedly had his arm.[71] People also flocked to an image of St. George in Looe before the Reformation, and a pilgrim, William Kendal, noted that on the feast of the saint a crowd of over a hundred people came to see the image immediately before the religious upheavals of the sixteenth century. Kendal lived two miles away from the chapel at Looe, and he walked the distance to participate in the devotions.[72] In John Heywood's play *The Four PP* from the 1530s, a character's recitation of a list of well-known shrines in England includes "St. George in Suthwarke."[73] St. George's Chapel in Windsor was also a place of pilgrimage, and by the mid-fifteenth century, it claimed to possess St. George's two fingers, his arm, a piece of his skull, and his heart. In 1349, an effort was made to promote pilgrimages to Windsor by petitioning for an indulgence, and Pope Clement VI fulfilled the request by granting an indulgence to any pilgrim who visited the chapel on the feast of St. George. Even with this supernatural benefit, Windsor never became a major pilgrimage destination.[74]

The *Anglo-Saxon Chronicle*, a work documenting the history of the Anglo-Saxons, contains a small piece of evidence about St. George's Day. The chronicle began during the reign of Alfred the Great in the ninth century and was continuously updated until the twelfth century. One section mentions the death of Ethelred in 1016, and remarks, "He ended his days on St. George's Day."[75] This short reference to St. George's Day does not reveal much about the celebration of the feast, but it is significant because it uses St. George's Day in a new context as a marker of time. The *Anglo-Saxon Chronicle* is not a religious text,

---

[71] James Gairdner, ed., *Letters and papers, foreign and domestic, of the reign of Henry VIII* (London: Eyre and Spottiswoode, 1887), 10:139.

[72] Robert Whiting, *The Blind Devotion of the People: Popular Religion and the English Reformation*, Cambridge studies in early modern British history (Cambridge: Cambridge University Press, 1989), 54.

[73] Duffy, *The Stripping of the Altars*, 192.

[74] MacGregor, "Salue Martir Spes Anglorum," 218; William Henry Bliss, ed., *Calendar of Entries in the Papal Registers Relating to Great Britain and Ireland: Petitions to the Pope, A.D. 1342-1419* (London: Eyre and Spottiswoode, 1896), 1:265-66.

[75] *The Anglo-Saxon Chronicle*, ed. James Ingram, trans. James H. Ford (Texas: El Paso Norte Press, 2005), 110.

and it was written in the vernacular. The use of St. George's Day here reveals an increasing awareness of the feast outside of the religious world because of the expectation that the secular world would know the date of St. George's Day.

The early cult of St. George in England is shrouded in mystery, but a few conclusions can be drawn from examining the evidence. The date when St. George's Day became a national celebration occurred later than previously postulated. On the one hand, the two most cited pieces of evidence for an early celebration of St. George's Day are Bede's *Martyrology* and the declaration of the Synod of Oxford. In both cases, historians have argued convincingly that St. George's feast was not originally included in these documents, which nullifies their significance in determining the rise of St. George's Day. On the other hand, evidence from monastic calendars and liturgical works demonstrates that St. George's Day was celebrated in liturgies from around the end of the first millennium, but it was not until the fifteenth century that St. George's Day was elevated to a major feast day of national significance.

During the medieval period, the feast of St. George was celebrated primarily on the local level. The strongest cults to the saint centered on monasteries and churches dedicated to St. George, and these areas were probably the first to celebrate St. George's feast as a holiday. Southwest England had the highest concentration of religious institutions dedicated to St. George, but churches under his patronage were located throughout the country.[76] Variances in monastic calendars also demonstrate that the elevation of the feast was not accomplished in unison. Moreover, local church councils decided upon the level of feast days. The Synod of Oxford and the Convocation of Canterbury, for example, did not speak for the entire church in England, and thus, it is anachronistic to use their proclamations as

---

[76] Good, *The Cult of St. George*, 161.

evidence for the creation of April 23 as a national day. The religious feast accordingly does not provide evidence for English nationalism in the medieval period.

Lastly, St. George's Day was initially a religious holiday. The day was meant to commemorate the martyrdom of a saint and to ask for his intercession. Religious leaders celebrated the feast and promoted the holy day. Celebrations were marked by the recitation of prayers, attendance at church, and mandatory reprieve from work. Early festivities made no mention of the hallmarks of later celebrations, such as his military connection, his battle with the dragon, or his association with the English nation.

Chapter Two
A Royal Celebration:
St. George as Knight

During the course of the Crusades and the Hundred Years' War, the image of St. George transformed from a martyr to a knight. The new warrior image of St. George was most evident in accounts of his apparitions on the battlefield as he reportedly appeared numerous times in the thick of an engagement to aid English troops. The battle of Agincourt, one of England's greatest victories, was no exception. The "Carol of St. George" written in the middle of the fifteenth century retells the story of the battle:

> He keped the mad from dragon's dred,
> And fraid all France and put to flight.
> At Agincourt - the crownecle ye red -
> The French him see foremost in fight.
>
> In his virtu he wol us lede
> Againis the Fend, the ful wight,
> And with his banner us oversprede,
> If we him love with all oure might.[1]

St. George also allegedly came to the aid of the English in physical form at Antioch and Jerusalem during the Crusades. In this manifes-

---

[1] R. T. Davies, *Medieval English Lyrics: A Critical Anthology* (London: Faber and Faber, 1987), 185.

tation of a warrior saint, he became known as the protector and defender of England, and he rose to become one of the most called upon heavenly intercessors for the monarchy and army. Consequently, his feast expanded in significance throughout the Late Middle Ag-Ages.

Religious celebrations on St. George's Day continued in monasteries, churches, and cathedrals, but beginning in the fourteenth century, the warrior class developed a parallel set of festivities, with the monarch and nobility of England taking the lead in promoting the feast day. The royal celebration emphasized the martial qualities of the saint but retained traditional religious elements as he was still viewed as a martyr and heavenly intercessor for those on earth. In other words, St. George's role as a warrior did not replace his status as a martyr, but the two functions, warrior and martyr, were combined in one saint, widening his appeal. The primary purpose of royal celebrations continued to be religious and consisted of venerating St. George in order to gain his protection for the monarchy and England.

This chapter explores the evolution of St. George's Day into a royal celebration focused on a warrior saint. The new role of St. George began with the Crusades when Western knights were exposed to the cult of Eastern warrior saints, and they repeatedly invoked the intercession of St. George on the battlefield. The role of the Crusades in the elevation of St. George's Day, however, has been overstated. English knights participated in the Crusades in a limited fashion, and evidence does support the reputed connection between Richard I and St. George. The growth of the cult of St. George should rather be attributed to Edward III and the Hundred Years' War. During the war, Edward created the Order of the Garter, and the feast of St. George was second only to Christmas in the royal household. Outside of the Garter, St. George's Day was also the occasion of royal marriages, burials, plays, and processions.

St. George's transition to a military saint led to an increased devotion to him in the Late Middle Ages, and the Crusades provide the most likely explanation for initiating this shift. St. George had been revered as a military saint in the East before the Crusades due to his status as a soldier in the Roman army, and the Crusaders brought the warrior image of St. George back from the East when they returned home. Moreover, devotion to St. George increased as a result of numerous apparitions of the saint during key battles.

However, the first of these reported apparitions occurred prior to the Crusades. Before reclaiming the Holy Land, Norman armies fought Muslims in Sicily, and St. George is said to have appeared to the Normans at the battle of Cerami in 1063. According to *The Deeds of Count Roger* (1090s) by Geoffrey Malaterra: "A certain knight, magnificent in his armor, mounted on a white horse and carrying a white standard with a splendid cross on it tied to the tip of his lance" appeared and led the army to victory.[2]

Indirect evidence also suggests that St. George was revered as a knight in England before the Crusades. Orderic Vitalis in *The Ecclesiastical History* (early twelfth century) described the activity of the cleric Gerold: "He made a great collection of tales of the combats of holy knights, drawn from the Old Testament and more recent records of Christian achievements, for them to imitate. He told them vivid stories of the conflicts of Demetrius and George, of Theodore and Sebastian, of the Theban legion and Maurice its leader, and of Eustace, supreme commander of the army and his companions, who won the crown of martyrdom in heaven."[3] Gerold composed his collection of stories before the Crusades, yet he refers to St. George as a holy knight. The apparition of St. George in Sicily to the Normans might be responsible for this early Norman reference to St. George as a military saint in England. Prior to this reference, St. George was previously unknown as a knight in England. The apparition in Sicily is

---

[2] Geoffrey Malaterra, *The Deeds of Count Roger of Calabria and Sicily and of His Brother Duke Robert Guiscard*, trans. Kenneth Baxter Wolf (Ann Arbor: University of Michigan Press, 2005), 21.
[3] Orderic Vitalis, *The Ecclesiastical History*, ed. Marjorie Chibnall (Oxford: Clarendon Press, 1972), 3:217.

notable for introducing a warrior image of St. George into England, and it is also the first time St. George appeared to aid a Western army fighting a Muslim foe, which later became a familiar theme. St. George's pre-Crusades status as a knight is also evident in the Anglo-Norman *Laudes Regiae*, a litany chanted on solemn feast days to seek the intercession of the saints. Versions of the litany composed by the Normans in the late eleventh century invoke St. George with Sts. Maurice and Sebastian as the protectors of all lords and soldiers of England.[4]

The Crusades provided additional opportunities for St. George to be portrayed as a warrior saint. When the Crusaders traversed the Byzantine Empire, they were introduced to the older cults of the Eastern warrior saints: Demetrius, George, Theodore, and Maurice. These saints were known in Western Europe as demonstrated by Gerold's list of warrior saints and the Anglo-Norman *Laudes Regiae*, but their cults were not as developed as in the East, nor were they primarily seen as military figures. The Crusaders needed new models of holy warriors for intercession during their battles, and they looked to Eastern warrior saints for inspiration. Traditionally, saints in the West were limited to martyrs of the Roman persecution and confessors that practiced heroic asceticism, but the restrained suffering and death of the early martyrs and confessors were incompatible with the undertakings of Christian warriors of the eleventh century. The void was filled by the Crusaders with Eastern warrior saints, and in particular, St. George stood out for veneration during the First Crusade.

As previously stated, the inspiration for devotion to St. George emerged from a series of miraculous apparitions of the saint during battles. After passing through Constantinople, the Crusaders took the city of Antioch in 1098, following a long and difficult siege. As soon as the city was taken, a relieving army attacked the Crusaders at Antioch. The anonymous *Gesta Francorum* contains a description of the fighting. During the heat of the battle, "Appeared from the moun-

---

[4] MacGregor, "Salue Martir Spes Anglorum," 62-63.

tains a countless host of men on white horses, whose banners were all
white. When our men saw this, they did not understand what was
happening or who these men might be, until they realized that this
was the succor sent by Christ, and that the leaders were St. George,
St. Mercurius and St. Demetrius."[5] The heavenly spirits are described
as inspiring the knights of the Crusades to victory. The *Gesta Francorum* also recounts that the Crusaders visited the town of Ramleh,
and that they believed in the town's church rested "the most pre-
cious" body of St. George. In their reverence for the saint, the
Crusaders selected a bishop for the town to "protect and build up"
the church.[6]

Stories associated with St. George and the Crusades appeared in
two popular twelfth-century English works, even though few English
knights participated in the First Crusade. William of Malmesbury's
Gest Regum Anglorum and Henry of Huntingdon's *Historia Anglorum*
contain *Gesta Francorum*'s account of St. George's apparition and the
visit to Ramleh with only slight variations. At about the same time,
the first visual representations of St. George appeared in English
churches. A church in Hardham, Sussex, has wall paintings of St.
George in battle, dating from around 1135. A carving in the church of
Fordington in Dorset contains a scene of St. George's apparition at
Antioch, and Damerham, Hampshire has an image thought to be St.
George on horseback trampling a fallen foe. By the mid-twelfth century, this evidence suggests that the English were aware of the events
of the First Crusade, and St. George was increasingly revered as a
military saint in England.[7]

Epic poems produced after the military engagements augmented
the role of St. George in the Crusades. These romances extended and
embellished the apparitions of St. George, and they helped extend

---

[5] *Gesta Francorum The Deeds of the Franks and the Other Pilgrims to Jerusalem,* ed. Rosalind Hill,
Oxford medieval texts (Oxford: Oxford University Press, 1972), 69.
[6] *Gesta Francorum,* 87.
[7] Good, *The Cult of St. George,* 77; Riches, *St. George,* 20, 23-24.

devotion to St. George beyond the halls of the cloister to the general public. The Crusade cycle written in old French—*Chanson d'Antioche* and *Chanson de Jerusalem*—particularly increased the role of St. George. Graindor de Douai composed the editions that we know today in the late twelfth century, but these themselves were based on works from the early twelfth century.[8]

In *Chanson d'Antioche*, St. George is said to have made three appearances, rather than the single apparition in the chronicles: at the battle of Doryleum, en route to Antioch, and during the defense of Antioch. In addition, the role of St. George changed from bystander to more active participant, and even leader of the heavenly force. The account includes additional information about devotion to St. George, recounting that Robert of Flanders, a leading Crusader, acquired a relic of the arm of St. George and went by the title, "Files saint Jorje."[9] *Chanson de Jerusalem* recounts the taking of Jerusalem in 1099 from Islamic forces. This account is the first to include St. George in the siege and battle for Jerusalem, and thus it fundamentally differs from all previous versions of the engagement. In *Chanson de Jerusalem*, St. George reportedly appeared three times in the story: at a battle in Lydda before Jerusalem is captured, while defending Jerusalem after it is captured, and at the battle of Ramla. The account is also unique because in it the Crusaders are said to have prayed to St. George before the battle. In earlier chronicles, St. George appeared without any invocations, but in later works, the Crusaders actively sought his intercession.[10] St. George also appeared in the *Chanson d'Aspremont*, a version of the Song of Roland composed in 1190, in which he led and assisted Roland in battle.[11] This reference in *Chanson*

[8] Geoffrey Meyers, "The Manuscripts of the Old French Cycle," in *The Old French Crusade Cycle: Volume I*, eds. Emanuel J. Mickel and Jan A. Nelson (Tuscaloosa: University of Alabama Press, 1977), xv.

[9] *La Chanson d'Antioche*, ed. Jan A. Nelson, (Tuscaloosa: University of Alabama Press, 2003), 124, 142, 254, 338; MacGregor, "Salue Martir Spes Anglorum," 87-89.

[10] *The Old French Crusade Cycle Volume VI: La Chanson De Jérusalem*, ed. Nigel Thorp (Tuscaloosa: University of Alabama Press, 1991), 52-54, 167, 232, 245-46.

[11] *La Chanson d'Aspremont*, trans. Michael A. Newth, (New York: Garland Publishing, 1989), 203-6; MacGregor, "Salue Martir Spes Anglorum," 93-94.

d'Aspremont, which is *not* from the Crusades, demonstrates that St. George's status as the archetypical warrior saint extended beyond the battles in the Holy Land, and his popularity had increased due to the stories of heavenly aid in battle. Although he appeared with other warrior saints, St. George typically led the heavenly forces, and therefore, his cult spread more than other warrior saints in the West.

One common misconception about the cult of St. George is that he acquired the role of protector of England and the English monarchy during the Third Crusade. Unlike the First Crusade, the English had a large contingent in the Third Crusade, and an English king, Richard I, known as the Lionheart, was one of its leaders. The French chronicler, Ambroise, documented only three references to St. George in his narrative of the crusade. Twice during the battle of Arsuf, knights, not Richard, called out for St. George's aid. They invoked the saint once before the battle, and again at the beginning of the battle. Richard only made one remark in reference to the saint, "The king, in the name of St. George, had the horses fed with barley."[12]

Later works overstate the importance of St. George during the reign of Richard. One event often associated with the Third Crusade is St. George's apparition to Richard during the siege of Acre in 1191. The vision, however, is not in any of the contemporary accounts, and the story first appeared in a historical work during the reign of Henry VIII in the sixteenth century. The story was most likely a fabrication for political purposes.[13] A possible source for the vision is *Richard Coer de Lyon*, a French romance composed in the middle of the thirteenth century and later translated into English. It relates how Richard praying for assistance before the battle of Arsuf, experienced a vision of St. George charging into battle that renewed his planned attack.[14] A

---

[12] Ambroise, *The History of the Holy War*, trans. Marianne Ailes (Woodbridge: Boydell Press, 2003), 118, 170.
[13] Laborderie, "Richard the Lionheart and the Birth of A National Cult of St. George," 45-47.
[14] MacGregor, "Salue Martir Spes Anglorum," 102.

second link between Richard and the cul'
ard reputedly rebuilt the church of St. C
saint's tomb. Undoubtedly, the Crusade.
and they were aware of the location of his .
recount that Richard was in Lydda for six wee.
Crusade. However, no contemporary accounts menu
of the church, and it seems unlikely that such a feat coula
plished in six weeks, the length of Richard's stay in Lydda.[15]

The Crusades had a lasting impact on the cult of St. George in th.
West. In particular, the reported apparitions of St. George helped
refashion him into the ideal knight, and his popularity rose dramatically among the martial classes of medieval England. The Crusades,
however, did not cause St. George to become patron of England, and
the role of Richard and the Third Crusade in the promotion of St.
George's cult was minimal.

Royal devotion to St. George rose to the forefront during the Hundred Years' War (1337-1453), and more specifically, during the reign
of Edward III (r. 1327-1377). The central vehicle for devotion to St.
George was the Order of the Garter, founded by Edward around
1348. The principal reason for the founding of the Garter was to
unite the nobles behind the monarchy and guarantee their loyalty in
the war with France. This knightly fraternity was the most prestigious
in England, and St. George was its principal patron.

The romantic story about the founding of the Garter is often repeated in popular works on chivalry. In the story, a lady at court,
often the Countess of Salisbury, had her garter fall to the ground. She
was quite embarrassed, and Edward wished to save her honor. He
took the garter, fastened it on his leg, and then proclaimed that he
would use the garter as the symbol of his new order of knights. He
then issued the famous phrase, "Honi soit qui mal y pense" (dishonored be he who thinks evil of it), which became the motto of the

---

[15] Laborderie, "Richard the Lionheart and the Birth of A National Cult of St. George," 43.

This highly romanticized account was first recorded in Joanot ell's *Tirant lo Blanc,* written in the late fifteenth century, and it urther developed in Polydore Vergil's *Anglica Historia,* published 1534. The story serves as an interesting legend, but limited evidence supports its veracity. The actual events surrounding the origins of the Garter are hard to discern because of a lack of sources. Official records for the order are not available until 1416, when Henry V ordered the start of an official register.[16] Before this date, historians must rely on contemporary chronicles and chance references in accounts of the wardrobe and exchequer.[17]

Edward's first attempt to found a knightly order came in 1344. At a great tournament at Windsor in January of that year, the king announced that he was going to found an order based on King Arthur and the Knights of the Round Table. The plan outlined by Edward called for a brotherhood of 300 knights and a major expansion of Windsor castle to serve as the home for the order. The plans for the knightly order stalled because the war against France consumed the monarch, and over the next two years, Edward campaigned continuously on the continent. When he returned to England and resumed the project, he made some fundamental changes to the structure of the order.

The exact date of the founding of the new order, the Order of the Garter, is unclear because of the dearth of sources. Researchers have been able to piece together some information using chance references to the order.[18] According to these references, the first evidence for a new order was in 1348. Letters patent from August 6, 1348, state that

---

[16] Preserved in John Anstis, *The Register of the Most Noble Order of the Garter: Usually Called the Black Book* (London: John Barber, 1724).

[17] Hugh Collins, *The Order of the Garter 1348-1461: Chivalry and Politics in Late Medieval England* (Oxford: Clarendon, 2000), 270-71.

[18] See Collins, *The Order of the Garter;* Juliet Vale, *Edward III and Chivalry: Chivalric Society and Its Context, 1270-1350* (Woodbridge: Boydell Press, 1982); D'Arcy Jonathan Dacre Boulton, *The Knights of the Crown: The Monarchical Orders of Knighthood in Later Medieval Europe 1325-1520* (Woodbridge: Boydell, 1987); Peter J. Begent and Hubert Chesshyre, *The Most Noble Order of the Garter* (London: Spink, 1999).

the chapel at Windsor was rededicated to St. George and the college of St. George was established. The first meeting of the Garter took place, at the very latest, in 1349, for Hugh de Courtenay, one of its original knights, died in September 1349. In addition, receipts from 1349 mention the purchase of twenty-four robes with garters.[19]

One important change from the original concept was a shift away from an Arthurian emphasis, to a religious order with St. George as the principal patron. Initially, the Garter fell under the patronage of the Virgin Mary, St. Edward, and St. George, but soon after its founding, St. George became its primary patron. At first, St. George does not appear to be the likely choice for the patron of the preeminent knightly order in England. The selection of a native of England, such as St. Edward, St. Edmund, or St. Thomas Beckett should have been more appealing. Why, then, did Edward select St. George as the principal patron for this prestigious order? Evidence suggests that most importantly, St. George was a warrior saint, and as such, an apt patron for a chivalric order. Furthermore, his cult as a warrior grew due to the Crusades, with knightly orders dedicated to him in Hungary, Aragon, Genoa, Burgundy, Holland, and Germany.[20] Elias Ashmole detailed St. George's role as universal patron of knights in his seventeenth-century history of the Garter, in which he argued that Edward selected St George as patron of the order because the saint was "the principal patron of the affairs of Christendom, and a tutelary guardian of military men, yet among all Christians the English did excel, and in this nation the founder of the order, in making choice of such an approved expert captain and patron."[21] In the fourteenth century, St. George was, therefore, not exclusively the patron of English knights, but all Christian knights. Furthermore, Edward was also inspired by John, duke of Normandy (later John II of France), who was planning a fraternity of knights dedicated to St. George and the Virgin Mary.

---

[19] Vale, *Edward III and Chivalry,* 83-84.

[20] Fox, *Saint George,* 100.

[21] Elias Ashmole, *The Institution, Laws and Ceremonies of the Most Noble Order of the Garter* (London: T. Dring, 1693), 130.

Similarities between the structure of John's planned order and that of
the Garter points to some level of borrowing by the English monarch. St. George was later abandoned by the French as a patron, when
the Order of the Star was founded in 1352.[22] Thus, the selection of St.
George as patron of the Garter is only understandable in an international, and particularly French, context.[23] Lastly, the replacement of
Arthur by St. George introduced a religious element into the Garter,
with the saint providing intercessory power for members of the Garter in the afterlife and for English knights on the battlefield.

The use of the garter as the symbol of the order was another innovation. The romantic version of the story emphasizing the
monarch's chivalry in dealing with a lady was likely a later invention,
and the true origin of the symbol lay in Edward's campaigns in
France. In this case, the garter was more of an arming buckle used in
battle to identify combatants than a piece of female underwear, and
the knot on the garter was a symbol of knightly unity. Edward frequently used the garter as a symbol, and after his resounding victory
at Crecy, he probably decided to incorporate it into his new order.
The relationship between the garter and the campaigns in France is
further demonstrated by its color and the motto of the fraternity. The
garter was blue and gold, the royal colors of France, and the motto,
"dishonored be he who thinks evil of it," referred to the English
claim for the throne of France, not the appearance of an article of
female underwear in public.[24]

The tradition of wearing blue on St. George's Day almost certainly started due to the color of the garter. The old custom of wearing
blue is first referred to in Lording Barry's play *Ram Alley* from 1611.

---

[22] Boulton, *The Knights of the Crown*, 174-77.
[23] D. A. L. Morgan, "The Banner-bearer of Christ and Our Lady's Knight: How God became
an Englishman revisited," in *St George's Chapel, Windsor, in the Fourteenth Century*, ed. Nigel Saul
(Woodbridge, Suffolk: Boydell Press, 2005), 51-62; D. A. L. Morgan, "The cult of St George
c.1500: national and international connotations," *Publications du Centre Européen d'Etudes Bourguignonnes* 35 (1995): 151-62.
[24] Collins, *The Order of the Garter*, 11-12.

One of the characters, Captain Face, remarks, "By Dis I will be knight, wear a blue coat on great St. George's Day, and with my fellows drive you all from Paul's." Thomas Freeman's *The Second Bowle* (1614) similarly mentions, "With's eorum nomine keeping greater away, Than a Court blew coat on St. George's Day."[25] The knights of the Garter's practice of wearing blue on St. George's Day thus spread to other segments of the population, and subsequently, created a new tradition.

The structure of the Garter was simpler than the originally planned Knights of the Round Table. The size of the project had to be scaled back due to the financial demands of the wars with France and the chaos caused by the Black Death. Edward also changed the planned meeting area for the knights of the Garter, deciding to rededicate the chapel at Windsor, rather than build a new meeting hall. The chapel, built in honor of St. Edward, was rededicated to St. George and the Virgin Mary in 1348, and the chapel became the center of activity for the order. The number of knights was also reduced to twenty-six from the original three hundred knights, which included the monarch and Prince of Wales. A college of St. George was also established to provide for the religious needs of the Garter. In residence at Windsor, the college was composed of a dean, twelve canons, thirteen vicars, four clerks, six choristers, and an usher. Their purpose was to pray for the members of the Garter, say Masses for deceased members, and officiate at liturgies during the annual feast of St. George. Eventually, twenty-six veteran knights were also in residence at Windsor. The number of veteran knights corresponded to the number of companions of the Garter.[26]

The Order of the Garter held their annual feast on St. George's Day in honor of their patron. They met every April 23, and barring a specially called meeting, St. George's Day was the only time members of the order officially gathered. If the feast fell within fifteen days of

---

25 Thomas Henry Dyer, *British Popular Customs, Present and Past* (London: G. Bell, 1900), 193.
26 Collins, *The Order of the Garter*, 29.

Easter, it was moved to another date. The companions of the order were required to attend, and if a knight failed to attend, a fine or penalty would be levied against him. The gathering lasted three days, starting on the eve, and ending the morning following the feast. The festivities included formal meetings of the knights, religious ceremonies, and great banquets.[27]

The knights assembled at Windsor on the eve of the feast of St. George. After gathering, a formal procession filed to the chapter house. Members then discussed the order's internal business, including issues surrounding elections, members' behavior, and disciplinary action against any offenders. Following the close of business, the congregation moved to the chapel to hear vespers. The religious ceremonies were presided over by the bishop of Winchester, the prelate of the Garter. Finally, the eve of the feast ended with a public banquet.

The climax of the assembly was the feast of St. George. The members gathered in the morning, and once assembled, they processed to the chapter house. Another meeting was held to discuss matters of the order and solve disputes between members. The congregation then moved to the chapel for a morning service, after which the knights assembled for the grand procession, which involved processing in state within the chapel of St. George or in the lower courtyard of the castle. During the reign of Henry VIII, the procession moved in the following order: veteran knights, officers of the Garter, prelate with a reliquary containing the heart of St. George accompanied by four men holding a canopy and torches, the sovereign in grand attire, and finally a collection of royal officials and notable lords and ladies. After the procession, high Mass was celebrated in the chapel, and an offertory was made by all present. The offering started with the king, who processed to the altar, knelt down,

---

[27] Collins, *The Order of the Garter,* 195-200; also see Nicholas Harris Nicolas, *History of the Orders of Knighthood of the British Empire* (London: J. Hunter, 1842), 400.

offered gold and silver, received a blessing, and then returned to his
stall. The process was repeated by all the knights of the Garter. The
religious service concluded with the singing of the *Te Deum*. The
knights then returned with the sovereign to his private chambers.
They later congregated in the great hall for a lavish banquet attended
by the knights and members of the royal household. There was ample
food, a call for largesse, orations, and entertainment. The confraterni-
ty then returned to the chapel for vespers, and the day concluded with
supper.[28]

The morning following the feast, the knights gathered again for a
formal procession to the chapter house where they discussed any
matters unresolved in previous meetings. During this session, an individual elected into the order would be summoned and invested with
the garter. The knights then proceeded to the chapel for the final religious ceremony, a requiem Mass offered for deceased members of the
Garter. Following Mass, they made an offering of gold and silver using the same format as the day before. These services concluded the
celebrations for St. George's Day.

The clothing of the knights of the Garter formed an important
and expensive aspect of the yearly gathering. Among the few records
that survive from the founding of the Garter are the accounts of the
Great Wardrobe. These accounts recorded the purchase of material
needed for elaborate costumes worn on the celebration of St.
George's Day. Early records include purchases of velvet, wool cloth,
taffeta, silk, and furs.[29] Every year a new livery was produced for the
festivities, consisting of a surcoat and a hood worn over a mantle. The
cloth was initially woolen but later changed to silk or velvet, and the
most commonly used colors were white, blue, sanguine, and scarlet.[30]
In addition to the knights, the ladies of the Garter, the canons, the
alms knights, and members of the royal household periodically re-

---

[28] The rules for the feast can be found in Ashmole, *The Institution, Laws and Ceremonies of the Most Noble Order of the Garter*, 465-612.

[29] Collins, *The Order of the Garter*, 204.

[30] Boulton, *The Knights of the Crown*, 162; Nicholas Harris Nicolas, *History of the Orders of Knighthood of the British Empire* (London: J. Hunter, 1842), ii, 341-46.

ceived special robes and mantles. Those members of the Garter who could not attend the yearly gathering still had to wear the mantle of the Garter on the feast of St. George.[31]

The knights' livery was only one of the major expenses of the festivities. Others included the sending of letters and messengers to all the members of the Garter and leading lords of England requesting their attendance at the celebration. The chapel, chapter house, and great hall needed to be decorated. Accommodations also had to be made for the royal family, the knights, and all the guests attending the feast. The largest expense for the festivities was the buttery, which purchased the wine, mead, and ale; the kitchen, which paid for the food, had the second highest total. The last major expense was entertainment, consisting of payments to minstrels, dancers, and players.[32]

The total expense of St. George's Day festivities reveals the importance of the holiday to the royal household. In *The Order of the Garter* (2000), Hugh Collins examined the diet books of the royal household and compared the expenses of St. George's Day to other holidays. According to his calculations, the average daily expense for the feast of St. George's Day was £150, compared to £20 - £40 for non-feast days. The only feast that rivaled the spending on St. George's Day was Christmas. In 1373, £161 15s 7d were spent on St. George's Day, and £236 15s 6d on Christmas. In 1404, the sum for St. George's Day was £211 11s, which was close to the £224 18s spent on Christmas. The next closest holiday was Easter, with an expenditure of £160 2s 10d. The three costliest celebrations of 1437 were Christmas at £145, St. George's Day at £144, and Pentecost at £77. In purely monetary terms, the celebration of St. George's Day in the late fourteenth and early fifteenth centuries was the second most important holiday, surpassed only by Christmas.

---

[31] Collins, *The Order of the Garter*, 27.
[32] Collins, *The Order of the Garter*, 204-7.

The Garter regularly celebrated St. George's Day even during wars and the absence of the monarch. The regular yearly gatherings followed the outlined formula for the festivities, but occasions such as the installation of a new member or the presence of a distinguished guest called for an elevated celebration. One grand celebration of the order took place in 1358 when John II of France was present as a prisoner. As mentioned previously, as Duke of Normandy, he had planned to form an order of knights under the patronage of St. George, and his model may have served as inspiration for the English order. In 1356, he was captured at the Battle of Poitiers in the Hundred Years' War and brought back to England as a prisoner. While imprisoned, he was treated as a royal figure and participated in gatherings of the Garter. In light of his special guest, Edward III wanted a truly extravagant celebration. Before the feast, a proclamation was sent throughout England inviting an extensive list of guests. According to the chronicles, "The duke of Brabant, the queen of Scotland, and an infinite number of knights and ladies of all nations, were present on the splendid occasion."[33] The king gave £500 to his wife, Philippa, to prepare her attire for the feast of St. George. John, the prisoner guest, said in scorn, "That he saw never so royal a feast, and so costly made, with tallies of tree, without paying of gold and silver."[34]

The greatest celebration of the feast of St. George under the auspices of the Garter, however, occurred in 1416. The distinguished guest was Emperor Sigismund of Germany, who was on a diplomatic trip attempting to broker a peace agreement between the French and English. The feast was postponed because of its proximity to Easter, which fell on April 19 that year. The emperor arrived in Dover on May 1, and his procession from the coast to London lasted until May 7. Greeted by numerous members of the royal family, important nobles, and church officials along the way, he was accompanied by a

---

[33] George Frederick Beltz, *Memorials of the Order of the Garter* (London: William Pickering, 1841), 5.
[34] Beltz, *Memorials of the Order of the Garter*, 5.

distinguished retinue, including 800 imperial cavalry. Henry V (r. 1413-1422) received Sigismund when he reached London. Towards the end of May, the knights of the Garter gathered to celebrate their annual feast. During the festivities, Sigismund was elected a knight of the Garter and invested with the symbols of the order. Henry even gave Sigismund the first place of honor at the festival table. Contemporaries described the feast, "The finery of the guests, the order of the servants, the variety of the courses, the inventions of the dishes, with the other things delightful to the sight and taste, whoever should endeavour to describe could never do it with justice."[35] Sigismund also brought the alleged heart of St. George and a large piece of his skull to Windsor Chapel as a gift. From this point, the relics became a central element of the devotion to St. George at Windsor, and they were carried in procession on the feast of St. George until the reign of Henry VIII.[36]

The festivities of 1416 included the presentation of three pastries, known as sotelties, detailing the legend of St. George. The following is a summary of the three: "And the first *Sotelte* was our Lady arming saint George, and an angel putting on his spurs; the second *sotelte* was saint George riding and fighting with the Dragon, with his spear in his hand; the third *sotelte* was a castle, and saint George and the king's daughter leading the lamb in at the castle gates. And all these *sotelties* were served to the Emperor and to the King, and no further, and other lords were *served* with other *sotelties* after their degrees."[37] For generations, historians have debated the nature of the sotelties. Some nineteenth-century historians of theater thought they were dramatic performances, and numerous works on St. George have repeated this error.[38] Sotelte can be most likely translated as subtlety, an ornate

---

[35] Robert S. Rait, *Royal Palaces of England* (New York: James Pott & Co, 1911), 111.

[36] "The Emperor Sigismund at Windsor," in *The Retrospective Review*, vol. 2 (London: John Russell Smith, 1854), 233-249.

[37] "The Emperor Sigismund at Windsor," 244.

[38] For example, see John Payne Collier, *The History of English Dramatic Poetry* (London: J. Murray, 1831), 20.

pastry or dessert. The banquet in 1416 probably had three courses of food, and each course was followed by a subtlety decorated with a scene from the life of Saint George.[39]

The royal family celebrated St. George in numerous other festivals outside the feast of the Order of Garter, the most well-known being the plays of St. George in Coventry. The city was famous for its pageants, and numerous members of the royal family attended the performances. Coventry is also connected to St. George as the legendary place of his birth, and it had a chapel in his honor and an annual procession to him. In 1456, Queen Margaret visited the city, and a pageant was held during her visit. Toward the end of the performance a great dragon appeared, but St. Margaret, not St. George, slew the dragon.[40] St. Margaret most likely replaced St. George in this play because St. Margaret shared her name with the queen. St. George, however, made a prominent appearance in the performances for Prince Edward and Prince Arthur. Prince Edward visited Coventry on April 28, 1474, only five days after the feast of St. George. The city put on a dramatic performance as part of the royal visit, and a detailed account was left of the plays. Near the end of the pageant, an armed St. George appeared. Before him were a young princess and a lamb threatened by a dragon, and above the saint, the father and mother of the princess watched the scene unfold. St. George defeated the dragon, and then he addressed Prince Edward:

> O mighty god oure all socoure celestiall;
> Wich pis Royme [d] hast gevn to dowere;
> To thi moder and to me George proteccion perpetall;
> Hit to defende from enemies ffere & nere;
> And as this mayden defended was here;
> Bi thy grace from this Dragon devoure;

---

[39] Riches, *St. George*, 110.
[40] The full pageant can be found in Thomas Sharp, *A Dissertation on the Pageants or Dramatic Mysteries Anciently Performed at Coventry* (Totowa, N.J.: Rowman and Littlefield, 1973), 146-151.

So lorde preserue this noble prynce and ever be his so-
coure.[41]

In his speech, St. George declared himself the protector of the
prince, stating that he will defend the prince as he defended the maid-
en. The pageant demonstrates St. George's distinctive role as patron
and protector of the royal family. A similar pageant occurred when
Prince Arthur visited Coventry on October 17, 1498. The performances started with speeches from King Arthur and the Queen of
Fortune. St. George then appeared and killed the dragon, most likely,
after a mock battle. Once the fighting finished, St. George gave a
speech:

That named am George your patron fauorable
To whom ye are & euer shalbe so acceptable
That in felde or Cite where so ever ye rayne
Shall I neuer fayle yewe thus is my purpose playn
To protect your magnyficence my self I shall endevour
In all thynges that your highnes shalt concerne
More tenderly then I sit did ever
Kyng duke yerle lorde or also berne
as ye be myn assistence in processe shall lerne
Which thurgh your vertue most amorous knygh
I owe to your presence be due & very right
like wyse as pis lady be grace I defended
That thurgh myschaunce chosen was to dye
fro this foule serpent whom I sore wonded
So ye in distresse preserue ever woll I
ffro all parell and wyked veleny
That shuld your noble persone in eny wyse distrayne

---

[41] R. W. Ingram, ed., *Records of Early English Drama. Coventry* (Toronto: University of Toronto Press, 1981), 53-54.

Which welcome is to lgis your Chambre & to me right fayn.[42]

The themes of the speech are similar to St. George's discourse to
Edward. St. George called himself the patron of the prince, and he
offered the prince protection. He stated that he will protect the prince
as he protected the lady and will deal with the prince's enemies as he
dealt with the dragon. The pageant provides further affirmation of the
growing connection between St. George and the royalty of England
as a heavenly intercessor.

Coventry was not the only city to welcome a member of the royal
family with a pageant of St. George. When Edward IV entered Bristol, a similar celebration ensued. On September 9, 1461, Edward
came to the city and was greeted by several actors. A performer playing William the Conqueror delivered a short address, and a great giant
presented the newly crowned monarch with the keys of the city. St.
George appeared next on horseback, and he engaged in a mock battle
with the dragon. In a castle above the scene, a king and queen
watched the combat, with their daughter and a lamb far below. St.
George killed the dragon, and after the battle, angels sang a song. In
the Bristol pageant, no record of a speech by St. George exists, but
the connection between the king and St. George is evident based on
the context of similar pageants.[43]

Another pageant of St. George was performed during Henry VII's
visit to Hereford in 1486. Henry arrived in Hereford on May 15 and
stayed for four days in the city as part of a provincial tour. The mayor
and horsemen greeted the monarch a mile outside of the city and
escorted him into the city. Once Henry entered the city, a grand pageant was performed with spoken parts by St. George, King Ethelbert,
and the Virgin Mary. Documents contain no description of a mock
battle with the dragon, but based on the tradition of other royal pag-

---

[42] Ingram, ed., *REED. Coventry*, 90.
[43] Mark C. Pilkinton, ed., *Records of Early English Drama. Bristol* (Toronto: University of Toronto Press, 1997), 7-8.

eants and the speech of St. George, most likely a battle occurred before the speech. St. George was the first to speak:

> Moost Cristen prince And frende unto the faith;
> Supporter of truth confounder of wickedness;
> As people of your Realme holy Reporth And saith;
> Welcome to this Citie Withoute eny feintenesse;
> And thinke verily as ye see her in likenesse;
> That this worme is discomfit by goddess [&] 'ayde' and myn;
> So shall I. be your helpe unto your lives fine;
> To Withstonde your Enemyes with the helpe of that blessed vir-
> gin;
> The Whiche loveth you Right wele I. dar plainly it say;
> wherfor ye be right Welcom I pray god further you in your way.[44]

St. George's speech contains the same offer of protection to the king
found in the other orations, and his address also includes a section
welcoming the monarch to the city because it was the first speech of
the pageant.[45]

St. George's Day was also selected as a date for significant events
in the life of England's royalty. Henry VI married Margaret of Anjou
on April 23, 1445, at the Abbey of St. Mary at Titchfield, Hampshire.[46] In a more somber event, the remains of Prince Arthur were
transferred on St. George's Day. The prince died on April 2, 1502, at
Ludlow Castle. On April 23, the feast of St. George, the body was
taken to the parish church, and then in a great procession, carried to
the Cathedral at Worcester. After a religious ceremony, the remains
were placed in a grave at the south end of the high altar of the cathe-

---

[44] David N. Klausner, ed., *Records of Early English Drama. Herefordshire, Worcestershire* (Toronto: University of Toronto Press, 1990), 144.

[45] Robert Withington, *English Pageantry; An Historical Outline*, (Cambridge: Harvard University Press, 1918), 1:159; Klausner, ed., *REED. Herefordshire, Worcestershire*, 12, 144.

[46] John N. King, *Tudor Royal Iconography: Literature and Art in an Age of Religious Crisis* (Prince-ton: Princeton University Press, 1989), 197.

dral.[47] April 23 was selected for royal events because it was the feast of St. George, and it remained a day for royal marriages and coronations even after the Reformation.

In the Late Middle Ages, the connection between St. George and the sovereign of England expanded. As we have seen, the Crusades and the Hundred Years' War transformed St. George first into a patron of the English military, and then the English monarchy. The Garter and royal activities revolved around St. George's Day, and St. George slowly became associated with more royal symbols. The saint's banner was adopted as the flag of England, his name was shouted on battlefields, and his image graced the coins of England.

One tradition of the English military was to use St. George's name as a battle cry. Froissart's *Chronicles*, which documents the Hundred Years' War, has many references to St. George. At the Battle of Blanchetaque in 1346, Edward III sent his troops into battle "in the name of God and Saint George."[48] At the Siege of Breteuil in 1356, the English garrison shouted, "St. George, Loyalty and Navarre."[49] Edward, the Black Prince, during the Battle of Poitiers in 1356 declared, "Advance, banner, in the name of God and of Saint George."[50] In addition, the chronicler, Thomas of Walsingham, recorded that "at the siege of Calais in 1349 Edward III moved by some sudden impulse drew his sword calling out 'Ha St. Edward! Ha St. George!'"[51] Shakespeare immortalized St. George as part of a battle cry in the play *Henry V* (1599), when the king screamed out to his troops at Harfleur, "God for Harry, England, and Saint George!"[52]

The monarchs of England also began to use the banner of St. George, a red cross on white background, as the flag of England. The

[47] W. Willis-Bund and William Page, *The Victoria History of the County of Worcester* (London: James Street Haymarket, 1906), 2:108.

[48] Jean Froissart, *Chronicles*, trans. Geoffrey Brereton (Harmondsworth: Penguin, 1968), 80.

[49] Froissart, *Chronicles*, 121.

[50] Froissart, *Chronicles*, 136.

[51] William George Smith and Henry Wace, *A Dictionary of Christian Biography, Literature, Sects and Doctrines* (London: J. Murray, 1877), 467.

[52] William Shakespeare, *King Henry V*, ed. T. W. Craik (London: Routledge, 1995), 204.

cross had been used as a military symbol since the time of Constantine, and a red cross was an early Christian symbol that represented either a martyr or the resurrected Christ. The adaptation of the red cross as an English symbol has a complex history, and as with every aspect of the history of St. George, is intertwined with myths. For instance, John Selden, writing in the seventeenth century, claimed with no supporting evidence that King Arthur bore the banner of St. George.[53] The adoption of the banner of St. George by the English was much later, and it occurred through a long and piecemeal process. The English's acceptance of the red cross might have been inspired by the Crusaders' use of the flag, or they may have borrowed it from Genoa, which also used a red cross. The first time English troops carried a red cross into a military engagement was at the battle of Evesham in 1265, during the reign of Henry III. The flag may have been used to contrast with the white cross carried by the opposition, led by Simon de Montfort, and therefore, it might not have been St. George's cross per se.[54] In preparation for Edward I's campaign against the Welsh in 1277, the roll of accounts recorded the purchase of red and white cloth for the manufacture of pennoncels and bracers in the form of the arms of St. George. This is the first explicit reference to the use of the cross of St. George as such in battle.[55] Furthermore, the articles of war drawn out by Richard II in 1385 mandate the wearing of the arms of St. George: "Every man of what estate, condition, or nation he may be, so that he be of our party, shall bear a large sign of the arms of St. George before, and another behind, upon peril that if he be hurt or slain in default thereof, he who shall hurt or slay him shall suffer no penalty for it; and that no enemy shall bear the said sign of St. George, unless he be a prisoner upon

---

[53] Fox, *Saint George*, 71.

[54] Riches, *St. George*, 103.

[55] William Gordon Perrin, *British Flags, Their Early History, and Their Development at Sea; With an Account of the Origin of the Flag As a National Device* (Cambridge: University Press, 1922), 37.

pain of death."[56] These articles of war were the first instance of the whole army being fitted with St. George's cross. The use of St. George's banner was further extended in the reign of Henry V. When Harfleur was captured in 1415, the banner of St. George was displayed alongside royal banners over the town gates. After the battle of Bosworth, Henry VII processed through the streets of London to St. Paul's Cathedral and presented three banners, including that of St. George. For the occasion, he ordered six yards of crimson velvet to construct a cross of St. George. [57] The English's use of St. George's cross, however, was not universal in the Middle Ages. English armies carried the banners of St. Peter of York, St. John of Beverley, and St. Wilfred of Ripon at the Battle of the Standard (1138); the banner of a dragon at Lewes (1216), Crecy (1346), and Bosworth Field (1485); the banner of St. Cuthbert during the Scottish wars of Edward I (1300); and the banners of St. Edmund and St. Edward during the Welsh war of Edward I (1277) and the battle of Carlaverock (1300).[58] During the reign of Henry VIII, the banner of St. George finally eclipsed those of other saints to become the principal flag of England. A painting depicting Henry VIII meeting Emperor Maximilian has the cross of St. George as the only banner of the English. In other sixteenth-century paintings, the English army likewise features only the banner of St. George.[59]

The chapel of St. George at Windsor, the spiritual center of the Garter, was another key element to the royal cult. Originally dedicated to St. Edward, Edward III rededicated it in 1348 to St. George, St. Edward, the Holy Trinity and the Virgin Mary. Soon after the rededication, its other patrons were abandoned in favor of St. George. The chapel was rebuilt by Edward IV starting in 1475 at the yearly cost of a thousand pounds. Edward had recently regained his throne and may have rebuilt the chapel as a sign of thanksgiving to the saint and to

---

[56] William Winthrop, *Military Law* (Washington, D.C.: W. H. Morrison, 1886), 2: Appendix 6.
[57] Riches, *St. George*, 110, 113-14.
[58] Perrin, *British Flags*, 34.
[59] Bengtson, "Saint George and the formation of English nationalism," 332.

cement the legitimacy of his reign.[60] Work on the chapel continued under the new Tudor dynasty, by Henry VII after the War of the Roses, to provide a resemblance of continuity to a situation which otherwise had very little. The image of St. George also began to appear on other royal objects. Henry VIII introduced the George noble, which was a gold coin minted during his reign. It had a depiction of St. George slaying the dragon on one side and Henry VIII on the reverse.[61]

In the fourteenth and fifteenth centuries, the English monarchy adopted St. George as its patron. Subsequently, St. George's Day became one of the most important days in the royal calendar. As argued above, the role of Richard I was minimal in the promotion of St. George. Edward III, the first great royal patron of St. George, was most responsible for increasing the cult of St. George. Henry V and the early Tudor kings were also devoted to St. George. The revised timeline highlights the importance of the Hundred Years' War and diminishes the Crusades as the era when St. George became the main intercessor of the English army and monarchy.

During the Late Middle Ages, English monarchs celebrated St. George's Day as one of their principal holidays, and they built upon the religious feast, which was first celebrated by members of the clergy. The royal celebrations continued many of the elements of religious holy days. The annual meetings of the Garter included Mass, vespers, and prayers for the dead. Conversely, St. George's connection with the military and monarchy was the main reason that the feast was elevated within the religious realm. The English victory at Agincourt, for example, prompted the elevation of the feast of St. George to a double major feast in 1415. Therefore, the rise of St.

---

[60] Bengtson, "Saint George and the formation of English nationalism," 327-28.
[61] Mary Ellen Snodgrass, *Coins and Currency: An Historical Encyclopedia* (Jefferson, N.C.: McFarland, 2003), 147.

George's Day as a religious feast directly correlated to the closeness of St. George and the English monarchy. The feast also provided an opportunity for important religious rituals, such as royal marriages and burials.

The feast continued to emphasize St. George as a heavenly protector. In the religious ceremonies, St. George was referred to as a martyr, and the aim of veneration was to seek his aid in reaching the afterlife. Royal celebrations continued to ask for his intercession and in many ways, those celebrating the feast continued to pray for the deceased to reach heaven. In particular, the Garter was similar to other medieval religious guilds that offered Masses for members who passed away. St. George was also invoked in a new manner as a warrior, and his assistance was sought to bring victory in war. In the pageants, he offered his protection to members of the royal family. On the battlefield, his name was invoked to lead the English to victory, and apparitions of the saint helped defeat enemy forces. St. George, though in a new guise, still acted as a heavenly intercessor, but his popularity increased with the warrior class because he was thought to provide supernatural protection.

The celebration of St. George's Day also gave the monarchy an element of legitimacy. After the reign of Edward III and Henry V, St. George's Day developed into an important royal feast, and future monarchs wanted to continue the tradition in order to appear legitimate. The desire for continuity was particularly true during the chaotic time of the War of the Roses, 1453–1487. The House of Lancaster and the House of York both had devotees to St. George. Edward IV was particularly committed to St. George and was responsible for rebuilding St. George's chapel. After the conflict settled, the Tudors under Henry VII and Henry VIII continued to promote the cult of St. George. The Tudors realized that St. George was not tied to one king or even one family, but St. George was the patron of the English monarchy in general. If they wanted to establish their legitimacy and maintain unity, then they would have to continue venerating the saint and celebrate his feast day. St. George's association with the monarchy also grew, as historian Jonathan Good pointed out, by mere chance that "successful" monarchs—Edward I, Edward III, and Henry V—were devoted to St. George and "unsuccessful" ones—Edward II, Richard II, and Henry VI—were not. Good argues, "St. George, therefore, became a figure that people could use to acknowledge someone as king, or to rebuke a king for not ruling well. Savvy kings came to realize that venerating St. George was expected of them to be taken seriously."[62]

Many advantages accrued to the monarchy from celebrating St. George's Day. The feast unified the kingdom. The Garter helped ensure loyalty among leading nobles in England, and annual celebrations at Windsor facilitated the connection between the sovereign and the most powerful individuals in the realm. Later, English monarchs invested foreign monarchs in the Garter for similar purposes. The monarchy also connected with the people of England through the celebration of St. George. The mock battles of St. George and the dragon were extremely popular with the peasants of medieval England, and commoners produced the pageants of St. George for their ruler. Therefore, St. George and the celebrations of April 23 were an important vehicle that connected the people of England with their sovereign.

---

[62] Good, *The Cult of St. George*, 52.

Chapter Three
A Popular Celebration:
St. George as Dragon-Slayer

J acobus de Voragine's *Legenda Aurea* popularized the familiar story of St. George and the dragon. According to this thirteenth-century source, St. George happened upon an area dominated by a dragon. To abate the monster's fury, defenseless locals gave the beast two sheep every day. When the supply ran low, they transitioned to one human chosen by lot and one sheep. On the day St. George arrived, the king's daughter had been selected for sacrifice. The monarch begged the people to spare his daughter, but they would allow no exceptions. While the princess awaited her fate, St. George came upon her, and inquired why she was so distraught. She informed him about her imminent death, and St. George vowed to protect her. When the dragon appeared, St. George wounded it and asked the princess to place her girdle around the dragon's neck, using it as a leash to bring the dragon into the city. St. George then instructed the townspeople in the Christian faith, and after baptizing them en masse, the triumphant saint slew the dragon and left without any compensation.[1]

In the Late Middle Ages, St. George's Day evolved from a religious and royal feast to a popular holiday. Peasants across England participated in celebrations along with the clergy and nobles. The key ingredient in the development of the popular celebration was the

---

[1] Jacobus de Voragine, *The Golden Legend: Selections*, trans. Christopher Stace (London: Penguin Books, 1998), 116-120.

transformation of St. George into a dragon-slayer as described in the *Legenda Aurea*. Most people today think that St. George and the dragon were always associated, but St. George was revered as a martyr without the dragon story for nearly eight centuries. The image of St. George as a dragon-slayer combined with his status as a martyr and knight produce the famous three faces of the patron of England. The dragon story profoundly impacted the popular celebration of St. George's Day, but peasants and artisans across England still viewed him primarily as a saint. They venerated him on his feast to be healed of illness, to be protected from natural disasters, and most importantly, to avoid punishment in the afterlife. Though the encounter with the dragon changed the composition of the festivals on April 23, the underlying religious meaning remained consistent with earlier celebrations.

The legend of the dragon made St. George a popular figure with the peasants of England, and the story remains a key element in celebrations of St. George's Day to the present day. Yet, it is still not clear how St. George acquired a dragon after eight hundred years without one. Individuals most likely confused the story of St. George with Eastern saints often associated with dragons. The story of St. Michael, who frequently is depicted killing a dragon that symbolizes the devil, could be one source of inspiration. St. Theodore is still another saint frequently portrayed killing a dragon. Eusebius also recorded that Constantine, though not a saint, was often shown with a slain dragon below his feet.[2]

The dragon could be related to the biblical serpent symbolizing the devil, sin, and evil. The Bible contains the story of the serpent in Genesis, in which the beast deceived Eve and was responsible for bringing original sin into the world.[3] Additionally, the Book of Reve-

---

[2] Elder, *George of Lydda*, 20; Fox, *Saint George*, 30, 40; MacGregor, "Salue Martir Spes Anglorum," 78.
[3] Genesis 3: 1-7.

lation relates the story of the dragon which threatened a woman and child, but was defeated by St. Michael and hurled down from heaven.[4] The dragon could also symbolize the king who martyred St. George. Some early accounts of the saint's martyrdom referred to the king as a dragon, centuries before the introduction of the dragon story. For instance, the account attributed to Pasicrates referred to Emperor Galerius as a "dragon," and in the Syriac version, King Dadianus was called the "serpent viper" and "foul and evil dragon."[5] Furthermore, early collections of miracles associated with St. George include the death of Diocletian. According to the accounts, an official of the emperor visited the shire at Lydda, but after breaking a glass lamp before an icon of St. George, he developed leprosy and died. Diocletian then went to Lydda, but the shire was protected by St. Michael, and the emperor was blinded and soon after died. Diocletian's alleged death at the shire of St. George thus provides further evidence for the connection between the dragon and emperor. Early images of St. George also depicted the saint killing a man, not a dragon.[6] Lastly, medieval authors could have been writing about a "real" dragon. Medieval literature has countless stories about dragons and legends of battles with dragons. Individuals living during the medieval period may have believed in dragons and thought St. George's dragon was real, not allegorical.[7]

The story of St. George and the dragon was possibly influenced by stories outside the Christian tradition. Ancient societies have countless stories of heroic figures slaying a beast. In ancient Babylon, Marduk killed Tiamat, and in the Persian tradition, Mithras fatally fought with Ahriman. The Egyptians told the story of Ra killing the monster Apophis. The Anglo-Saxon story of Beowulf chronicles his killing of Grendel. In Germanic legends, the monster-slayer was Siegfried. The Greeks had many myths in the hero-and-beast milieu,

---

[4] Revelation 12: 1-9.
[5] Elder, *George of Lydda*, 20.
[6] Walter, "The Origins of the Cult of St. George," 317.
[7] Fox, *Saint George*, 33.

including Zeus and Typhon, Apollo and Python, and Heracles, who killed Geryon and Hydra.[8] Of all the ancient legends, St. George is most often associated with the Greek legend of Perseus and Andromeda. In that story, Poseidon sends a sea monster to attack the kingdom of Ethiopia. To pacify the monster, Andromeda, the king's daughter, is offered as a sacrifice. Perseus kills the sea monster, saves Andromeda, and then marries her. The similarities between St. George and Perseus are numerous with both killing a monster terrorizing society and saving a princess. The two legends are also connected geographically. St. George's cult was centered at Lydda, not far from the traditional place where Perseus battled with the monster at modern day Jaffa.[9]

To claim St. George is only a Christianized version of these ancient myths would be an overstatement. The gap of eight hundred years between the martyr St. George and the dragon-slayer St. George suggests that the saint was more than a mythical figure adopted by Christians, but some elements of St. George's story might have been borrowed from those pagan legends.

The first evidence of St. George's encounter with the dragon is found in images. Early representations of St. George often depict him as a warrior. One sixth-century image in Bawit, Egypt, shows a cuirass under the saint's cloak and sword on his side, but without a dragon. Early works found in Georgia, though, had St. George on horseback spearing a man, conceivably representing a pagan emperor. The first image of St. George killing a dragon dates from the early eleventh century and is located in the Church of St. Barbara, Soganli Valley, Cappadocia.[10] A coin from the reign of Roger I, prince of Antioch from 1112 to 1119, also depicts St. George on horseback attacking a dragon, and a Greek inscription confirms that the individual is St. George. Moreover, the coin provides the first evidence of Crusader

---

[8] Fox, *Saint George*, 40.
[9] S. Baring-Gould, *Curious Myths of the Middle Ages* (London: Longmans, Green, 1914), 301-2.
[10] Walter, "The Origins of the Cult of St. George," 317-20.

knowledge of St. George as a dragon-slayer.[11] The earliest written account of the dragon story is an eleventh-century Georgian manuscript.[12] Greek versions of the story circulated during the eleventh century are based on the older Eastern tradition, and the earliest Western manuscript with the dragon story is dated to after 1170.[13]

Popularization of the dragon story is attributed to the pastoral guides of the thirteenth century. The thirteenth century gave rise to the mendicant orders of the Dominicans and Franciscans, and those orders placed a greater emphasis on preaching to lay people. To guide local priests in preaching, the mendicants published numerous pastoral guides. The most famous was the *Legenda Aurea*, written by the Dominican Jacobus de Voragine around 1266, and the first copies made their way to England by 1290. Jacobus' work greatly influenced the cult of St. George due to its inclusion of St. George's martyrdom, the assistance St. George provided to the Crusaders, and the dragon story, uniquely containing all three accounts. The *Legenda* was one of the best-sellers of the medieval period; some scholars claim that scribes only produced more copies of the Bible. The abundance of surviving copies, more than 800 Latin manuscripts, demonstrates the wide distribution of the text. The guide was initially intended for the clergy, but soon the *Legenda* was translated into the vernacular and disseminated among the laity. Early versions appeared in French, Spanish, Italian, Dutch, German, Bohemian, Provençal, and many other languages. The *Legenda* was translated into English by an anonymous author in 1438, and famously by William Caxton in 1483.[14] The popularity of the *Legenda* helped create a standard version of St. George's life, and the work placed the episode with the dragon at its center. The *Legenda* thus permanently altered the way St. George was portrayed by emphasizing his chivalry in addition to his faith. In the

---

[11] MacGregor, "Salue Martir Spes Anglorum," 79.
[12] Walter, "The Origins of the Cult of St. George," 321.
[13] MacGregor, "Salue Martir Spes Anglorum," 109.
[14] Sherry L. Reames, *The Legenda Aurea: A Reexamination of Its Paradoxical History* (Madison: University of Wisconsin Press, 1985), 3-4.

first records of the encounter with the dragon, he kills the dragon
with the sign of the cross. In the *Legenda*, the dragon is injured by a
lance and later killed by the sword. Jacobus stressed St. George's martial skills in subduing the dragon and also in his aid offered to the
Crusaders, casting him as a model knight. The work also influenced
the celebration of St. George's Day. Organized chronologically, one
purpose of the book was to provide material for sermons. The section
on St. George in the *Legenda* was read on April 23 in churches and
monasteries across Europe, and thereby, the story in the *Legenda*
spread far beyond the clergy and educated laity, to even the illiterate
masses.

The *South English Legendary*, written at the end of the thirteenth
century, was another popular collection of the lives of the saints.
Composed in the vernacular and meant for the laity, the text was
popular, considering that more than sixty manuscripts exist from before the sixteenth century.[15] The *Legendary* contains a short life of St.
George, primarily focused on his martyrdom.[16] Oddly, it does not
mention that St. George was a warrior, or that he assisted in the Crusades. The introduction states that many people greatly desire to hear
of the battles of kings and knights, but these stories are mainly ficti-
tious.[17] The unknown compiler might have neglected the military
aspects of St. George as a reaction against contemporary interest in
knights supplanting the cult of martyrs and saints. The *Legendary*, similar to the *Legenda*, was used for sermons on feast days, and the work
provides additional evidence that the people of England probably
heard the story of St. George on a yearly basis. The *Legendary* additionally includes a prayer offered by St. George, also found in the *Old
English Martyrology*, to protect people from sickness, hunger and pesti-

---

[15] Anne B. Thompson, *Everyday Saints and the Art of Narrative in the South English Legendary*
(Aldershot: Ashgate, 2003), 3.
[16] *The South English Legendary. Vol. 1, Text*, eds. Anna J. Mill and Charlotte D'Evelyn (London:
Oxford University Press, 1956), 155-59.
[17] *The South English Legendary*, 3.

lence, or on a journey by land or sea, if they keep his feast day. The fourteenth century, thus, had two competing accounts of St. George: the knight version found in the *Legenda,* and the martyr version found in the *Legendary.* In the end, the knight and dragon-slayer proved more popular than the martyr.[18]

The *Legenda* influenced future pastoral guides, including the *Speculum Sacerdotale.* Only an early fifteenth-century manuscript of *Speculum Sacerdotale* survives, and it contains the story of St. George's martyrdom and his battle with the dragon. It relied heavily on the *Legenda* for the story of the dragon, but was influenced by other works for its account of the martyrdom.[19] Another pastoral guide influenced by the *Legenda* was John Mirk's *Festial.* Mirk, an Augustinian canon, composed the work between 1382 and 1390 as a manual written in the vernacular to aid with preaching. The use of the vernacular made it popular with clergy unskilled in Latin. Shorter than the *Legenda, Festial* was cheaper and more accessible. Twenty-six manuscripts exist of *Festial,* which is evidence of its widespread use.[20] Mirk is thought to have relied heavily on the *Legenda* as the source of his lives of the saints. In its section on St. George, *Festial* includes the dragon story, the martyrdom, and assistance during the Crusades.[21] The dragon story and the account of the Crusades are almost exactly the same as those found in the *Legenda.* However, the story of the martyrdom of St. George in *Festial* differs from other pastoral guides. Unlike earlier English accounts, a canonical version forms the basis of the martyrdom in *Festial.* Canonical accounts were common in the East, but *Festial* was the first canonical version that appeared in England. In other words, Mirk attempted to remove the more fantastic elements from the martyrdom. The most rational explanation is that concern over the spread of the Lollards, a heretical movement in England,

---

[18] MacGregor, "Salue Martir Spes Anglorum," 116-17.

[19] *Speculum Sacerdotale,* ed. Edward H. Weatherly (London: Oxford University Press, 1936), 129-33.

[20] Sarah Salih, *A Companion to Middle English Hagiography* (Cambridge: Brewer, 2006), 59-60.

[21] John Mirk, *Mirk's Festial: a collection of homilies,* ed. Theodor Erbe, Early English Text Society no. 96 (London: K. Paul, Trench, Trubner & Co., 1905), 132-35.

might have convinced Mirk to record a more orthodox account of the passion of St. George.[22]

The popularity of the *Legenda* prompted its translation into English. The first English version, known as the *Gilte Legende*, was translated in the early fifteenth century. It was translated from a French version, not from the original Latin, and thus, some small alterations to the text occurred. The most famous translation into English was William Caxton's late fifteenth-century translation, the *Golden Legend*. He first published his work in 1483, coincidently publishing Mirk's *Festial* the same year. The *Golden Legend* stayed in print until 1527, and *Festial* was in print until 1532.[23] Caxton relied on French, Latin, and English versions for his edition, though he followed the French edition most closely. Caxton also added a paragraph to the end of the entry on St. George: "This blessed and holy martyr S. George is patron of this realm of England and the cry of men of war. In the worship of whom is founded the noble order of the garter, and also a noble college in the castle of Windsor by kings of England... Then let us pray unto him that he be special protector and defender of this realm."[24] Caxton's addition suggests that by the end of the fifteenth century, St. George was considered to be the patron and protector of England.

More than any other institution, religious guilds organized popular celebrations on St. George's Day. A guild, in the most general terms, was a medieval organization of individuals tied together for economic, social, or religious reasons. The earliest guilds were organized for economic practices. Merchant guilds helped facilitate trade between different locations, and craft guilds organized skilled workers within

---

[22] MacGregor, "Salue Martir Spes Anglorum," 123; Judy Ann Ford, *John Mirk's Festial: Orthodoxy, Lollardy, and the Common People in Fourteenth-Century England* (Cambridge: D.S. Brewer, 2006).

[23] MacGregor, "Salue Martir Spes Anglorum," 127.

[24] Jacobus de Voragine, *The Golden Legend, or, Lives of the Saints as Englished by William Caxton*, ed. Frederick Startridge Ellis (London: J. M. Dent & Sons, 1900), 3:133-34.

their trades. Bakers, blacksmiths, entertainers, and other professional groups formed guilds to control entrance into their professions, to fix prices and production, and train new members. Later in the medieval period, religious guilds appeared, and their primary goal was neither economic nor occupational, but spiritual. By the fifteenth century, every parish had on average three religious guilds, with an estimated 30,000 guilds in England alone. Guilds thus formed a key element in the cultural and religious life of late medieval society.[25]

The main purpose of religious guilds was to pray together to gain merit for the afterlife, thereby avoiding eternal damnation in hell and limiting temporary suffering in purgatory. Medieval theology dictated that sins committed by a person on earth determined the destination of the soul after death. God's justice sent great sinners to hell, where there was no hope of salvation, but individuals with limited sins were sent to purgatory. Akin to hell because it was a place of great suffering, purgatory differed from hell in that it was temporary. The soul, through suffering in purgatory, was purged of sin and made ready for heaven. Suffering in purgatory could be reduced or completely avoided through actions taken by the person while still alive, or by a living person in place of the suffering individual. Furthermore, intercessory actions could be offered for a person while he was alive or after his death.[26]

Religious guilds focused on intercessory actions. The most effective means to mitigate the suffering of a soul was by offering Masses for the individual. Guilds paid priests to say Masses for their members, and these clerics typically offered Masses once a year on the feast of the guild, or after one of the members of the guild had died. Wealthier guilds hired a permanent chaplain to celebrate Masses on a regular basis for its members. Members of guilds also attended Mass together on Sundays and feast days. Recitation of devotional prayers was another way to earn merit. People frequently recited litanies in-

---

[25] Good, The Cult of St. George, 105.
[26] Edward Hanna, "Purgatory," in The Catholic Encyclopedia (New York: Robert Appleton Company, 1910).

voking the saints or the rosary in honor of the Blessed Virgin Mary.
Guilds were very active in organizing devotional prayers and processions dedicated to Jesus, Mary, and the saints. Lastly, guilds gave alms
to the church and to the poor. Donations to the church included
money for the building of churches, candles to be burned on altars,
the maintenance of a side chapel or altar, the purchase of a statue or
windows, and so forth. These donations to the church often resulted
in an indulgence or remittance of sins.[27]

Guilds also selected special patrons to intercede for them in heav-
en. As the popularity of St. George increased in the fifteenth and
sixteenth centuries, a significant number of guilds associated with St.
George emerged in England. Some of the guilds dedicated to St.
George were tied to a parish church as purely religious institutions,
and others were craft and merchant guilds which had selected St.
George as their patron. The guilds of St. George went by a variety of
names, such as the Brotherhood of St. George, the Fraternity of St.
George, and the Wardens of St. George. These guilds existed
throughout England in every region of the country. No systematic
catalog of medieval England guilds exists, but Richard II's inquiry
into the nature of the guilds in 1388 provides a glimpse into the distribution of medieval guilds.[28] Five hundred guilds responded to the
inquest, and ten were dedicated to St. George—Littleport, Lincoln,
Springthorpe, Lynn (2), Norwich, Great Yarmouth (2), Bury St. Ed-
munds, and Warwick, and thus, 2 percent of guilds were dedicated to
St. George. The cult of St. George, however, was only beginning to
appear at the end of the fourteenth century, and numerous other
towns developed religious guilds dedicated to St. George after the
1388 inquest.[29]

[27] Duffy, *The Stripping of the Altars,* 141-54.
[28] H. F. Westlake, *The Parish Gilds of Medieval England* (London: Society for Promoting Christian Knowledge, 1919), 137-238.
[29] Anthony, Ashburton, Banwell, Barnstaple, Braunton, Bridgewater, Bristol, Bodmin, Boston, Chagford, Chichester, Coventry, Dublin, Dunster, Exeter, Golant, Launceston,
Leicester, Liskeard, London, Lostwithiel, Lydd, New Romney, North Petherwin, Northamp-

Guilds often had a sacred location that served as a focal point of devotion to their patron saint. Many guilds constructed and maintained chapels, altars, statues, and images of St. George. In St. Nicolas Church, New Romney, a fraternity dedicated to St. George erected an image of St. George in the parish church in 1481. A religious guild associated with St. George in All Saints Church in Lydd maintained an image of St. George until it was sold in 1549. The Brotherhood of St. George in St. Clement's Church in Sandwich had an image of St. George in the south aisle of the church.[30] In St. Martin's Church, the largest in Leicester, the guild of St. George constructed its own chapel in the west end of the south aisle. The chapel contained a statue of St. George in full armor and on horseback.[31] The proliferation of St. George's guilds, consequently, resulted in an increase of his images, exposing the general public further to his cult.

Guilds also hosted celebrations for the feast of their patron saint. Guilds dedicated to St. George commemorated April 23 with elaborate processions, Masses, and prayers to the saint. Fairs and church ales formed part of the celebrations, and still other guilds reenacted the story of St. George in pageants and plays. The climax of the celebration of St. George's Day was the ridings of St. George, a slow moving procession with limited dramatic performances. Processions were an important part of medieval culture, with the elaborate festivities on Corpus Christi providing the most familiar example.[32] The ridings usually moved through the town, and at various stages, performers reenacted the legend of St. George and the dragon. These processions frequently occurred with other religious services, such as

---

ton, Nottingham, Morebath, Morton, Peterborough, Plymouth, Oxford, Sandwich, Salisbury, South Petherwin, Southwark, Stratton, Totnes, and York; see Good, *The Cult of St. George,* 168-70.

[30] James M. Gibson, ed., *Records of Early English Drama. Kent: Diocese of Canterbury,* (London: British Library, 2002), 1:xc.

[31] Dudley Baxter, *The Reformation at St. Martin's, Leicester* (London: Catholic Truth Society, 1898), 2.

[32] Miri Rubin, *Corpus Christi: The Eucharist in Late Medieval Culture* (Cambridge: Cambridge University Press, 1991), 243-70.

communal prayers or Mass, and the feast day retained a strong religious element. The procession, in some cases, also had an important civic function, with political leaders of the town playing a significant role.

St. George's Day formed an important part of the ceremonial calendar of the city of Bristol. The city contained a chapel dedicated to St. George, and each year, on the feast of St. George, a procession was held. Records from the city demonstrate that the local government helped finance the festivities throughout the fifteenth century and early part of the sixteenth century. The city often contributed two torches for the procession; paid for the service of waytes, a small body of musicians; and provided funds for drinking.[33]

A procession on St. George's Day also took place in medieval Canterbury. The town had many processions, with the five largest held for St. Thomas Beckett, the Annunciation, the Nativity, the Assumption, and St. George. The town had a church dedicated to St. George and an image of the saint. According to an inventory taken during the Reformation, Canterbury possessed a relic of the leg of St. George, thus making it a place of pilgrimage for the saint.[34] Accounts from the Reformation also state that the saint's image "was borne in procession on St. George's Day in the honor of God and the King, with Mr. Mayor, the aldermen, their wives, with all the commons of the same going in procession."[35]

Richard Johnson's account of St. George in *The Famous Historie of the Seven Champions of Christendom* (1596-7) claimed that Coventry was the birthplace of St. George. While Johnson's claim is false, the town had several significant representations of St. George. A chapel of St. George near the Gosford Gate contained a late fifteenth-century sculpture of St. George on horseback in full armor and trampling a

33 Pilkinton, ed., *REED. Bristol,* 7, 10, 26, 29-32.
34 Cunningham Geike, *The English Reformation: How It Came About, and Why We Should Uphold It* (New York: D. Appleton and Co, 1879), 74.
35 Gibson, ed., *REED. Kent,* 1:lxxviii, 1:xc.

dragon. Other artistic representations include a sculpture on the tower of St. Michael's Cathedral, an image with a relic housed at the Cathedral Priory, and a tapestry of St. George at St. Mary's Hall. [36] Coventry marked the feast of St. George with a grand procession. According to city records, St. George's Day was one of the main procession days along with Corpus Christi, the Ascension, and Whitsunday. Starting in the late fifteenth century and ending in 1539, records document townspeople bearing a cross and candlesticks on St. George's Day. The procession probably included some form of mock battle between a dragon and St. George similar to the performances during the royal visits to Coventry in the fifteenth century.[37]

Exeter, in Devon, was another town with a pageant on April 23. Evidence for the procession comes from the records of Holy Trinity Church and the guild of St. George tied to the parish. In the second half of the fifteenth century, the records show the purchase of "scogens" or scutis for St. George, and the sale of a sword owned by the guild.[38] The evidence also includes payment to mimes for St. George's Day and entries for "St. George gathering money." Historians assume the arms purchased for St. George were not merely decorations, but were used in primitive plays reenacting the battle of St. George during the "gathering" time.[39]

An elaborate procession took place in Leicester on the feast of St. George. Records of the riding come from the churchwarden accounts of the church of St. Martin, the largest church in Leicester and home to the town's two most important guilds, the guilds of Corpus Christi and St. George. The guild of St. George had a chapel in the west end of the south aisle, containing a statue of St. George in full armor and on horseback. The trappings around the altar were mentioned in a

---

[36] Alan Somerset, "Mysteries End: Edam, Reed, and the Midlands," *Medieval and Renaissance Drama in England* 16 (2003): 20-21.

[37] Ingram, ed., *REED. Coventry*, 113-14, 151; Peter Clark and Paul Slack, eds., *Crisis and Order in English Towns, 1500-1700; Essays in Urban History* (Toronto: University of Toronto Press, 1972), 72-79.

[38] John Wasson, "The St. George and Robin Hood Plays in Devon," *Medieval English Theatre* 2:2 (1980): 66-69.

[39] Wasson, "The St. George and Robin Hood Plays in Devon," xxxviii.

receipt of sales in 1551, which detailed the "sale of candlesticks, bells, stoups, the vente over St. George's altar."[40] The guild also possessed its own hall near the eastern end of St. Martin's churchyard. The riding of St. George was one of grandest events of the year. The riding did not always fall on the feast of St. George, but occurred sometime between his feast and Whitsunday. Local gentry and nobles attended the ridings, and the mayor and other officials presented them with gifts on the feast day. Local officials mandated in 1467 that all the townspeople must attend the festivities. The town also helped the guild finance the riding, and in 1498, forty-eight officials were required to pay the guild: chamberlains 6d per year and non-chamberlains at least 4d. Several decades later in 1523, the town government took steps to impose a penalty of £5 upon the master of St. George's guild if the riding did not take place according to the ancient custom. The mayor and chamberlain were also fined if they failed to enforce the law. Limited evidence chronicles the details of this riding of St. George. A single piece of evidence in the chamberlain's accounts suggests a dragon took part in the procession, which in 1536 stated that the chamberlains "paid for the dressing of the dragon."[41] Perhaps other characters were included in the riding, but the lack of sources limits our knowledge of the procession in Leicester.[42]

Lostwithiel, Cornwall, also hosted a riding of St. George directed by the guild of St. George, established around 1414 at the church of St. Bartholomew. Along with the Corpus Christi guild, it was one of two religious guilds in Lostwithiel. The guild had its own chaplain, cared for a shrine, and administered land dedicated to St. George. The religious activities of the guild included dirges for the dead, annual

---

[40] Baxter, *The Reformation at St. Martin's,* 11.
[41] William Kelly, *Notices Illustrative of the Drama, and Other Popular Amusements, Chiefly in the Sixteenth and Seventeenth Centuries, Incidentally Illustrating Shakespeare and His Contemporaries Extracted from the Chamberlains' Accounts and Other Manuscripts of the Borough of Leicester* (London: J.R. Smith, 1865), 47.
[42] Baxter, *The Reformation at St. Martin's,* 1-2; William Kelly, *Notices Illustrative of the Drama,* 36-51.

Masses, and funerals of guild members. The central event for the guild was the riding of St. George on his feast day. The parade focused on the figure of St. George, and a member of the guild dressed as the saint with a crown, scepter, sword, and armor. Great care went into preparing for the riding, and numerous payments detail the cleaning of the armor before the feast day. Accounts from the year 1536 note, "3*d* paid for the scouring of the armour and 4*d* for grease and oil as well as 4*d* for two dowsen."[43] In the procession, St. George rode on horseback as the prince of Cornwall, and a mounted retinue tended to the saint. Musicians were also present, as one year a piper received payment for his services. After leading the procession through the streets, St. George arrived at the town church, where he greeted the parish priest. The party then entered the church to participate in the Divine Office for the dead. A feast followed at which St. George received all the honors of a prince of Cornwall. The next day the local priest celebrated a requiem Mass for the brethren of the guild who had died.[44]

The small town of Morebath in Devon had a St. George's Day celebration, but the records are not clear whether a play or procession took place. The parish church in Morebath was dedicated to St. George and contained numerous images of the saint. In 1528, payments were recorded for a streamer with St. George on both sides, and a banner with St. George on one side and St. Sidwell on the other. In 1529, a new St. George (possibly a statue) was bought and the following year an image of St. George was purchased. In 1531, an expense for a "new horse to our dragon" was documented.[45] The format of the celebration has to be deduced from a series of payments for items and services. The first clear evidence for a play about St. George is from 1540. In that year, boards and trestles were bought, a city in the churchyard was built, and a payment "for stoffe

[43] Evelyn Newlyn, ed., *Records of Early English Drama. Cornwall and Dorset* (Toronto: University of Toronto Press, 1999), 412.

[44] Newlyn, ed., *REED. Cornwall and Dorset,* 106.

[45] Wasson, "The St. George and Robin Hood Plays in Devon," 66.

and Dressyng for the same" were made.[46] Payments were marked for revel Sunday, which fell during St. George's tide or the closest Sunday to April 23, and they included payments for church ales and musicians to provide entertainment. The last pieces of evidence consisted of payments to clean the churchyard in 1538: "For swepyn of [b]e churche yerde a gaynste for revyll Sunday," and several entries in the 1540s: "For clenssyng of [b]e churche yerde a gayn sent iorge tyde."[47] The cleaning of the churchyard would be an appropriate preparation for a play or celebration. On the one hand, this piecemeal evidence points to a limited and irregular, though existent, celebration of St. George's Day. On the other hand, in his study of Morebath, Eamon Duffy argued that a large annual festival in honor of St. George directed by a guild at Morebath is "largely fantasy."[48]

In some towns, only limited evidence points to a riding of St. George. When the guild of St. George was disbanded in Plymouth during the Reformation, the city council bought a harness of St. George. In 1542 they paid "for skowryng [scouring] of S Georgez harnez" and bought a barrel to "putt the same harneyz yn." While the evidence of a harness of St. George does not prove the existence of a riding, it does provide one of the basic elements.[49] In Newcastle, records refer to payments for the construction of a dragon out of canvas and timber. The chamberlain accounts from April 18, 1510, record payment for the "canwes to the dragon" and "nallis to the dragon." The entry for the next day includes "beldyng the dragon" and "payntting the dragon."[50] Building a dragon April 18-19, in close proximity to the feast of St. George, is similarly recorded by towns with known St. George processions. Therefore, it can be assumed

[46] Wasson, "The St. George and Robin Hood Plays in Devon," 66.

[47] John M. Wasson, ed., *Records of Early English Drama. Devon* (Toronto: University of Toronto Press, 1986), xxv, xxv, 209-11, 448-49.

[48] Eamon Duffy, *The Voices of Morebath: Reformation and Rebellion in an English Village.* (New Haven: Yale University Press, 2001), 66.

[49] Wasson, ed., *REED. Devon*, xxv, 230.

[50] J. J. Anderson, ed., *Records of Early English Drama. Newcastle Upon Tyne* (Toronto: University of Toronto Press, 1982), 13,

that a celebration around St. George's Day in Newcastle, limited though it might be, took place.[51] The town of Dartmouth also presents circumstantial evidence for a riding of St. George. A payment for "the getheryng mony of Seynte george" was recorded in 1533, and two entries in 1541 and 1542 mention "the showryng of S. georges swerd and salett."[52] The fact that the armor of St. George had to be scoured in consecutive years implies that it was used for more than hanging in a church, and the money set aside for the gathering of St. George provides additional confirmation for a riding.

The town of Sandwich, Kent, shared many of the common elements of the popular celebrations of St. George's Day. The main institution behind the procession was the guild of St. George associated with the church of St. Clement. The church had an altar to St. George in the south aisle, and the altar contained an image of St. George. The image was carried in procession on the feast of the saint, and the wardens of St. George had a yearly payment "toward the charge of beryng of saint George this yere."[53] In some years, the procession extended beyond Sandwich and past St. George's Day. In 1535, accounts in Dover included payments for "men of Sandwyche that dauncyd the Mores on seint Markes daie [April 25] at the beryng of Seint George."[54]

One of the later and more elaborate processions took place at Stratford. Holy Trinity Church in Stratford had two depictions of St. George, a wood carving from between 1430 and 1440, and a sixteenth-century wall painting. The painting depicted St. George in armor on horseback swinging his sword at a dragon. The town held an annual riding of St. George on Ascension Day. As the Ascension falls forty days after Easter and thus could be celebrated from late April to early June, it falls in the same calendar period as St. George's Day. The town's Bridge Wardens financed the celebrations from 1542

---

[51] Anderson, ed., *REED. Newcastle Upon Tyne*, xv, xxxviii.
[52] Wasson, ed., *REED. Devon*, xxv, 63.
[53] Gibson, ed., *REED. Kent*, 1:xc.
[54] Gibson, ed., *REED. Kent*, 1:xc, 1:xliv.

to 1547, and from 1553 to 1557. The records indicate payments to have the armor scoured, which implies that the armor was worn and scuffed. It also needed leathering, which meant the addition of buckles or straps. St. George rode on horseback, and payments indicate that two men carried a dragon in procession. The costume of the dragon also needed mending and dressing. The wardens purchased bells and gloves, perhaps for jesters or dancers, and gunpowder to produce a fire-blowing dragon. The repairs indicate an active pageant with an armed engagement as the yearly maintenance of the costumes must have resulted from damage during mock battles between the dragon and St. George.[55]

The three ridings with the most historical documentation are from Norwich, York, and Dublin. The case of Dublin is interesting because it is outside of England, but medieval Dublin had many English traditions as it was the center of English rule in Ireland. The cosmopolitan nature of medieval Dublin was reflected in its festival calendar. The largest processions in Dublin occurred on St. George's Day, St. Patrick's Day, and Corpus Christi. Dublin had numerous connections to St. George besides the procession. A church built in the city was dedicated to the saint in the late twelfth century, and the city also had a guild to St. George. The mayor and council of Dublin requested a patent to establish a fraternity of the Guild of St. George, and Henry VI consented to their request on June 27, 1426. The guild was associated with the Dublin Civic Assembly. Outgoing members of the assembly became officers of the guild, and the mayor of the previous year became the guild master.[56]

The procession was very elaborate, and historians are fortunate to have a detailed description of the pageant from the first half of the sixteenth century. The original report no longer exists, but a seventeenth-century copy has survived. The procession started with actors

---

[55] Somerset, "Mysteries End," 21-22.
[56] Alan J. Fletcher, *Drama, Performance and Polity in Pre-Cromwellian Ireland* (Toronto: University of Toronto Press, 2000), 131, 138.

portraying an emperor attended by two doctors, and an empress attended upon by two knights and two maidens. St. George followed on horseback, accompanied by four mounted men carrying the pole-ax, standard, and sword of St. George, and the sword of the emperor. Behind St. George, a maiden leading a dragon and four trumpeters processed. The queen and king of the Dele were next in the parade. Two knights led the queen, and two maidens behind the queen carried her train. The procession made its way through the streets of Dublin, and likely stopped at various points to reenact scenes from the legend of St. George as was typical in similar processions. Repeated payments for the mending of the dragon suggest St. George fought the dragon at one point during the riding. Finally, the collection of actors arrived at the terminus of the procession, St. George's chapel, which was decorated for the feast day with cushions, hangings, and rushes. After the procession, participants attended a liturgy in honor of St. George.[57]

The politics behind the procession in Dublin were twofold. First, the ceremonial life of Dublin was meant to promote unity. The three processions reflected the political elements of life in Dublin: St. George's Day represented English influence, St. Patrick's Day signified local traditions, and Corpus Christi reflected universal religious unity. In his examination of the three processions, Alan Fletcher argued that the diverse community of Dublin stayed together by celebrating together.[58] Second, the procession was a vehicle to demonstrate power relationships in sixteenth-century Dublin. Attendants carried the swords of St. George and the emperor in the procession, and the mayor and Lord Deputy, the representative of the English king, were the only two individuals in Dublin who had swords carried for them during ceremonies throughout the year. The mayor's connection with St. George is further exemplified by the fact

---

[57] Fletcher, *Drama, Performance and Polity*, 138.
[58] Alan Fletcher, "Playing and Staying Together: Projecting the Corporate Image in Sixteenth-Century Dublin," in *Civic Ritual and Drama*, ed. A. F. Johnston and W. Hüsken (Amsterdam: Rodopi B.V., 1997), 15-37.

that he was responsible for finding an individual to play St. George, and the mayor's sergeant often took the role. It has been argued that the figure of St. George stood for the mayor and the power of the corporation, and the figure of the emperor stood for the Lord Deputy and the state. The procession thus symbolically displayed the two powers in Dublin working together to maintain control over the hostile Irish forces surrounding them, but also being independent from each other.[59]

The guild of St. George in Norwich organized the most famous riding of St. George during this period. The city, the second largest in early sixteenth-century England, had a long tradition of devotion to St. George. The guild of St. George was founded in 1385 as a religious guild with the typical functions of charitable works, prayers for deceased members, and celebration of the saint's day. According to the certificate that the guild filed in 1388, early celebrations were fairly limited. Members gathered on the feast of St. George to hear Mass and evensong in the cathedral and make an offering of a candle and halfpenny. The following day, a requiem Mass was celebrated for deceased guild members.[60] For the next thirty years, the guild disappeared from the records, but it reappeared in 1417, when the guild received a charter from Henry V. From this point, fairly extensive guild records are available; annual account rolls, which detail membership and activities, are preserved from 1420. The guild was altered in the early part of the fifteenth century; some changes included creating a governing body, providing members with a livery, holding an annual feast, and hiring a priest to celebrate daily Mass for the members.[61] A list of ordinances was composed soon after the charter was granted explaining the new elements. From this docu-

---

[59] Fletcher, *Drama, Performance and Polity*, 138-45.
[60] Ben R. McRee, "Religious Gilds and Civil Order: The Cast of Norwich in the Late Middle Ages," *Speculum* 67 (1992): 74.
[61] McRee, "Religious Gilds and Civil Order," 76; Mary Grace, ed. *Records of the Gild of St. George in Norwich, 1389-1547*, Norfolk Record Society 9 (Norwich: Norfolk Record Society, 1937), 28-29.

ment, a picture of the elaborate riding held at Norwich can be recon-structed.

The ordinance dictated that St. George's Day be kept as a holiday. If it fell within three days of Easter, another day would be selected for the feast. A meeting before St. George's Day began preparations for the celebration by assigning roles in the procession. The procession started with an individual carrying the guild's banner and two individ-uals carrying candles. A man bearing St. George's wooden sword preceded the saint, and the handle of the sword was carved to repre-sent the head of a dragon. According to tradition, Henry V gave this sword to the guild as a gift. St. George came next in the pageant; the person who played the saint was selected from the guild members. A dragon was not mentioned in the ordinances, but account records starting in 1420 point to the presence of one.[62] Even later, Lady Mar-garet, representing the princess, was added to the procession. She followed St. George on horseback, clad in purple and red satin with a chain of jewels and a gold flower set with pearls. The remaining members of the guild followed on horseback wearing the livery of the guild. The men alternated yearly between red gowns and red hoods, but the women always wore red hoods. The procession navigated its way through the city, ending at the cathedral to hear Mass and make an offering of candles and a halfpenny. At the end of the liturgy, the guild held a great feast, followed by evensong and a dirge service of-fered for their founder Henry V and the souls of brothers of the fraternity. The next day a requiem Mass took place for deceased members. Following Mass, officers were elected for the next year at a meeting, including two individuals to organize the feast for the fol-lowing year and to purchase the livery.[63]

The feast day also helped achieve unity in the city of Norwich. The ordinances twice warned guild members to refrain from argu-

---

[62] McRee, "Religious Gilds and Civil Order," 77.
[63] McRee, "Religious Gilds and Civil Order," 77; Grace, ed. *Records of the Gild of St. George*, 33-38; Joshua Toulmin Smith, *English Gilds* (London: N. Trubner & Co, 1870), 443-453; David Galloway, ed., *Records of Early English Drama. Norwich, 1540-1642* (Toronto: University of Toronto Press, 1984), xxvi-xxviii.

ments on the feast day. A diverse group of individuals composed the guild in its early years, with members coming from a full range of backgrounds, including the city elite, members of the government, and also more modest members of society. Liberal admission policies resulted in the guild's remarkable growth in the 1420s and 1430s, admitting almost 250 members.[64]

Feast day celebrations became part of the infighting which affected Norwich in the middle of the fifteenth century. The controversy centered on Mayor Thomas Wetherby, and his dissatisfaction following a disputed election in 1433. In the aftermath of the disturbance, he lost his aldermanship and was fined. He later regained his aldermanship with the help of the Earl of Suffolk. This power struggle in Norwich resulted in riots and the suspension of civic liberties in 1437 and 1443. In the last case, the city lost civic liberties for four years. During the fighting, the guild of St. George became entwined in the controversy. Wetherby and Suffolk were members of the guild of St. George, and many of their followers flocked to the guild. Ben McRee, a historian of Norwich, maintained that the annual procession took on a "partisan layer of meaning," with Suffolk representing St. George.[65] St. George and Suffolk were both outsiders, and Suffolk's actions of saving Norwich from infighting were similar to St. George saving the princess from the dragon. The dispute was resolved several years later when the city regained its liberties, and the guild was reformed. A plan to restructure the guild by restricting membership to government officials and limiting the master of the guild to the mayor or his immediate predecessor failed. In 1452, the guild reorganized, remaining open to all citizens, but requiring the outgoing mayor to become the chief officer of the guild and all aldermen to become guild members. Additionally, St. George and the dragon disappeared

---

[64] McRee, "Religious Gilds and Civil Order," 77-79.
[65] Ben McRee, "Unity or Division? The Social Meaning of Guild Ceremony in Urban Communities," in *City and Spectacle in Medieval Europe*, eds. Barbara Hanawalt and Kathryn Reyerson (Minneapolis: University of Minnesota Press, 1994), 198.

for fifteen years, only reappearing after Wetherby's last opponent died in 1467.[66] The guild, which could have been dissolved because of the infighting, instead helped unify the city through the riding.[67]

The last late medieval city with an elaborate St. George's Day celebration was York. The city had a chapel dedicated to St. George and a guild in his honor. The guild, founded in 1447, was initially dedicated to St. Christopher, but St. George became co-patron with St. Christopher around 1470. The guild started and maintained the celebration of St. George's Day in York. Unfortunately, no records from the time period of the guild document the celebration of the feast day in detail. The only records for the festivities come from the revival of celebrations between 1554 and 1558, after the guild was dissolved in 1549. Surviving records from the Marian Restoration provide us with a picture of what the celebration might have looked like during an earlier period.[68]

St. George's Day in York was divided into two parts. The first section focused on spiritual elements, which included a procession, Mass, and sermon. The second half centered on a riding and a play about St. George. Typically, the procession and riding were combined into one element, but in York, the procession existed as a religious ritual distinct from the riding. Documents mention both a procession and a riding and indicate that Mass and a sermon separated the procession from the riding. Moreover, the procession, being a solemn affair in preparation for the liturgy, brought people to St. George's chapel for the service, and the riding left from St. George's chapel after the service. Services were held at St. George's Chapel, but in 1556 the cleric delivered the sermon outside at an area called St. George's Close. In that year, a pulpit was taken out to the field for the preacher.[69]

---

[66] McClendon, "A Moveable Feast," 14-15.
[67] McRee, "Religious Gilds and Civil Order," 67.
[68] Eileen White, "Bryngyng forth of Saynt George: The St. George Celebrations in York." *Medieval English Theatre* 3:2 (1981): 114-21.
[69] White, "Bryngyng forth of Saynt George," 114-21.

The remainder of the day's festivities focused on the riding of St. George. St. George in armor led the riding followed by a king, a queen, their daughter, and a dragon. The procession also included St. Christopher, co-patron of the guild, and the city waytes, hired to play music. Records mention the play of St. George, which was associated with the riding, but the exact arrangement is unclear. Chamberlain accounts included costs for the canvas of a pageant wagon and for men to transport a pageant with a dragon and St. Christopher. Based on the evidence, a pageant wagon could have carried the characters, and at appointed stops along the riding, the wagon could have served as a stage for scenes from the life of St. George. Payment to the actors is further evidence for a play. The "king and queen that playd" were given 12*d*, and John Stamper was paid 3*s* 4*d* for "for playng St. George."[70] The payments imply that the actors did more than simply walk through the town. No documents provide the dialogue of the play, but the characters mentioned in the riding are the essential elements to recreate the basic story of the saint's encounter with the dragon and rescue of the princess.

The majority of evidence for the York riding dates from the reign of Mary, after the guild of St. George and St. Christopher was suppressed, but some references point to a longer tradition of the celebrations and an association with the guild. The first record of a riding comes from the will of Sir William Todd in 1503: "Also I wil my fine Salett to Saynt Christofer gyld and my will is it be vsed euere at the Ridyng of Saynt George with in the said Citie."[71] This piece of evidence shows that in the early part of the sixteenth century a yearly riding of St. George occurred in York and the guild partook in it. Furthermore, a memorandum notes that the riding was canceled because St. George's Day fell on Good Friday in 1546, three years before the guild was dissolved and eight years before the riding was

---

[70] Alexandra F. Johnston and Margaret Rogerson, eds., *Records of Early English Drama. York* (Toronto: University of Toronto Press, 1979), 1:318-19.
[71] White, "Bryngyng forth of Saynt George," 118.

revived in 1554. Finally, when the riding was brought back in 1554, officials wanted to follow "the auncient Custome" of celebrating St. George's Day. [72] It is unclear what is meant by "ancient custom," but it is safe to say that the ridings of St. George occurred well before 1554 in York.

Numerous folk traditions influenced the development of St. George's Day. Notably, mummers' plays were often associated with the celebration of St. George's Day. Mummers' plays appeared in three basic formats. The first and most common was the hero-combat play, which included a battle between two adversaries, the death of one combatant, and the resurrection of the slain character by a doctor. The second version was the sword dance play, and it shared many elements with the hero-combat version, but the death was carried out by a group. The last and least common type was the wooing ceremony. Combat remained in the wooing ceremony, but it was secondary to the winning of a girl by a clown. Early theorists of mummers' plays believed the plays were based on pre-Christian rituals. They speculated that performances celebrated battle between the seasons, and the two combatants represented winter and summer. The yearly battle was won by summer, but winter was resurrected to fight once again. The resurrection also signified the rebirth of nature in spring. [73]

At first, numerous connections appear between mummers' plays and the ridings of St. George. The most apparent is that St. George, also in the form of Prince George or King George, was the most common character in the hero-combat version of the play. The death and resurrection theme of the play also mirrors closely the story of St. George's martyrdom, early versions of which contained several deaths

---

[72] Johnston and Rogerson, eds., *REED. York*, 1:310.

[73] Early theorists of these plays draw from the Cambridge School of classical anthropology outlined by James Frazer. For early works on the mummer plays see: Reginald John Elliott Tiddy, *The Mummers' Play: With a Memoir*, ed. Rupert Spens Thompson (Oxford: Clarendon Press, 1923); E. K. Chambers, *The Mediaeval Stage* (Oxford: Clarendon Press, 1903); E. K. Chambers, *The English Folk-Play* (Oxford: Clarendon Press, 1933); Withington, *English Pageantry*.

and resurrections. Lastly, mumming season, the end of winter and start of spring, coincides with St. George's Day.

In the first part of the twentieth century, historians generally accepted that mummers' plays symbolized seasonal combat and the celebration of rebirth. Even as late as 1961, a theorist argued that "the St. George and Dragon and similar mummeries which still characterize European calendar festivals and whose ultimate origin in a primitive ritual is universally conceded."[74] Yet in the past few decades, the idea that mummers' plays were based on primitive rituals has been discredited. The main concern is that proponents of the survival thesis neglect a gap of over a millennium. The first written records of mummers' plays come from the eighteenth century, and the earliest record is a four line section of the Exeter play from 1737. A chapbook from Newcastle containing the mummers' play *Alexander and the King of Egypt* can be dated to between 1746 and 1769. A copy of a play performed in 1779 at Revesby exists, and records survive of a play performed at Islip, Oxfordshire, around 1780. Furthermore, no record of the form, text, or characters of the folk plays has been found before the time of printed records.[75] This lack of records distinguishes mummers' plays from other folk traditions such as Morris dancing, which is referred to throughout the medieval period. Based on the lack of evidence, historians of mummers' plays conclude that the plays are an early modern creation with roots in the fifteenth and sixteenth centuries.[76] Therefore, the connection between popular celebrations on St. George's Day and mummers' plays must be reevaluated. In the early twentieth century, Robert Withington, a historian of pageants, wrote in reference to sword dances: "We may, I think safely, assume that it was from the folk custom that St. George

---

[74] E. T. Kirby, "The Origin of the Mummers' Play," *Journal of American Folklore* 84 (1971): 276.

[75] Georgina Smith, "Chapbooks and Traditional Plays: Communication and Performance," *Folklore* 92:2 (1981): 210.

[76] Stephen D Corrsin, *Sword Dancing in Europe: A History* (Enfield Lock, Middlesex: Hisarlic Press, 1996), 10.

appeared in pageantry. The natural current is from folk-custom to pageantry, rather than in the other direction."[77] The conclusion that mummers' plays developed in the early modern period reverses the direction of causation argued by Withington and others. The ridings or pageants of St. George are older than the mummers' plays, and thus, the ridings influenced the development of the plays.

Rogation processions, another folk tradition, have a close association to St. George's Day. The Rogation festival is divided into two traditions. Minor Rogation developed during the fifth century in France, and it is celebrated on the Monday, Tuesday, and Wednesday before the Ascension. The Roman feast of Major Rogation takes place on April 25 and dates from the sixth century. The practice spread to England from the continent, and gained popularity during the medieval period. The term "rogation" comes from the Latin *rogare*, which means "to ask." The feast was an opportunity to ask for a bountiful growing season, and the central ritual included a procession marking the boundaries of the parish and the blessing of the fields. Traditionally, a dragon was carried in procession, and the *Legenda Aurea* states the following about the festival: "In some churches, and especially in them of France, is accustomed to bear a dragon with a long tail filled full of chaff or other thing. The two first days it is borne before the cross, and on the third day they bear it after the cross, with the tail all void, by which is understood that the first day tofore the law, or the second under the law, the devil reigned in the world, and on the third day, of grace, by the passion of Jesus Christ, he was put out of his realm."[78] The ridings of St. George and Rogation processions were not directly connected, but the proximity of St. George's feast to the Rogation Days and the shared battle with the dragon might have reinforced the early celebration of the saint's day.

St. George's Day had many traditional celebrations of which the ridings were the most evident. In addition to these festivities, St. George's Day was also a day to hold less distinctive celebrations.

---

[77] Withington, *English Pageantry*, 14.
[78] Jacobus, *The Golden Legend*, 126.

Work was prohibited on April 23, making it possible to hold fairs, church ales, weddings, and other social events. The town of Chichester held a fair every year on St. George's Day, starting around 1500. The town's prosperity grew in the Late Middle Ages because of its markets and fairs. The connection between the town fair and the feast of St. George was likely related to the merchant guild in Chichester and its growth in power throughout the medieval period. In the twelfth century, the merchants formed a guild, and a century later, they had gained control of the government. By the fourteenth century, the merchant guild became associated with the religious guild of St. George, and in essence, the business and political elite gained control of the religious guild of St. George, with the mayor serving as the guild master. The guild, however, was still primarily concerned with religious and charitable works. The selection of the feast of St. George's Day for a fair in 1500 demonstrates the desire of the guild to commemorate the feast of their patron. According to their records, the guild spent money on entertainment, including jugglers and performers for the celebration. Only one entry specifically states St. George's Day: "Paid on St. George's Day to the prince's bearward [keeper of bears]."[79] Many other towns had fairs on April 23 as well; for example, fairs were held at Fordington in Dorset on the feast of St. George as well as the days before it and after it.[80]

By the end of the Middle Ages, St. George's Day was celebrated across England, becoming one of the most important days in the English calendar. St. George was not associated with one particular location in England, however, as St. Thomas Beckett was associated with Canterbury, which allowed his cult to develop across the country. Advocates of St. George included people from diverse backgrounds. He was deeply entrenched in the liturgical life of the

---

[79] Cameron Louis, ed., *Records of Early English Drama. Sussex* (Toronto: University of Toronto Press, 2000), ix, xxiv, xxxix, 18, 231.
[80] Newlyn, ed., *REED. Cornwall and Dorset*, 64.

religious as a martyr and patron saint of England. Kings and nobles were devotees of St. George as a warrior saint who came to their aid in the Crusades and Hundred Years' War. Lastly, peasants were fascinated with St. George as a romantic dragon-slayer. The three segments of King Alfred's famous Three Orders of medieval society—those who pray, those who fight, and those who work—were thus devoted to St. George in three distinct guises.[81]

Celebrations of St. George's Day, though widespread, were not universal or uniform by the end of the medieval period. As documented in this chapter, each town celebrated the feast its own way. The format of the ridings depended on local traditions and the resources of the local guilds. The importance of St. George's Day varied from town to town, when compared to other holidays. In York and Norwich, the feast was the climax of the festive calendar, but in other areas, notably London, it was commemorated without much significance. In medieval England, St. George's Day was a collection of numerous autonomous and local festivals, not a national holiday.

The popular celebration of St. George rose in prominence on the eve of the Reformation, and thus, the ridings of St. George were a late medieval creation. The story of the dragon was not popularized until the appearance of the *Legenda Aurea* around 1270. Religious guilds devoted to St. George appeared in the fourteenth century, and the ridings were not instituted until the fifteenth and sixteenth centuries. The high point of the ridings came in the decades before the Reformation, and in some cases, such as York, during the Marian Restoration after the start of the Reformation. The periodization of the ridings coincides with the revisionist school of the Reformation, which holds that religious guilds, devotion to saints, and reverence of relics and images were all thriving on the eve of the Reformation.[82]

The late date marking the beginning of popular devotions to St. George makes any connection with pre-Christian practices impossi-

---

[81] Timothy Powell, "The 'Three Orders' of society in Anglo-Saxon England," *Anglo-Saxon England* 23 (2007): 103.
[82] Duffy, *The Stripping of the Altars*; Haigh, *The English Reformation Revised*.

ble. Seven hundred years fall between the Christianization of England and the appearance of St. George and the dragon. Moreover, no evidence of a hybrid ceremony during those seven hundred years exists to bridge the gap between pagan rituals and the St. George ridings. The mummers' plays and sword dances that *might* have been hybrid ceremonies between pagan rituals and the ridings were, in fact, developed after the ridings. In other words, popular celebrations of St. George developed within the world of medieval Catholicism, and the annual rituals across England reinforced traditional religious practices. Plays and processions focused on the veneration of St. George, and Masses, prayers for the death, the offering of candles, and other religious rituals constituted the principal activities on April 23. St. George's battle with the dragon may have captured the imagination of the peasants, but they venerated him primarily because of his intercessory power as a great saint.

Popular celebrations of St. George's Day were a peculiar mix of religion, politics, and entertainment. The feast still carried a powerful religious element. Yet, the holiday was not purely religious. As the cases of Norwich and Dublin demonstrate, politics played an important part in the ridings. Figures in the procession and the individuals who played them either challenged or affirmed power structures within local politics. In addition, guilds controlling the ridings participated in local political struggles. Besides religion and politics, the last element of the popular celebration was entertainment. Mock battles between the patron of England and the dragon were a great attraction in medieval England. The peasant community eagerly awaited the ridings and strongly resisted attempts to suppress them. In addition to the mock battle, revelers enjoyed music, dancing, and drinking that accompanied the annual celebration.

Lastly, the fifteenth and first half of the sixteenth centuries marked the climax of the popularity of St. George in England, when celebrations of St. George's Day were the greatest and most widespread. After the Reformation, the popularity of St. George's Day entered a long and steady decline. Periods of revival existed, but the festivities never reached the level of the Late Middle Ages.

Chapter Four
Decline of the Day:
The Reformation and Beyond

In 1541, a young Edward VI, after attending a service on St. George's Day, gathered with knights of the Order of the Garter, and inquired of them, "My lords, I pray you, what saint is St. George that we here so honour him?" The question perplexed the lords, but eventually, the Lord Treasurer answered, "If it pleases your majesty, I did never read in any history of St. George, but only in 'Legenda Aurea,' where it is thus set down: That St. George out with his sword and ran the dragon through with his spear." The response allegedly caused the monarch to break into laughter, responding in jest, "I pray you, my lord, and what did he with his sword the while?" The Lord Treasurer replied, "That I cannot tell your majesty." The veracity of the story is doubtful, considering Edward must have known of St. George when his government altered the statutes of the Garter, but it correctly portrays the dislike religious reformers had for St. George, his battle with the dragon, and the celebration of his feast day.[1]

Observation of St. George's Day began to diminish after the Reformation, declining from its high point in the fifteenth century to its lowest point in the eighteenth century. Popular celebrations were nearly eliminated, and the few that persisted bore no resemblance to their medieval predecessors. The holy day was reduced in rank, and at

---

[1] John Foxe, *The Acts and Monuments of John Foxe: A New and Complete Edition*, eds. Stephen Reed Cattley and George Townsend (London: R. B. Seeley and W. Burnside, 1837), 6:351-52.

a certain point, abolished completely. The royal feast lasted longer because of the Garter and the support of the Stuart monarchs, but it, too, was lost by the end of the eighteenth century. The post-Reformation era, however, helped create a new image of St. George, but unlike the medieval transformations of the saint that added new elements, religious reformers and Enlightenment thinkers successfully undermined belief in St. George as a real person and martyr, stripping an essential feature of the medieval cult. St. George survived as a mythical knight and dragon-slayer, reinvented as a native of England. In late sixteenth-century literature, St. George, under his new persona, represented the ideal Englishman, and this new representation of St. George, created as a result of the Reformation, became the focus of modern celebrations on April 23.

The celebration of saints' days played a significant role in the culture of late medieval England as the celebratory calendar was marked by a constant cycle of holy days. Sundays formed the mainstay of religious celebrations, but throughout the medieval period, an increasing number of days were remembered as holy. By the late medieval period, forty to fifty days were considered *festa ferianda* in England, but the exact number is difficult to calculate because the list of holy days varied from region to region. A day designated *festa ferianda* required the same reverence as Sunday, and mandated a prohibition of labor and attendance at matins, Mass, and vespers. In addition to feasts, days of penance and fasting formed an integral part of the liturgical calendar. Penitential periods included the seasons of Advent and Lent, Ember Days, and eves of high feasts, and in total, close to seventy days every year required some level of fasting. With each passing decade, the English Church elevated more days to feasts and fasts, with England's liturgical calendar reaching its pinnacle in the fifteenth and sixteenth centuries.[2]

---

[2] Duffy, *The Stripping of the Altars*, 41-42.

The festive year consisted of a cycle of holidays commemorating events in the life of Jesus, the Virgin Mary, and the saints. The festive year began with Christmas, followed by the Feast of the Circumcision and Epiphany. The Purification of Mary, also known as Candlemas, was celebrated on February 2. Spring contained the great movable feasts surrounding the passion and death of Jesus. Shrove Tuesday was a feast held the day before Ash Wednesday, which marked the start of a penitential period. Lent followed, consisting of the forty penitential days (non-Sundays) from Ash Wednesday to Easter. The festivities of Holy Week composed the highpoint of the liturgical year. Palm Sunday, celebrated with processions, marked the beginning of Holy Week. Maundy Thursday commemorated the night of the Last Supper, and Good Friday observed the death of Jesus. Easter, the greatest of the feasts, celebrated Jesus' resurrection. The time surrounding Easter contained the fixed feasts of the Annunciation on March 25, St. George on April 23, St. Mark on April 25, and Sts. Philip and James on May 1. Following Easter were the celebrations of Rogation, Ascension, Whitsunday (Pentecost), Trinity Sunday, and Corpus Christi. The Feast of the nativity of St. John took place on June 24 and merged with the celebration of Midsummer. Scholars consider the first half of the year from Christmas to Midsummer to be the festive part of the year, for it contained the most important festivals of the year, maintaining that the remainder of the year from Midsummer to Christmas composed a secular time. This division of the year is anachronistic because medieval writers did not divide time in such a manner. Furthermore, the divide is also inaccurate, for religious feasts were held throughout the year. Numerous saints popular in England had feasts in the second part of the year: the translation of the relics of St. Thomas Beckett on July 7, St. James on July 25, St. Michael on September 29, All Saints on November 1, St. Martin on November 11, and St. Hugh on November 17.[3] Many Marian feasts

---

[3] Works on the liturgical year in England include: Ronald Hutton, *The Rise and Fall of Merry*

fell on dates in late summer and fall: the Assumption on August 15, Nativity on September 8, and Immaculate Conception on December 8. In short, religious feasts dotted the majority of the medieval calendar of England, and thus, drove the festive culture of the period.

The cycle of religious events coincided with many non-religious aspects of life. Writers used religious feasts as dates in letters and diaries. Landowners typically collected rent on Lady Day and Michaelmas. Legal terms were based on the religious feasts of Easter, Trinity Sunday, Michaelmas, and St. Hilary. Agricultural activities corresponded with holy days in the calendar, with one farmer recording, "Lambs conceived at Michaelmas would be born before Candlemas, that ploughing should be over by Andrewmas."[4] Feasts of saints were designated days for commercial activities like fairs and markets. Even in medicine, days for bloodletting and taking a laxative concurred with religious feasts. In a way, every task had a proper time, and the church, through the religious calendar, arbitrated when that was.[5] No separation existed between the religious and the non-religious, and thus, the religious calendar intertwined with civil, astronomical, pagan, agricultural, and legal events. According to Eamon Duffy, no other option besides the religious calendar existed: "It is not difficult to understand the importance of the liturgical calendar for late medieval people. There was, in the first, no alternative, secular reckoning of time: legal deeds, anniversaries, birthdays, were reckoned by the religious festival on which they occurred."[6]

It is an oversimplification to state that the calendar was purely a religious entity, for many feasts had origins tied to pagan or astronomical events. Christmas occurred near the winter equinox, St.

England: The Ritual Year, 1400-1700 (Oxford: Oxford University Press, 1994), 5-49; Ronald Hutton, *Stations of the Sun: A History of the Ritual Year in Britain* (Oxford: Oxford University Press, 1996); David Cressy, *Bonfires and Bells: National Memory and the Protestant Calendar in Elizabethan and Stuart England* (Berkeley: University of California Press, 1989), 13-34; Edward Muir, *Ritual in Early Modern Europe* (Cambridge: Cambridge University Press, 2005), 66.
[4] Cressy, *Bonfires and Bells*, 15.
[5] C. John Sommerville, *The Secularization of Early Modern England: From Religious Culture to Religious Faith* (New York: Oxford University Press, 1992), 34.
[6] Duffy, *The Stripping of the Altars*, 41, 49.

John's nativity took place on the summer solstice, and Sts. Philip and James were celebrated on May Day. Then again, feasts were not entirely inspired by pagan festivals, but they likely borrowed and merged with more ancient traditions. Moreover, religious feasts consisted of more than spiritual activities. The prohibition of work allowed individuals to attend Mass and other religious services, but time was also available for bonfires, dancing, and drinking. Several religious reformers lamented that the excessive number of holy days provided an opportunity for laziness and immoral revelry.[7]

The English Reformation brought about an end to the popular celebrations on St. George's Day. The Reformation moved in a slow and piecemeal fashion under Henry VIII (r. 1509–1547), but escalated during the short reign of Edward VI (r. 1547–1553). A short revival of traditional practices occurred under Mary I (r. 1553–1558), but the celebration of St. George's Day never regained its pre-Reformation prominence. The celebration went into a long and permanent decline starting under Elizabeth I (r. 1558–1603). The condemnation of St. George's Day was part of a wider shift away from medieval Catholicism and traditional religious practices. Religious authorities censured feast days, images, processions, pilgrimages, and religious guilds during the sixteenth century. As a result, the popular celebrations of St. George's Day celebrated throughout England came to an end, or were fundamentally altered by the end of the century.

In 1536, Henry VIII issued an injunction reducing the number of holy days, offering several reasons for the need to reduce the number of feasts. The number of holy days had "excessively grown" and was likely to continue increasing. The time off from work allowed for "sloth and idleness, the very nurse of thieves, vagabonds" and "licentious vacations and liberty." Peasants refused to work during feasts in harvest time, and thus food rotted in the fields. Lastly, God only

---

[7] Sommerville, *The Secularization of Early Modern England,* 34-35.

mandated the Sabbath as a day of rest; other holy days were created by man. The injunction also moved the celebration of the patron saint of the parish to the first Sunday in October. The numerous churches dedicated to St. George, thus, had to celebrate the feast of their patron in October, rather than on April 23. The injunction also significantly reduced the number of feast days. With only a few exceptions, holy days during harvest time, from July 1 to September 29, and all feasts falling in the Westminster law terms were abolished. Henry spared the feasts of the Virgin Mary, the Apostles, the Nativity, the Ascension, All Hallows Day, Candlemas, Easter, St. John the Baptist, St. Michael, and St. George. The act was a brash move by Henry, completely altering the ritual year. The selection of St. George as one of the few saints to maintain a feast day, the only non-biblical saint, points to his special status as patron of England, the Order of the Garter, and the monarchy. Numerous other popular saints had their feasts abrogated, such as St. Martin, St. Mary Magdalene, St. Anne, St. Cuthbert, St. Augustine of Canterbury, St. Edmund, St. Edward the Confessor, St. Alban, and St. Thomas Becket (translation of his relics).[8]

Through a series of injunctions and acts, Henry also moved against the cult of saints in images, pilgrimages, and relics. Leaders of the reforming faction, Thomas Cromwell, and later Thomas Cranmer, advised Henry in this direction. The Ten Articles set forth the first formulation of the theological positions of the English Church after its break with Rome in 1536. The last five articles dealt with religious ceremonies and defined positions on the cult of saints, praying to saints, and images. The document warned against abuses related to images, and counseled that proper instruction was needed to avoid falling into idolatry. Moreover, it advised that saints may be honored, but not with the "confidence and honour which are only due unto God." Praying to saints was to "be done without any vain superstition, as to think that any saint is more merciful, or will hear us sooner

[8] Duffy, *The Stripping of the Altars*, 394-95.

than Christ, or that any saint doth serve for one thing more than another, or is patron of the same."[9]

The same year, the king issued an injunction, composed by
Thomas Cromwell, elaborating on the Ten Articles. This injunction
declared that the clergy "shall not set forth or extol any images, relics,
or miracles for any superstition or lucre, nor allure the people by any
enticements to the pilgrimage of any saint, otherwise than is permitted
in the Articles lately put forth by the authority of the king's majesty."[10] Traditional practices also came under attack in *The Institution of a
Christian Man* of 1537, known as the Bishop's Book. A further elabo-
ration of the Ten Articles issued by bishops, it was not authorized by
the monarchy. Still another injunction appearing in 1538 took a hard
stance against images, relics and pilgrimages, attacking "wandering to
pilgrimages, offering of money, candles, or tapers, to images or relics
or kissing, or licking the same" as superstitions. In particular, "feigned
images" that were the source of pilgrimages and devotions should be
taken down and "suffer from henceforth no candles, tapers, or images
of wax to be set afore any image or picture."[11]

These declarations forced many churches and guilds to sell or destroy their images of St. George. The images in many cases formed
the center of an altar to St. George, which received special devotion
during his feast day and were carried in procession on April 23. Subsequently, the destruction of the images of St. George greatly altered
the celebration of his feast day. A detailed account chronicles the
destruction of the image of St. George carried in procession on the
saint's feast day in Canterbury, illustrating the connection between the
suppression of feast days and removal of images. When the Archbishop of Canterbury, Thomas Cranmer, received the order from

---

[9] Ten Articles found in Gerald Lewis Bray, ed., *Documents of the English Reformation 1526-1701*
(Cambridge: James Clarke, 2004), 171-72.
[10] Injunction found in Henry Gee and William John Hardy, *Documents Illustrative of English
Church History* (London: Macmillan, 1896), 271.
[11] Injunction found in Gee and Hardy, *Documents Illustrative of English Church History*, 277.

Henry to destroy St. George's shrine, he immediately put the order into effect. The commissary, Nevison, who was married to the niece of Cranmer, ordered that the saint be taken down, and the curate and churchwardens carried out Nevison's orders. Afterwards, the commissary questioned them about the image, and they responded that they had taken the image down. Nevison then ordered, "It is not only the King's Majesty's pleasure to have such images abused to be pulled down, but also to be disfigured, and nothing of such images to remain." One of the churchwardens protested that St. George was the patron of England and the church. The commissary responded, "We have no patron but Christ." The parson concluded that the cause for the destruction of the image was "he was borne in procession on St. George's day in the honor of God and the King, with Mr. Mayor, the aldermen, their wives, with all the commons of the same going in procession."[12]

Henry disrupted traditional practices in a limited and uneven manner. Execution of the Ten Articles and the injunctions was not carried out in a uniform fashion but varied from diocese to diocese, region to region, town to town, and church to church depending on the disposition of the clergy and the people. Some churches hid images and refused to destroy them as a form of limited resistance to the theological changes. A full scale revolt, the Pilgrimage of Grace in 1536-7, was motivated in part by the abrogation of holy days. Henry's religious policy became more conservative later in his reign with the Six Articles, the King's Book, and the fall of Cromwell; therefore, aggressive tactics used against the cult of saints were relaxed.

When Edward VI came to power after the death of his father in 1547, the reforming party had complete control of the monarchy. The Duke of Somerset, regnant for the boy king, and Archbishop Cranmer, the spiritual leader, actively promoted religious change. Edward's short reign had a tremendous impact on the popular celebration of St. George's Day. Cranmer released a set of injunctions that repeated

---

[12] Gairdner, ed., *Letters and papers, foreign and domestic, of the Reign of Henry VIII*, 2:309.

many of the principles laid out during Henry's reign involving relics, images and pilgrimages. In addition, the documents prohibited processions: "They shall not from henceforth, in any parish church, at any time use any procession about the church or church-yard, or other place."[13] Cranmer maintained that the main reasons for eliminating processions was to reduce the amount of confusion and strife in the parish, so that people might hear the prayers in a more quiet and edifying manner. The prohibition focused on processions before Mass on Sunday, but the injunction affected all religious processions, including those on Candlemas, Corpus Christi, Palm Sunday, and St. George's Day.

The second area impacted by Edward was the dissolution of the religious guilds, which had begun with the Chantries Act of 1545, released late in the reign of Henry. A large survey of chantries was carried out in 1546, but only a few of their assets were confiscated before the king died. Edward released a new act in 1547, replacing the one issued by Henry. The new decree had the same intent as the earlier document but a more ideological motive. Whereas Henry needed the money to fight wars in France and Scotland, the Chantries Act of 1547 argued that chantries should be closed because they were based on faulty theological reasoning. The act dissolved religious colleges, chantries, hospitals, free chapels, fraternities, brotherhoods, and guilds and seized the property and money controlled by them. The main purpose of chantries was to hire priests to say Mass for the dead in purgatory, and religious reformers opposed this practice on theological grounds. Chantries, however, had numerous other purposes as they supported education, provided Mass and sacraments in areas far from parishes, and directed the ceremonial life of towns. As a result of the closing of the guilds, these other functions, along with the Masses for the dead, came to an end. Many of the guilds dedicated to

---

[13] Thomas Cranmer, *Miscellaneous Writings and Letters of Thomas Cranmer*, ed. John Edmund Cox (Cambridge: Cambridge University Press, 1846), 2:502.

St. George were dissolved during this time. For instance, the guild of St. Christopher and St. George in York was surveyed in 1546, and plans were made to sell the property which it controlled. The land was sold after the second Chantries Act in 1548-9. The chapel of St. George was purchased and turned into St. George's House, used as a work house for the poor, and later a house of correction.[14]

The vast impact of Edward's short reign, 1547-1553, resulted from the rigorous implementation of the injunctions. Cranmer and his allies actively implemented the resolutions passed by the government. Commissioners surveyed the country to confirm that images were taken down and destroyed in churches, chapels, and homes; old religious books and vestments were sold; chantries were shut down and their wealth confiscated; and traditional religious ceremonies were brought to an end. The *Chronicle of the Grey friars of London* records that the Bishop of London in 1552 commanded that St. George's Day "shulde not be kepte, and no more it was not."[15] In Leicester, the mayor sold the horse which St. George rode and the floor and vault holding St. George in 1547.[16] The decorations surrounding the altar to St. George, also in Leicester, were sold, and accounts of the parish in 1551 contain the "sale of candlesticks, bells, stoups, the vente over St. George's altar, painted cloth, etc."[17] In 1548 at Morebath, banners, candlesticks, and cloths for the altars of Sts. Sidwell and George were sold without commission.[18] At Holy Trinity Church in Exeter, St. George was taken down in 1548, and at St. Lawrence Church, a silver image of St. George on horseback was removed in 1549. St. George was confiscated at Ashburton in 1547-8, and in Stratton, St. George and his horse were taken down in 1547-8.[19] At Crediton, an image of

---

[14] Eileen White, *The St. Christopher and St. George Guild of York* (York: Borthwick Institute, 1987), 19-21.

[15] John Gough Nichols, *Chronicle of the Grey Friars of London* (London: Camden Society, 1852), 74.

[16] William, *Notices Illustrative of the Drama,* 50.

[17] Baxter, *The Reformation at St. Martin's, Leicester,* 11.

[18] Whiting, *The Blind Devotion of the People,* 21.

[19] Whiting, *The Blind Devotion of the People,* 77.

St. George was listed with others as defaced or burned.[20] Though the destruction of images was directed from above, many individuals, including priests, complied with governmental orders due to desire for money and political favors or out of fear.[21] Throughout England, images and altars of St. George were destroyed or dismantled during the reign of Edward.

After the death of Edward, Mary I briefly revived the popular celebrations of St. George's Day as she reunited the Church of England with Rome and reversed the religious policies of the previous two Tudor kings. Some of the images that survived the period of turmoil were restored. An image of St. George, for example, returned to its place in Braunton in 1557-8.[22] The annual procession was revived in Leicester, for in 1554, an expense reads, "Item pd for dressing & hesyng sent George harness."[23] The best recorded revival was in York, discussed in the previous chapter. The guild at York was dissolved in 1549, but the procession was revived in 1554 and continued sporadically throughout the rest of the decade. The restoration under Mary was short-lived. After her death, her sister Elizabeth I came to the throne, and shared more in common with her father than her half-sister. She broke ties with Rome and reinstituted many of the religious changes favored by the reforming party. During her long reign, the traditional ceremonial year of medieval England disappeared and was replaced by a new national, secular calendar.

By the end of the sixteenth century, annual celebrations on St. George's Day were no longer taking place. The dissolution of the religious guilds, the attack on the cult of the saints, and the reform of the calendar successfully brought an end to the peasant celebrations on April 23. The only exception was in Norwich, where a much al-

---

20 Whiting, *The Blind Devotion of the People*, 81.
21 Ethan H. Shagan, *Popular Politics and the English Reformation* (Cambridge: Cambridge University Press, 2003).
22 Whiting, *The Blind Devotion of the People*, 79.
23 William, *Notices Illustrative of the Drama*, 50.

tered celebration lasted until the nineteenth century. The guild of St. George escaped the Chantries Acts because it had a royal charter from Henry V declaring it a permanent institution. The guild renamed itself the Company and Citizens of Saint George and divorced itself from religious practices associated with medieval Catholicism. The company continued to celebrate the feast of St. George, but most of the traditional elements were no longer present.[24] The festivities contained no representations of St. George and the dragon, no mock battle, and no procession. The celebration consisted of evensong on the eve of the feast, a banquet and divine service on the feast day, and a sermon and election of officers on the following day. Moreover, religious ceremonies no longer focused on deceased members of the fraternity or the intercessory power of the saint.[25]

The Marian revival partially restored the traditional festivities in Norwich. The name changed to Guild of St. George, replacing the Company and Citizens of Saint George, and the annual feast regained some of its former glory. Strangely, the date of the feast moved from April 23 to the Sunday after Trinity Sunday. It is unclear why the feast shifted, given that Mary restored the ceremonial calendar of the medieval period.[26]

Elizabeth's ascension brought new challenges to the celebration in Norwich, but members of the guild persisted. Once again, the guild was renamed to the Company and Fellowship of St. George, and the feast began to lose its connection with St. George. The town continued to hold annual feasts, but the celebrations never returned to April 23. The image of St. George also temporarily disappeared, for in 1559, the records for the feast state, "neyther George nor Margett. But for pastyme the dragon to com In and shew hym self as in other yeares."[27] In the absence of St. George, the procession and feast took on a new political meaning, focusing on civil authorities. In 1574, the

24 Muriel C McClendon, "Against God's word: government, religion and the crisis of authority in early Reformation Norwich," *Sixteenth Century Journal* 25 (1994): 353-69.

25 McClendon, "A Moveable Feast," 18; Galloway, ed., *REED. Norwich*, 23.

26 McClendon, "A Moveable Feast," 19-20.

27 Galloway, ed., *REED. Norwich*, 47.

political leaders in Norwich moved the celebration to the Sunday before Midsummer, with the installation of the mayor on the Tuesday
preceding Midsummer, thus linking the two events. The connection
between the new holiday and the installation of the mayor is confirmed by the minutes of the Company that labeled the feast as "the
feast of the mayor, shreves and company." The celebration was
moved again, to the Tuesday after the feast of St. Peter, but continued
to be celebrated in June. According to one historian of Norwich,
Muriel McClendon, the feast completely fused with the installation of
the city's mayor in the seventeenth century, and the city chamberlain
started financing the annual festivity. As holdovers from the past, the
dragon continued to make appearances in the expense accounts, and a
George returned between the years 1619 and 1632.[28]

The transformation of Norwich's celebration is revealing on a political and religious level. First, the mayor over time replaced the
figure of St. George. The heavenly protector and intercessor was no
longer needed in a more secular worldview; rather, civil authorities
protected and defended the people. Second, the transformation of the
dragon also demonstrates an altered religious orientation. The dragon
in the story of St. George represented evil, but in the seventeenth
century, the new dragon was less dangerous and more playful than the
medieval version. He was affectionately named "snap" and was preceded by a fool and pair of whifflers. The new dragon was a danger
that could be handled and controlled by a worldly official, and thus,
no supernatural intercessor such as St. George was needed. The procession in its new form continued for several centuries. It was
curtailed during the Civil War, and the Company of St. George was
dissolved in 1732. However, the dragon remained part of the mayor's
inauguration until the passage of the Corporation Act in 1835. Although the celebration continued past the Reformation, the meaning
of the procession completely changed in the early modern period with

---

[28] McClendon, "A Moveable Feast," 22.

the removal of religious elements and civil authorities' use of the ritual to affirm their power.[29]

The Reformation also altered liturgical ceremonies held on St. George's Day. When Henry VIII severed ties with the Roman Church, most traditional liturgical practices remained in place. Changes were limited to his reform of the Sarum breviary, introduction of a new English litany used in processions, and sanctioning of reading the bible in English. For the most part, medieval liturgical books remained in use, albeit with prayers to the pope and St. Thomas Beckett eliminated. Cranmer directed the process of creating a new liturgical guide, starting in the reign of Henry, but not coming to fruition until the time of Edward. Cranmer's work was influenced by the Sarum Rite, which dominated England in the late medieval era, but he drew upon reforms from other leading clergymen, including the reform of the breviary by Spanish Cardinal Francis Quiñones, and the church reforms of Hermann von Wied, Archbishop of Cologne. Cranmer's synthesis resulted in the *Book of Common Prayer* (BCP) of 1549. It contained a new English formula for the Liturgy of the Hours, Mass, baptism, confirmation, matrimony, visitation of the sick, burial, and the purification of women. A monumental achievement, the work created new liturgical services to parallel the theological shift of the Reformation.[30]

The religious experience of the ceremonies in the BCP differed noticeably from pre-Reformation liturgies. Most apparent was the transition from Latin to English as the primary language of the liturgy. Included in this liturgical shift, the BCP dramatically reduced the religious celebration of saint days. Cranmer's opposition to non-biblical saints and a new way of organizing the religious calendar led to a decreased number of feast days. The BCP sought to universalize the liturgical calendar across England, and the preface of the work critiqued the cacophony of liturgical books used at the time: "Some

---

[29] McClendon, "A Moveable Feast," 23.
[30] *The First and Second Prayer Books of Edward Sixth* (London: J.M. Dent & Sons, 1910), vii-ix.

folowyng Salsbury use, some Herford use, some the use of Bangor, some of Yorke, and some of Lincolne." With the BCP, "the whole realme shall have but one use." The universal nature of the BCP altered the celebration of St. George's Day because the feast began on the local level and rose in rank in a piecemeal fashion, and the BCP did not accommodate local customs in parishes dedicated to St. George or local areas with a substantial cult of St. George. Moreover, the BCP simplified the method used to select biblical readings for the Lord's Supper, Morning Prayer, and Evening Prayer. The preface lamented that the reading of the Bible in liturgies was "altered, broken, and neglected, by planting in uncertein stories, Legendes, Respondes, Verses, vaine repeticions, Commemaracions, and Synodalles, that commonly when any boke of the Bible was began: before three or foure Chapiters were read out, all the rest were unread." The BCP contained a calendar and a system of tables that allowed for reading Bible passages "in ordre, without breakyng one piece therof from another." The new tables reduced the number of feast days and assigned no special readings to most feast days to facilitate reading the Bible in order. Thereby, the number of feast days with selected readings greatly diminished.[31]

The BCP of 1549 also contained a new calendar of feasts. The fixed feasts included events in the life of Jesus and Mary—Circumcision, Epiphany, Purification of St. Mary the Virgin, Annunciation, Christmas—and feasts of biblical figures.[32] The BCP had twenty-five fixed holy days, a reduction from the Sarum Rite, which celebrated one hundred fifty-six fixed feast days in 1514. A noticeable omission from the BCP was the feast of St. George on April 23. All twenty-five of the feasts had Collects, Epistles, and Gospels selected

---

[31] *The First and Second Prayer Books of Edward Sixth*, 3-4.

[32] Conversion of St. Paul, St. Mathias, St. Mark, Sts. Philip and James, St. Barnabas, St. Peter, Nativity of St. John the Baptist, St. James, St. Mary Magdalene, St. Bartholomew, St. Matthew, St. Michael, St. Luke, Sts. Jude and Simon, All Saints, St. Andrew, St. Thomas, St. Stephen, St. John, and Holy Innocents.

for the Lord's Supper celebrated on the feast. In future revisions of the BCP in 1552, 1559, and 1561, many saints were added to the calendar, but none were added to the list of days with Collects, Epistles and Gospels.

A revision of the BCP appeared late in the reign of Edward as Cranmer came increasingly under the influence of more radical reformers, including Martin Bucer, an exiled German reformer; Peter Martyr, an Italian with Zwinglian tendencies; John Hooper, a reforming bishop; and Jan Laski, a Polish reformer. The 1552 revision, however, added some holy days to the calendar, including St. George, St. Clement, St. Lawrence, and the feast of Lammas. The revision removed St. Mary Magdalene and St. Barnabas, but St. Barnabas' removal from the calendar likely resulted from the fault of the printer because the Collect, Epistle and Gospel were retained for his feast. The feast of St. George was added in the BCP as a lesser feast, listed in black ink instead of red, without any particular readings from the Bible selected for the day.[33] The inclusion of St. George's Day in a more Protestant book appears contradictory and begs the question: why was it added? The same year that the new BCP was introduced an act was passed in parliament dealing with holy days and fasting days. The seventh paragraph of the act dealt exclusively with St. George's Day and specifically allowed the Order of the Garter to celebrate the feast. One can conclude that the presence of the feast of St. George was likely due to his association with the powerful order, and not for religious reasons.[34]

Use of the BCP temporarily came to an end under Mary I, but the work returned early in the reign of Elizabeth, who introduced a more conservative version of the 1552 BCP in 1559. The calendar had minor changes, with the feast of St. Clement removed and St. Barnabas

---

[33] *The First and Second Prayer Books of Edward Sixth*, 338; the readings for Morning Prayer were 1 Kings 30 and Acts 20, and the readings for Evening Prayer were 1 Kings 31 and 2 Peter 2.
[34] Archibald John Stephens, *The Statutes Relating to the Ecclesiastical and Eleemosynary Institutions of England, Wales, Ireland, India and the Colonies with the Decisions There* (London: John W. Parker, 1845), 336.

restored.[35] The feast of St. George was elevated to a red letter day in the 1559 text and thus celebrated with greater solemnity. Yet, the readings for April 23 remained the same as the 1552 edition.[36] In 1560, an unofficial Latin version of the BCP was published for private use in universities and colleges; it differed greatly from the English version, giving greater attention to the veneration of saints and listing a saint for nearly every day of the year.[37] St. George's Day was celebrated as a red letter day in this text.[38] A revised calendar of the English version of the BCP appeared in 1561, continuing the emphasis on saints found in the Latin text. A commission, including Archbishop Parker, Bishop Grindal, Dr. Bill, and Walter Haddon, the compiler of the Latin calendar, added fifty-seven traditional feasts to the calendar.[39] The 1561 calendar downgraded the feast of St. George from a red letter day to a black letter day.[40]

The Elizabethan edition remained in force until the English Civil War (1642–1651). The only change occurred when James I altered the calendar in 1604 by adding the feast of St. Enurchus on September 7. James was not devoted to the saint, but he wanted to honor the birth of Elizabeth on September 7.[41] Puritan success in the English Civil War brought an end to the use of the BCP and its calendar. In 1645, the Westminster Assembly issued the *Directory for the Public Worship of God*, which included this short statement on the Christian year: "There is no day commanded in scripture to be kept holy under the

---

[35] Tables for feasts in 1549, 1552, 1559 in John Henry Blunt, *The Annotated Book of Common Prayer: Being an Historical, Ritual, and Theological Commentary on the Devotional System of the Church of England* (London: Longmans, Green and Co., 1907), 127.

[36] William Keatinge Clay, *Liturgical Services: Liturgies and Occasional Forms of Prayer Set Forth in the Reign of Queen Elizabeth* (Cambridge: Cambridge University Press, 1847), 48.

[37] David N. Griffiths, *The Bibliography of the Book of Common Prayer, 1549-1999* (London: British Library, 2002), 19-20.

[38] Clay, *Liturgical Services*, 316.

[39] Blunt, *The Annotated Book of Common Prayer*, 128.

[40] Clay, *Liturgical Services*, 447; the readings from the Old Testament were also altered with 2 Kings 19 for Morning Prayer and 2 Kings 20 for Evening Prayer.

[41] "St. Enurchus – A Liturgical Problem" in Vernon Staley, *Liturgical Studies* (London: Longmans, Green, and Co., 1907), 58-65.

gospel but the Lord's Day, which is the Christian Sabbath. Festival days, vulgarly called Holy-days, having no warrant in the word of God, are not to be continued."[42] All holy days, even Christmas and definitely St. George's Day, were prohibited. The restoration of the monarchy under Charles II brought back the BCP. The 1662 version contained some changes to the calendar, adding the feasts of St. Alban and Ven. Bede as black letter days and the martyrdom of King Charles as a red letter day. St. George's Day remained a black letter day.[43] The Church of England used the 1662 version of the BCP as the main liturgical book until the twentieth century, and it is still authorized for liturgical functions.

The introduction of new liturgical works impacted the religious celebration of St. George's Day. The period between the 1549 edition and the 1662 edition was a time of great fluctuation. St. George went off the calendar, returned as a black letter day, was elevated to a red letter day, and then downgraded to a black letter day. It has remained a black letter day in the BCP, and as such, it does not merit special readings or prayers for Morning Prayer, Evening Prayer, or the Lord's Supper. All editions of the BCP contain no mention of St. George outside of the calendar. The only holy days celebrated with special prayers were the red letter days, restricted to Jesus, Mary, saints in the Bible, and King Charles. In short, St. George's Day was not eliminated as a religious feast due to the Reformation in England, but its liturgical significance was greatly diminished.

The Catholic Church also revised its celebration of St. George's Day. During the period of Catholic reform, the church sought to address some of the issues which had brought about the rise of Protestantism. Erasmus, who remained in union with the Catholic Church, was highly critical of St. George. Furthermore, Pope Clement

---

[42] James F. White, *Documents of Christian Worship: Descriptive and Interpretive Sources* (Louisville: John Knox Press, 1992), 37.

[43] *The Book of Common Prayer: From the Original Manuscript Attached to the Act of Uniformity of 1662, and Now Preserved in the House of Lords* (London: Eyre & Spottiswoode, 1892), 35; the readings from the Old Testament changed to 2 Kings 28 for Morning Prayer and 2 Samuel 29 for Evening Prayer.

VII, (r. 1523–1534), ordered the dragon story to be removed from all missals and breviaries, preferring St. George be mentioned only as a martyr. The Council of Trent reviewed the question of devotion to saints, and in response to Protestant attacks, it affirmed the traditional practices related to images, pilgrimages, and relics. The council also reviewed the historicity of some of the more fantastic saints, and St. George survived the new vigorous criteria put forth by the Catholic Church because of his ancient cult.[44] The Tridentine Calendar issued in 1568 as part of the revised Roman Missal included the feast of St. George as a semi-double feast, which was higher than a simple feast, but lower than a double feast. St. George's Day remained a semi-double in the Catholic calendar of saints until semi-double feasts were eliminated in 1955.[45] Pope Benedict XIV (r. 1749–1758) recognized St. George as protector of England, and his feast was elevated to a double feast day in England, making it a holy day of obligation for all English Catholics until it reverted back to a simple day of devotion for Catholics in 1778.[46]

The Order of the Garter continued to meet through the reign of Henry VIII. Some alterations to the Garter occurred because of the changing religious views of the Reformation, but no major revision of the order took place during Henry's reign. In 1540, one change was made: money formerly used to say Masses for a dead companion was to be used to repair roads and help the poor.[47] Under Edward VI, the Garter needed to be reformed to remain consistent with the radical religious changes taking place. The government under Edward dis-

---

[44] Peter Burke, "How to Become a Counter-Reformation Saint," in *The Counter-Reformation: The Essential Readings*, ed. David Martin Luebke (Malden, Mass.: Blackwell, 1999), 131.
[45] Baring-Gould, *Curious Myths of the Middle Ages*, 30-31. The readings for the feast were 2 Tim 2: 8-11 and 3:10-13, and John 15:1-8. The Collect for St. George's Day was "God who makest us glad through the merits and intercession of blessed George the martyr mercifully grant that we who ask through him Thy good things may obtain the gift of Thy grace."
[46] Alban Butler, David Hugh Farmer, and Paul Burns. *Butler's Lives of the Saints: April* (Collegeville, Minn.: The Liturgical Press, 1999), 163.
[47] Beltz, *Memorials of the Order of the Garter*, xcii.

solved hundreds of religious guilds, but the Garter was not affected because it was a royal institution. Nevertheless, the Garter shared many characteristics with religious guilds. Furthermore, it was dedicated to St. George, and Edward opposed devotion to non-biblical saints. A royal ordinance issued on April 20, 1548, substantially altered the Garter's ceremony on the feast of St. George. First, it eliminated the procession of knights around the churchyard and directed that reverences in church be made to the sovereign only. Sec-Second, the ordinance abolished the requiem Mass, and mandated that Masses said on St. George's Day and the following day follow the rubric found in the new BCP. George Frederick Beltz, a Victorian historian of the Garter, remarked that "these injunctions were regarded as a virtual abrogation of the grand festival of the Order which had been annually celebrated at Windsor from the period of the foundation: that solemnity was not observed during the remainder of Edward's reign."[48]

In 1552, a piece of legislation, Keeping Holy-Days and Fasting Days, devoted a full paragraph to allowing the Garter to keep St. George's Day as a feast:

> Provided always, and be it enacted by the authority aforesaid that it shall be lawful to the knights of the right honourable Order of the Garter, and to every of them to keep and celebrate solemnly the feast of their order commonly called St. George's feast, yearly from henceforth the xxij, xxiij, and xxiv days of April, and at such other time and times as yearly shall be thought convenient by the king's highness, his heirs and successors, and the said knight of the said honourable order, or any of them, now being, or hereafter to be; any thing in this act heretofore mentioned to the contrary notwithstanding.[49]

---

[48] Beltz, *Memorials of the Order of the Garter*, xcv.
[49] Stephens, *The Statutes Relating to the Ecclesiastical and Eleemosynary Institutions.* 336.

The document demonstrates the importance of the feast of St. George to the Order of the Garter. Even with the onslaught directed against the veneration of saints, the companions of the Garter were able to celebrate the feast of their patron.

On St. George's Day in 1550, the knight's chapter agreed to examine the structure of the Garter and to reform it. The king developed three drafts to alter the organization between 1550 and 1551, and the new reforms broke all ties with the patron saint. The name of the Garter was changed: "The Order should from thenceforth be called the Order of the Garter and not of St. George lest the honour due to God might seem to be given to a creature." Likewise, the image of St. George and his red cross was removed from the badge. At first, Edward wanted the badge to depict him, but the image selected was of a nameless "armed knight sitting on horseback." The feast was moved from St. George's Day to Whitsun-eve, Whitsunday, and Whitmonday. The solemnity of the feast was greatly reduced and consisted of Morning Prayer, Evening Prayer, and Holy Communion. The knights also discussed matters in chapter and ate supper and dinner together. [50] The reforms of Edward, however, never came to be, for he died in July 1553.

The ascension of Mary to the throne reversed the path of the Garter. She abrogated the statutes passed under her half-brother and restored the great feast of the Garter to St. George's Day. The Queen's husband, Philip, was installed as a member of the Garter, and he presided over the ceremonies and chapters, personally leading the procession of the Garter on St. George's Day in 1555.[51] When Elizabeth came to the throne, she did not undertake the overhaul which her half-brother attempted. Rather, the feast of St. George continued during her reign but in a subdued fashion. One major alteration took place on April 23, 1567, when she decreed that the feast

---

[50] The statutes are in Beltz, *Memorials of the Order of the Garter*, xcvii-xcix.
[51] Hutton, *Stations of the Sun*, 216; Beltz, *Memorials of the Order of the Garter*, c-ci.

was not necessarily to be held at Windsor, but wh
was present. After that, only a few celebrations we?
on St. George's Day, only for the appointment of
son to the Garter or with the sovereign's permission.[52]

The death of Elizabeth brought an end to the Tudor line and began that of the Stuarts, whose early monarchs were devoted to
restoring the grandeur of St. George's Day. They reinstated many of
the ancient customs of the Garter, including representations of St.
George on important symbols, the ladies of the Garter, and the grand
feasts at Windsor. The activities of the Garter were suspended during
the Civil War, but rejuvenated with the restoration of Charles II. In
April 1661, twenty knights were installed on the feast to restore the
reduced number of knights following the Civil War. Though the devotion of the Stuarts to St. George was strong, the annual feast on
April 23 was discontinued after the Restoration. From 1667 onward,
the records of the Garter make no reference to an annual feast on St.
George's Day.[53] Knights continued to be elected and invested in the
Garter, but rarely on or around April 23.

Several of the Stuart kings selected St. George's Day for their
coronation. Charles II was crowned in England on April 23, 1661;
James II's coronation occurred on April 23, 1685; and Anne's coronation was April 23, 1702.[54] The connection between St. George and the
Stuarts remained even after the Hanoverian line came to power.
Crowds assaulted George I with the shouts of "St. George for England, no Hanoverians." The son of James II, James Francis Edward
Stuart, held as the real heir to the throne by the Stuarts, went by the
title, "Chevalier of St. George" or "the knight of St. George." When
he invaded Ireland in 1715 in order to reclaim the throne, supporters
rioted for James across the British Isles on St. George's Day. Ten

[52] Beltz, *Memorials of the Order of the Garter*, ciii-civ.
[53] Beltz, *Memorials of the Order of the Garter*, cxxxi.
[54] Anthony Hamilton, Philibert Gramont, and Walter Scott, *Memoirs of the Court of Charles the Second* (London: Henry G. Bohn, 1846), 335-38; Francis Sandford, *The History of the Coronation of King James II* (London: Thomas Newcome, 1687); Arthur Penrhyn Stanley, *Historical Memorials of Westminster Abbey* (London: Murray, 1886), 75-82.

ιousand people drank to the health of James in London, great bonfires blazed all over the city, and King George was burned in effigy
with William III and Oliver Cromwell. Those who did not support
James had their homes attacked, including the Lord Mayor.[55]

The Hanoverian monarchs realized the symbolic power of St.
George, and thus sought to reshape his image. Aided by the fact that
early monarchs and the patron saint shared the same name, the Hanoverians recast St. George into a Protestant image, a knight slaying a
papal enemy. One poem composed for the entrance of George I read,
"Their Popish dragon must now lose his Sting, Because St. George
our champion is, and King." Images also contained the new symbolism. A medal commemorating the coronation of George portrayed St.
George killing a dragon, and the painting, *The Landing of King George in
Greenwich*, depicted the king, accompanied by St. George, trampling
the dragon of popery.[56]

Knights of the Garter continued to celebrate St. George's Day after the Reformation. A great festival occurred when Henry, the earl of
Derby and knight of the Garter since 1574, visited Liverpool in 1577.
Festivities commenced on April 22, the eve of St. George's Day,
when the Earl attended a service at St. Nicholas Church accompanied
by an elaborate procession. After the liturgy, a mock battle was staged
with cannons and ships. On St. George's Day itself, the Earl processed in grand fashion to church, attended a service, and then
witnessed another mock battle. The sequence of events was repeated
again in the evening.[57] Sir Henry Sidney, invested in the Garter in
1564, had two grand celebrations on St. George's Day. In 1581, he
hosted a celebration at Shrewsbury that entailed welcomes, processions, sermons, ceremonies, banquets, orations, martial games, and

---

[55] Martin Haile, *James Francis Edward, the Old Chevalier* (London: J.M. Dent & Co, 1907), 153,
167.
[56] Hannah Smith, *Georgian Monarchy: Politics and Culture, 1714-1760* (Cambridge: Cambridge
University Press, 2006), 27-28.
[57] David George, ed., *Records of Early English Drama. Lancashire* (Toronto: University of Toronto Press, 1991), xxviii-xxix, 42-43.

farewells lasting three weeks. The following year he staged another celebration on St. George's Day in Ludlow.[58]

Some pageants of St. George continued after the Reformation in a limited fashion. In Wells, a reenactment of the battle of St. George and the dragon took place in 1607. The play formed part of a long celebration from May to June intended to raise money for the local church. The performances created tension with Puritan sympathizers, and a lawsuit was brought by the Puritan John Hole against the festivities' organizers. The case was heard in the Star Chamber, producing an ample amount of evidence for the plays in the form of court documents. The celebration included a "maypole, street dancing, ales, a Robin Hood, morris troupes, and shows and pageants by the city's six craft guild companies." The play of St. George took place on June 17, and possibly was staged again on June 25. The figure of St. George was played by David Trymme, with a company of about twenty to thirty men. St. George rode on horseback, armed with a spear and a sword, and he fought with the dragon. A poem written about the play also described the figures of the king and queen of Egypt, suggesting the performance may have been an elaborate affair with a king, queen, and princess.[59] The play was performed again in 1613 when Queen Anne visited Wells. The mayor ordered the craft guilds to put on a presentation for the queen, and for her visit, the Mercer's Company performed "a Morrice daunce of Younge children, The Giant and the Giantesse. Kinge Ptolomeus w/th his Queene & daughter was to bee devoured of the dragon. St. George w/th his knights who slew the dragon and rescued the virgin."[60] The list of characters implies that a sophisticated pageant of St. George took place.

---

[58] George, ed., *REED. Lancashire*, 85-86, 228-30, 394.

[59] James Stokes and Robert Joseph Alexander, eds., *Records of Early English Drama. Somerset* (Toronto: University of Toronto Press, 1996), 1:334, 1:340, 1:352, 2:709-10, 2:724; Bruce R. Smith, *The Acoustic World of Early Modern England: Attending to the O-Factor* (Chicago: University of Chicago Press, 1999), 133-35; David Underdown, *Revel, Riot, and Rebellion: Popular Politics and Culture in England 1603-1660* (Oxford: Oxford University Press, 1987), 55.

[60] Stokes and Alexander, eds., *REED. Somerset*, 1:372; David Underdown, Susan Dwyer Amussen, and Mark A. Kishlansky. *Political Culture and Cultural Politics in Early Modern England: Essays Presented to David Underdown* (Manchester: Manchester University Press, 1995), 150-51.

The town of Chester also revived the celebration of St. George's Day in the seventeenth century. Chester had celebrated St. George's Day in the past by providing gifts to prisoners, carrying a banner in procession, and riding the banns for the Whitsunday plays. The celebration of St. George's Day, however, was neglected for half a century after the ascension of Elizabeth and her repression of traditional devotions. Robert Amerye, a former sheriff, revived the festivities in Chester but in a different form from earlier celebrations. Instead of a procession, mock battle, or religious service, Amerye organized a horse race for April 23, 1610, with three silver cups to be distributed as prizes.[61] For the first celebration in 1610, Amerye penned "a triumph in honor of her prince." The triumph was for Prince Henry, the oldest son of James I, and the play was dedicated to the king, his heir, and "that Noble victor Saint George our aforesaid English Champion."[62] A procession composed part of the celebration and included a dragon and an individual representing St. George on horseback with a helmet and shield, accompanied by three attendants. A series of figures gave speeches including Fame, Mercury, Chester, Britain, Cambria, Rumor, Peace, Plenty, Envy, Love and Joy. Most of the speeches gave honor to the king, the prince, and the country. Cambria's speech mentioned St. George's Day: "Which day Saint George hath blissfully created, To Take his Birth-right; with such great joy, As such a day was never consecrated, To memorize which more than blissful feast."[63] Rumor's speech focused exclusively on honoring St. George and commemorated St. George as a great warrior and dragon-slayer.[64] Even sixty years after the suppression of the ridings, the achievements of the patron saint and his feast day were

---

[61] Frederic Shoberl, *Horse-Racing: Its History and Early Records of the Principal and Other Race Meetings: with Anecdotes, Etc.* (London: Saunders, Otley, and Co., 1863), 100-120.

[62] Richard Davies and Thomas Corser, *Chester's Triumph in Honor of Her Prince, As It Was Performed Upon St. George's Day, 1610, in the Foresaid Citie* (Manchester: Chetham Society, 1844), xxiii; Lawrence M. Clopper, ed., *Records of Early English Drama. Chester* (Toronto: University of Toronto Press, 1979), 258-62.

[63] Davies, *Chester's Triumph in Honor of Her Prince*, xxxv.

[64] Davies, *Chester's Triumph in Honor of Her Prince*, xxxv-xxxvi.

still remembered, but this celebration differed from previous pageants of St. George in that it focused mainly on the king and royal family. The triumph did not honor St. George but the prince, and the patron saint's importance came from his association and reaffirmation of the royal cult. Participants of the horse race consisted of elite gentlemen, and commoners were distant spectators, whereas, pageants of the pre-Reformation period had been primarily for the peasants. Lastly, the pageant was secondary to the horse race. The triumph was only performed at the first horse race in 1610, and no evidence exists for any further performances including St. George. In future years, the race was the sole event held during the St. George's Day celebration.[65]

Literature in the era after the Reformation transformed the image of St. George into a desacralized version of the medieval saint. Two popular romantic accounts guided the process of reinvention, Edmund Spenser's *The Faerie Queene* (1590), and Richard Johnson's *The Famous history of the Seven Champions of Christendom* (1596). Spenser's work was a Protestant retelling of the story of St. George. The main hero of the poem's first book is the Redcrosse Knight, who plays the role of St. George. The name of St. George is first mentioned in canto ii, but the Redcrosse Knight learns of his own identity in canto x. The text reveals his English roots and that he shall be known as St. George:

> For thou amongst those Saints, whom thou doest see,
> Shalt be a Saint, and thine owne nations frend
> And Patrone: thou Saint *George* shalt called bee,
> Saint *George* of mery England, the signe of victoree.[66]

The following two cantos retell the traditional story of St. George. According to the legend, he follows Una, a princess, to her parent's

---

[65] McClendon, "A Moveable Feast," 24-25; Underdown, *Revel, Riot, and Rebellion,* 69-70.

[66] Edmund Spenser, *The Faerie Queene, Book One* (Boston: Houghton, Mifflin and Company, 1905), 186.

castle, under attack by a dragon. He battles the dragon and is mortally wounded two times, but both times he is revived. The Redcrosse Knight finally kills the dragon after wounding the beast five times in three days. The king, pleased by the slaying of the dragon, offers Una to the Redcrosse Knight. The couple is betrothed, but the Redcrosse Knight serves the Faerie Queene for six years before marrying Una. The Redcrosse Knight, as St. George, introduced new elements into the legend of the saint. First, the Redcrosse Knight represented an indistinct person rather than a real, historical individual. The Redcrosse Knight's journey symbolized any person searching for truth because he had flaws and made mistakes; he was not a powerful heavenly intercessor. Second, the Redcrosse Knight was born in England, not in the Middle East. Therefore, he was a national figure, a representation of all of England. Third, the story of the Redcrosse Knight emphasized a dragon-slaying knight, and completely neglected St. George's martyrdom for the faith. Lastly, the story launched an assault on the Catholic Church. Spenser's view of Rome is revealed in the representation of the two female figures that pursue the Redcrosse Knight. The first is Una, who symbolized the Church of England and all that is good; and the second is Duessa, a witch who represented the Catholic Church and all that is evil. The juxtaposition of Protestantism as good and Catholicism as evil is an important theme of the work. The influence of *The Faerie Queene* was profound. It was well received at court and became one of the most popular English poems. The wide acceptance of the work gave it a lasting impact of the perception of St. George and the celebration of his day.[67]

Richard Johnson, a contemporary of Spenser, composed *The Famous history of the Seven Champions of Christendom*, a work equally influential in the formation of the new image of St. George. The book

---

[67] Elizabeth Heale, *The Faerie Queene: A Reader's Guide* (Cambridge: Cambridge University Press, 1987), 23-24.

relates the adventures of St. George of England, St. Andrew of Scotland, St. Patrick of Ireland, St. Denis of France, St. James of Spain, St. Anthony of Italy, and St. David of Wales. St. George's story, central to the book, portrayed him as a romantic knight. According to the tale, St. George is born in Coventry with birthmarks depicting a dragon, a cross on his hand, and a garter on his left leg. Kalyb, an enchantress, steals the boy, and raises him in the forest. As he reaches maturity, he begins to desire adventure, escapes from Kalyb, and frees the other six champions, also imprisoned by Kalyb. St. George goes to Egypt, battles with a dragon, and liberates the princess Sabra, daughter of King Ptolemy. Almindor, a suitor of Sabra, convinces the king to betray St. George, resulting in his imprisonment, but he immediately escapes. Upon his return to Egypt seven years later, he finds Sabra married to Almindor, but her virginity preserved. The couple reunites and is married in Greece. The seven champions came together once again and through battle conquer Persia, Egypt, and Morocco. St. George returns to Coventry with Sabra, and they have three sons. After Sabra dies, St. George leaves for a pilgrimage to Jerusalem. He returns home to battle another dragon in England, and in battle, he and the dragon are mortally wounded.

Johnson's depiction of St. George mirrored many of the changes in Spenser's work. St. George was born in England and portrayed as a knight and dragon-slayer. As with Spenser, the text did not mention the martyrdom of St. George, so essential to early Passions of the saint. Instead Johnson placed more emphasis on St. George's romance with Sabra and his three children. Lastly, the work did not directly attack Catholicism, but it indirectly challenged devotion to the saints. Johnson's liberal alteration of the life of St. George, borrowed heavily from the tale of Sir Bevis of Hampton, changed the saint into a purely romantic figure. Johnson's version of the saint became a popular inspiration for eighteenth-century chapbooks, and thus formed people's impression of St. George to the present day. In short, Johnson and Spenser portrayed St. George as a mythical English knight interested in warfare and princesses, undermining the image of St. George as a martyr and saint, thus diminishing religious devotion to him.[68]

Undoubtedly, medieval devotion to saints was one of the main targets of religious reformers, and the commemoration of feast days suffered as a result. In particular, saints of uncertain origins faced particularly harsh criticism. Opponents singled out St. George as one of the most controversial of saints due to his non-biblical roots, the church's condemnation of his early Passions, the dragons and maidens that filled his legends, and the limited historical records about him. Religious reformers had no shortage of material to assail veneration of St. George.

St. George came under suspicion in Desiderius Erasmus' satirical work, *The Praise of Folly*. Though Erasmus remained a Catholic, the work, written in 1509, helped ignite the Protestant Reformation. Erasmus included St. George, along with Sts. Barbara and Christopher, as saints whose lives were full of "feigned miracles and strangle lies" and were an "old wives' story." He continued, "If there be any poetical saint, or one of whom there goes more stories than ordinary, as for example, a George, a Christopher, or a Barbara, you shall see him more religiously worshipped than Peter, Paul, or even Christ himself... they have gotten a Hercules, another Hippolytus, and a St. George, whose horse most religiously set out with trappings and bosses there wants little but they worship; however, they endeavor to make him their friend by some present or other, and to swear by his master's brazen helmet is an oath for a prince."[69]

In his seminal sixteenth-century work, *Institutes of the Christian Religion*, John Calvin challenged the very existence of St. George. He

---

[68] Johnson, *The Seven Champions of Christendom*; Gordon Hall Gerould, *Saints' Legends* (Boston: Houghton, Mifflin and Company, 1916), 318-20; Riches, *St. George*, 179-82.
[69] Desiderius Erasmus, *The Praise of Folly* (Ann Arbor: University of Michigan Press, 1958), 66-67, 75.

referred to the saint in a section questioning intercessory prayer directed to saints:

> There is no mention of fictitious intercession, superstition having rashly adopted intercessors who have not been divinely appointed. While the Scripture abounds in various forms of prayer, we find no example of this intercession, without which Papists think there is no prayer. Moreover, it is evident that this superstition is the result of distrust, because they are either not contented with Christ as an intercessor, or have altogether robbed him of this honor. This last is easily proved by their effrontery in maintaining, as the strongest of all their arguments for the intercession of the saints, that we are unworthy of familiar access to God. This, indeed, we acknowledge to be most true, but we thence infer that they leave nothing to Christ, because they consider his intercession as nothing, unless it is supplemented by that of George and Hypolyte, and similar phantoms.[70]

Peter Heylyn, a defender of St. George, wrote in 1631 that St. George faced "a second persecution... a martyr, not in his person only, but in his history."[71] Heylyn cited, in addition to Erasmus and Calvin, the German Lutheran Martin Chemnitz in *Examinis concilii Tridentini* (1566-73), the English Puritan William Perkins in *A Warning against the Idolatrie of the Last Times* (1601), the dean of Canterbury John Boys, and Cardinal Robert Bellarmine, among others, who claimed that St. George did not exist.[72]

In addition to questioning St. George's existence, another scholarly challenge maintained that St. George was inspired by George, the Arian bishop of Alexandria. The first individual to propagate this

---

[70] John Calvin, *Institutes of the Christian Religion*, trans. Henry Beveridge (Edinburgh: Calvin Translation Society, 1845), 2:491.

[71] Peter Heylyn, *The Historie of That Most Famous Saint and Souldier of Christ Jesus, St. George of Cappadocia* (London: Henry Seyle, 1631), 41.

[72] Heylyn, *The Historie of That Most Famous Saint,* 45-47.

opinion was John Rainolds (often spelled Reynolds), a leading English churchman with strong Calvinist tendencies.[73] His theory concerning St. George is found in *De Romanae Ecclesiae Idolatria* (1596). The idea that St. George came from the Arian George gained increasing acceptance in the seventeenth and eighteenth centuries, and Edward Gibbon further popularized the theory in his work, *The History of the Decline and Fall of the Roman Empire* (1776-1789).[74] According to Gibbon, George was born at Epiphania in Cilicia and surnamed the Cappadocian. From humble origins, he accumulated a great deal of wealth by securing a contract to supply bacon to the Roman army. His business deals were "infamous" for their "fraud and corruption." Following his venture into business, he embraced the Arian faith with zeal. He was elevated to the bishopric of Alexandria, the seat of Athanasius, the great adversary of Arianism. He ruled with "cruelty and avarice" and oppressed the members of his dioceses, both pagan and Christian. The ascension of Julian the Apostate brought an end to George's reign. The pagan, Latin historian Ammianus Marcellinus recorded an account of his death:

> They fell upon George, howling and yelling, beat him about, trampled upon him, and finally spread-eagled him and finished him off... Not content with this, the brutal mob loaded the mutilated bodies [of George and his supporters] on camels and took them to the beach, where they burned them and threw their ashes into the sea, for fear that the remains might be collected and have a church built over them. This had happened in other cases, when men persecuted for their religion endured torture till they met a glorious death with their faith unspotted, and are now called martyrs. The wretched victims

---

[73] Not to be confused with Edward Reynolds, bishop of Norwich.

[74] Claims that St. George was an Arian bishop can be found in Amandus Polanus' *Syntagma theologiae christianae* (1609); Caesar Baronius' revision of the *Roman Martyrology*; Gibbon stated that the first reference that St. George was an Arian bishop was made by Isaac Pontanus.

of these cruel sufferings might have been saved by the help of their fellow-Christians had not the whole population been inflamed by universal hatred of George.[75]

Gibbon thus argued that the heroic death of George caused people to forget his life, and they remembered him as a martyr. Gibbon's assertion is reasonable, for the pagan mob took great care to destroy the body precisely to prevent the development of a cult. St. George, an Arian saint, the argument continues, was cleansed of his Arian roots and over time accepted by the Catholic Church. In particular, his identity merged with the nameless martyr in Eusebius' account of the persecutions under Diocletian. In Gibbon's words: "The odious stranger, disguising every circumstance of time and place, assumed the mask of a martyr, a saint, and a Christian hero; and the infamous George of Cappadocia has been transformed into the renowned St. George of England, the patron of arms, of chivalry, and of the garter."[76]

The claim that a corrupt Roman contractor and hated Arian bishop was the "real" St. George of England detracted greatly from the cult of St. George, and the theory found resonance among intellectuals due to the many similarities between the two individuals. Both figures shared the same first name, had a connection with Cappadocia, and thus, were known as George of Cappadocia. Their stories include a reference to the Roman army, one as a warrior and the other as a contractor. They both had a heroic "martyr's" death. In both stories, they battled with an Athanasius. The Arian George fought with St. Athanasius, and in the early Passions of St. George, he battled the magician Athanasius. Lastly, Pope Gelasius I condemned the legends of St. George for being produced by heretics and schismatics in the fifth century.

---

[75] The life and death of George of Cappadocia are described by Ammianus, Gregory Nazianzen and Epiphanius Heeres; quote from: Ammianus Marcellinus, *The Later Roman Empire: A.D. 354-378*, trans. Walter Hamilton (Harmondsworth: Penguin, 1986), 247.

[76] Gibbon, Edward. *The History of the Decline and Fall of the Roman Empire*. New York: Macmillan, 1914. 496-98.

George of Cappadocia was not the only individual claimed as the source of the "real" St. George. Thomas Salmon, divine and writer on music, asserted that the real patron of England was George, bishop of Ostia and papal legate to England in the eighth century. He elaborated his theory in *A New Historical Account of St. George for England* (1704).[77] John Byrom, poet, claimed St. Gregory the Great as the source of St. George, making St. Gregory the real patron of England. St. Gregory's connection to England consisted of his commissioning of St. Augustine of Canterbury to convert the English to Christianity. Byrom formulated his opinion in a poem, in which he pondered: "If Georgius ben't a Mistake for Gregorius." His argument never gained traction, and it remained peculiarly Bryom's view. He wrote the poem in the 1750s, but published it twenty years later.[78]

St. George had his defenders however. John Selden, one advocate, examined St. George and the Order of the Garter in *Titles of Honor* (1614, 2nd edition 1631). Selden argued that the antiquity of the cult of St. George demonstrated that he was a historical figure. The work also included a paragraph arguing against the connection between the Arian bishop and the patron saint of England. The greatest defender of St. George in the seventeenth century, however, was Peter Heylyn. His work, *The historie of that most famous saint and souldier of Christ Jesus, St. George of Cappadocia* (1631), provided the first full-length investigation of St. George. Heylyn, a staunch royalist and supporter of the conservative religious reforms of Archbishop Laud, found it necessary to defend St. George from the attacks of Puritans. The dedication of the work lamented that St. George was called a heretic and phantom, and explained that the honor of the king and the knights of the Garter motivated him to write the history of St. George. Heylyn

---

[77] Thomas Salmon, *A New Historical Account of St. George for England and the Original of the Most Noble Order of Garter* (London: R. Janeway, 1704); Salmon argued that the medieval St. George was inspired by the Arian bishop and was confused in England with George, the Bishop of Ostia.

[78] John Byrom, *The Poems of John Byrom*, ed., Adolphus William Ward (Manchester: Chetham Society, 1894), 472.

built on the contributions of Selden, but he investigated the sources more thoroughly. He collected what he thought were false statements about St. George in the first part of the book: the dragon story, St. George's English birth, the Arian question, and St. George's nonexistence. The second half of the work explained the development of the cult of St. George in the East and in the West. Heylyn's work served as the basis for countless other studies on St. George. Heylyn and Selden wrote to prove the ancient origins of the cult of St. George and to save St. George as patron of the English monarchy and the Garter. Their zeal, however, influenced the accuracy of their works. They were responsible for numerous mistakes repeated in future works, wrongly claiming that: (1) the cult of St. George originally focused on him as a warrior saint and not a martyr, (2) St. George was popular during the Anglo-Saxon period, (3) St. George was patron of England because of Richard I, and (4) the climax of his cult came during the Hundred Years' War.[79]

The controversy surrounding St. George became heated in the Society of Antiquaries of London. The Society, founded in 1707, was charged with "the encouragement, advancement and furtherance of the study and knowledge of the antiquities and history of this and other countries."[80] The society held its annual meetings on St. George's Day, and St. George was patron of the Society. They selected St. George's Day in honor of George II, founder of the Society and as the Sovereign of the Order of the Garter, and in honor of St. George.[81] Members of the Society who opposed the traditional view of St. George were first to assert their claims. Byrom, who claimed St. Gregory was the real St. George, sent his poem about the saint in a letter to Lord Willoughby, president of the Society. A fellow of the Society, John Pettingall composed the work, *A dissertation on the original of the equestrian figure of the George and of the garter* (1753), in which he

---

[79] MacGregor, "Salue Martir Spes Anglorum," 19; John Selden, *Titles of Honor* (London: R. Whittakers, 1631).

[80] David M. Evans, *The Remains of Distant Times: Archaeology and the National Trust* (Woodbridge, Suffolk: Boydell, 1996), 8.

[81] Received a Royal Charter in 1751.

argued St. George was the Arian bishop. Byrom's and Pettingall's attacks on St. George were answered by Samuel Pegge, another fellow of the Society. Pegge read a paper to the Society in defense of St. George on April 10, 1777, and it appeared in *Archaeologia*, the Society's journal, in 1779 as "Observations on the History of St. George, the Patron Saint of England." A controversial Catholic priest, John Milner, also defended St. George against those who held he was an Arian bishop in 1792. Milner produced a pamphlet, and the full title explains his motive: *An Historical and Critical Inquiry into the Existence and Character of St. George, Patron of England, of the Order of the Garter, and of the Antiquarian Society; in which the assertion of Edward Gibbon, Esq. and of certain other writers, concerning this Saint, are discussed, In a Letter to the Right Hon. George Earl of Leicester, President of the Antiquarian Society.* Scholars of the seventeenth and eighteenth centuries damaged St. George's reputation, causing the cult of St. George and the celebration of his feast day to suffer greatly. Religious reformers accused the patron saint of England of being a mythical knight with no real existence, and intellectuals during the Enlightenment argued that St. George was really a corrupt Arian bishop, among other things.[82]

The declining significance of St. George's Day occurred within a wider shift in the understanding of time. The medieval calendar was rooted in a cyclical view of the world. Every year repeated the same cycle of feast days and celebrations, with no alteration in the pattern and no anticipation of change. This concept of progress rested on the idea that eventually earthly time would come to an end when the world ceased to exist. The Protestant, and later Enlightenment, view of time emphasized progress in *this* world, believing in an advancement from one year to the next. The modern, linear concept of time conflicted with the cyclical medieval view. The modern idea also

---

[82] John Pettingal, *A Dissertation on the Original of the Equestrian Figure of the George and of the Garter.* (London: Samuel Paterson, 1753); Samuel Pegge, "Observations on the History of St. George," 1-32.

downplayed the importance of the timeless eternal and increased the importance of worldly time. This shift was reinforced by the movement away from an agrarian society tied to the cycles of the earth to an industrial society dependent on man.[83]

The secularization of the calendar existed as a corollary to the new understanding of time. Religious feasts composed much of the medieval calendar, and ecclesiastical leaders of the Catholic Church controlled the composition of the calendar. As shown in previous chapters, the feast of St. George was introduced into the calendar through martyrologies, church synods, and declarations of bishops. When the church became subject to the state in the English Reformation, the state seized control of the calendar. Leading Protestants advocated altering the religious calendar in the post-Reformation era, but they needed the approval of the monarchy and parliament. Moreover, the new calendar contained a proliferation of royal, secular feasts, and many of these new holidays replaced religious celebrations. According to historian David Cressy, the monarchs created "a new national, secular, and dynastic calendar centering on the anniversaries of the Protestant monarch."[84] National holidays commemorated the anniversary of the monarch's ascension to the throne and birthdays of the monarch and members of the royal family. Several royal holidays transcended the monarchs associated with them, surviving beyond their reign. The ascension of Elizabeth on November 17 remained an annual celebration even after her death. Guy Fawkes Day, the day James I survived an assassination attempt, on November 5 continues to be celebrated as a Protestant holiday. The martyrdom of Charles I, on January 30, became an important religious feast after the Restoration, and Royal Oak Day (Oak Apple Day) on May 29 celebrated the restoration of the monarchy after the Civil War. The calendar was also nationalized in the early modern period. Churches throughout England used the religious calendar in the *Book of Common Prayer*, and the state universally sanctioned secular holidays. The local feasts of

---

[83] Sommerville, *The Secularization of Early Modern England*, 33-34.
[84] Cressy, *Bonfires and Bells*, viii.

"Merry England" slowly fell into disuse. In short, this period witnessed a slow transition from a medieval, local, church-controlled
calendar to a modern, national, state-controlled one.[85]

The English, however, did not proceed as far as the French Revolutionary Calendar. The new French calendar, introduced in 1793,
based on a similar idea of secularization was far more radical. In an
effort to remove every vestige of Christianity, the French changed the
week to ten days, renamed the months, and marked the first year of
the Republic as Year One. The Christian week, Sunday, all holy days,
and the Year of Our Lord were all eliminated. Though England did
not experience as drastic a revision, the calendar slowly and similarly
was secularized and came under the control of the state.[86]

In the nineteenth century, Auguste Comte, a French thinker, developed the Positivist Calendar. In his new calendar, he named the
months and days, not after Catholic saints, but after great figures in
history. Though the calendar included religious individuals, it focused
mainly on non-religious figures like Aristotle, Charlemagne, Dante,
and Descartes. This calendar never became popular, but demonstrated increasing devotion to the "Great Men" of history. These figures
increasingly replaced saints as inspiration for holidays. St. George
shared his feast day with William Shakespeare, one of the greatest
individuals in English history. April 23 was the day of Shakespeare's
death, and by some accounts, the day of his birth. Shakespeare's baptism took place on April 26, 1564, but the exact date of his birth is
unknown. The birth of Shakespeare, without evidence, was celebrated
in later times on April 23, conveniently St. George's Day. Eighteenth-
century historians are to blame for the error. George Steevens' renowned biography of Shakespeare in 1773 noted his birthday was
April 23, and the inaccuracy spread from this authoritative account
into numerous other works. To further connect the great playwright

---

[85] Sommerville, *The Secularization of Early Modern England*, 33-44.
[86] Alan Aldridge, *Religion in the Contemporary World: A Sociological Introduction* (Cambridge: Polity Press, 2000), 152-53.

with St. George's Day, Shakespeare died on April 23, 1616.[87] As a result, the feast of St. George became intertwined with the celebration of the birth and death of Shakespeare. April 23 no longer belonged exclusively to St. George's Day, but to Shakespeare as well.

Celebration of St. George's Day entered a period of steady decline starting in the reign of Henry VIII. Popular celebrations such as the ridings and pageants abruptly ended in the early stages of the Reformation. The few that remained, as with Norwich, were completely altered and bore no connection to the saint. Royal festivities centered on the Order of the Garter lasted longer, slowly declining in grandeur and then fading from records in the late seventeenth century. The religious feast remained part of the Church of England, but the holy day was only a shadow of its former glory.

The decline in the celebration of St. George's Day can be attributed to several factors, a changing religious climate being the most important. Protestants targeted devotion to the saints, and they argued against praying to saints, honoring images of saints, celebrating their feast days, and every other form of devotion. As a result, St. George's Day diminished in importance. Those of a worldlier mindset also attacked St. George's Day. The first wave of dissenters claimed that St. George did not exist; they were followed by another group, most famously represented by Edward Gibbon, who claimed he was a corrupt Arian bishop. These accusations tarnished St. George's image and cult, and St. George's Day declined as a result of these challenges. Lastly, English monarchs began to dispute the importance of holy days, replacing the traditional ceremonial calendar of religious feasts with a calendar based on nationalistic holidays commemorating events in the life of monarchs. The triple assault of religious reformers, philosophers, and monarchs overpowered the supporters of St.

---

[87] S. Schoenbaum, *William Shakespeare: A Compact Documentary Life* (New York: Oxford University Press, 1987), 24-25; Anthony Holden, *William Shakespeare: The Man Behind the Genius: a Biography* (Boston: Little, Brown, 1999), 10-11.

George's Day, and by the late eighteenth century, the celebrations of the feast no longer took place in England.

The image of St. George was altered in an unimaginable way during the Reformation and Enlightenment. In the medieval period, he was primarily remembered as a martyr, but he also acquired the image of knight and dragon-slayer. From the sixteenth to eighteenth centuries, St. George as a martyr and saint was attacked rigorously, and he was reduced to a non-entity or Arian bishop of Alexandria. The representation of St. George as a knight and dragon-slayer lasted longer. In the popular imagination of the English, St. George became a mythical knight and dragon-slayer. During this time, few English thought St. George was a glorious martyr, and fewer still celebrated his feast on April 23.

Chapter Five
Resurgence of the Day:
St. George's Day in North America

W hen William Stephens was appointed president of the county of Savannah, Georgia in 1741, he encountered an ethnically divided settlement. In order to unify the settlers, he turned to the ceremonial calendar of the British Empire. He recorded in his journal the efforts he took to encourage the celebration of St. George's Day, St. Andrew's Day, St. David's Day, the Birthday of George II, and Pope's Day (Guy Fawkes Day). On April 23, 1742, Stephens ordered the flag hoisted, a couple gallons of wine to be distributed to the public, and a five gun salute "to Cherish that Humour, and promote Unity." The festivities, which previous records do not mention, were quickly and enthusiastically incorporated by the population of Georgia. By 1745, Stephens, "considering the many rejoicying days," thought to limit the festivities on St. George's Day.[1]

The pattern of the introduction of new holidays into North America by immigrant populations and then the enthusiastic incorporation and celebration of them by the local population, is a familiar

---

[1] William Stephens, *The Journal of William Stephens, 1741-1743,* ed., Ellis Merton Coulter (Athens: University of Georgia Press. 1958), 68 -69; Brendan McConville, *The King's Three Faces: The Rise & Fall of Royal America, 1688-1776* (Chapel Hill: University of North Carolina Press, 2006), 73-75; Part of this chapter appeared in Hanael P. Bianchi, "The St. George's Society of New York and the Resurgence of England's National Holiday," *New York History* 92 (Winter–Spring 2011): 53-64, and the material is being reprinted with permission; For recent scholarship on English associations in the United States see Tanja Bueltmanna and Donald M. MacRailda, "Globalizing St George: English associations in the Anglo-world to the 1930s," *Journal of Global History* 7, no. 1 (2013): 79-105.

theme. This chapter examines the transfer of St. George's Day across the Atlantic, and how, ironically, these celebrations grew in the empire as they declined in England. In North America, a resurgence of the celebration of St. George's Day occurred at the end of the eighteenth century, but these new celebrations differed from the religious, royal, and popular celebrations of the medieval period. They completely neglected St. George as a saint and real person. Rarely mentioning the patron of England, celebrants only referred to him as a representation of the nation. Celebrations instead focused on English nationalism over St. George, and the holiday was orchestrated by new institutions, ethnic societies focused on providing mutual benefit to members, that were more interested in promoting English ideals than seeking the intercession of a saint.

The upheaval of the Reformation and the Enlightenment adversely impacted the celebration of St. George's Day in England. Liturgical developments outlined in the *Book of Common Prayer* limited religious celebrations. Popular celebrations, with a few minor exceptions, were halted, and royal celebrations were irregular and on a small scale. Robert Hampton, in his work on medieval dates and customs, re-marked in 1841 that St. George's Day in England was "now passed over without notice."[2]

The revival of St. George's Day came from an improbable loca-tion as the British colonies in North America possessed many attributes that appeared hostile to the devotion and celebration of St. George. Many of the early settlers, in particular those in New Eng-land, were Puritans, and they called for the most radical overhaul of the calendar, including the elimination of all religious holidays except Sunday. Their disdain for the patron saint of England and his symbols is evident in a story from Cotton Mather's *Magnalia Christi Americana*

---

[2] Robert T. Hampson, *Medii Ævi Kalendarium; Or, Dates, Charters, and Customs of the Middle Ages* (London: H.K. Causton, 1841), 241.

(1702). Mather recorded an account of colonists who "cut the red-cross out of the king's colours, to testifie a zeal against the continu-ance or appearance of a superstition. This hot action met with a warm censure; and besides the mischiefs hereby occasioned among the trained soldiers, whereof some were loth to follow the colours which had the cross, least they should put honour upon a Popish idol."[3]

The religious disposition of the Puritan population was only one of many obstacles facing the revitalization of St. George's Day in North America. Isolation and low population density made it difficult to celebrate a uniform ritual year. As William Stephens found in Georgia, holidays were not celebrated in remote areas of the colonies. Nor was the population of North America solely English, but a het-erogeneous group with a variety of feasts and celebrations, forcing St. George's Day to compete with many holidays from outside the Eng-lish celebratory cycle. Lastly, the American population developed their own celebrations, and in some instances, the feasting took a distinc-tive anti-English tone. Yet amid this seemingly negative environment, St. George's Day was revived in New York, Philadelphia, Quebec, and countless other cities thousands of miles from England.

Flooding into America, English immigrants brought with them the cultural practices of England to their new homeland, including the celebration of St. George's Day. A trickle of English settlers came to the North American colonies in late sixteenth century, but the first successful permanent colony was Jamestown, established in 1607. The stream of English colonists steadily increased with time. English col-onists dominated early European immigration to North America, and in the 1790 census, 90 percent of the United States' white population was of English descent. By 1820, the English numbered 350,000, Irish followed at 60,000 and Germans and Scots were at 50,000. Africans, however, surpassed all immigrant groups with 400,000.[4] The influx of

---

[3] Cotton Mather, *Magnalia Christi Americana; Or, The Ecclesiastical History of New-England, from Its First Planting, in the Year 1620, Unto the Year of Our Lord 1698* (Hartford: S. Andrus & Son, 1853), 2:499.

[4] Roger Daniels, *Coming to America: A History of Immigration and Ethnicity in American Life* (New York: HarperCollins, 1990), 6.

non-English immigrants lowered the percentage of English in the white population of Americans from 90 percent (1790) to 60 percent (1820).[5] Between 1820 and 1914, immigration increased dramatically, but the percentage of individuals from England continued to decline. Germans, Italians, and Irish surpassed the number of English entering America, and of the thirty million Europeans that came to America between 1820 and 1914, only 2.6 million were English.[6] Immigrants to the new land had a myriad of reasons for embarking on the difficult journey across the Atlantic. A series of factors pushed certain segments of the population out of Europe, including religious and political persecution, economic hardship, famine, and population increase. The population of England, for example, increased from 5.8 million in 1751, to 8.7 million in 1801, to 16.7 million in 1851.[7] Other factors pulled immigrants to North America, including the promise of liberty, land, and economic prosperity.

The resurgence of St. George's Day in America occurred under the auspices of the St. George's societies founded across the continent. A nineteenth-century author wrote, "Happily the 23rd of April has become memorable on this continent by the establishment of the Saint George's Society."[8] These associations of English men sought to aid English immigrants and poor individuals of English descent. The development of such organizations did not occur in isolation, but rather the late eighteenth and early nineteenth centuries were the highpoint for fraternal organizations in the United States. Alexis de Tocqueville discussed the American affinity for associations in 1830: "Americans of all ages, all conditions, and all dispositions constantly form associations. They have… associations of a thousand other

---

[5] Daniels, *Coming to America*, 68.

[6] Daniels, *Coming to America*, 6.

[7] E. A. Wrigley and Roger Schofield, *The Population History of England, 1541-1871: A Reconstruction* (Cambridge: Cambridge University Press, 1989), 528-29.

[8] "St. George's Society in New York," *The Albion*, April 25, 1846, 5.

kinds, religious, moral, serious, futile, general or restricted, enormous or diminutive. The Americans make associations to give entertainments, to found seminaries, to build inns, to construct churches, to diffuse books, to send missionaries to the antipodes; in this manner they found hospitals, prisons, and schools."[9]

The origins of fraternal organizations stretch back to the religious confraternities and craft guilds of the medieval period. Medieval guilds, as we have seen, were the main force behind the popular celebrations of St. George's Day in the Late Middle Ages. After the collapse of the guilds, fraternal organizations reappeared in Britain in the early modern period. The rise of freemasonry was an important step in the advancement of modern associational life. Freemasonry's emphasis on secrecy clouds its history, but historians conclude the movement was founded in England or Scotland during the seventeenth century. This secretive fraternity probably originated from a craft guild of stonemasons, but it evolved to allow non-practicing masons to become members. Freemasonry became the model for other associations with its rituals, structure of lodges, and mutual assistance. Another progenitor of the St. George's societies was the friendly societies, which also appeared in the seventeenth century. A friendly society was a primitive insurance venture in which members paid a fee to a general fund that was distributed to members during a prolonged illness or to surviving family members after a death. The friendly societies, unlike freemasonry, focused on the poor, were not ritualistic or secretive, and were locally based. Immigrants from the British Isles, therefore, had a long tradition of forming associations for mutual benefit.[10]

The creation of ethnic societies for mutual assistance was not an English development, however. The English modeled their societies on those established by other ethnic groups. Ethnic societies first

---

[9] Alexis de Tocqueville, *Democracy in America* (New York: Vintage Books, 1945), 2:114.
[10] David T. Beito, "'This Enormous Army': The Mutual-Aid Tradition of American Fraternal Societies before the Twentieth Century," in *The Voluntary City: Choice, Community, and Civil Society*, ed. David T. Beito, Peter Gordon, and Alexander Tabarrok (Ann Arbor: University of Michigan Press, 2002), 182–203.

appeared in seventeenth-century London. The first to organize were
the Scottish, and they obtained a royal charter in 1665 for the creation
of a Scottish Hospital or Corporation. The Irish formed a charitable
society in 1704, and the Welsh initiated the Society of Ancient Britons
in 1715. From these humble origins, London in the eighteenth century had dozens of ethnic associations and clubs, and the celebration of
ethnic holidays—St. Andrew's Day, St. Patrick's Day and St. David's
Day—were common occurrences. Ethnic societies spread from London to the colonies in North America, and historian Peter Clark
argues, "The London model was undoubtedly influential" in the development of American societies.[11] The American counterparts
mirrored the structure and festivities of the organizations in England,
and moreover, some London societies, such as the Society of Ancient
Britons, directly inspired colonial branches.[12] As in London, non-
English groups had several reasons to create exclusive associations
based on ethnicity in North America. Colonial culture was distinctive-
ly English in its language, laws, and customs, causing other ethnicities
to feel isolated in this foreign world. Non-English ethnicities were
also minority groups, and thus they organized to deal with their dis-
advantaged position. Regardless of the reason, eighteenth-century
America witnessed the creation of numerous ethnic associations for
mutual assistance.

Philadelphia was one of the most diverse cities in North America
and serves as a good case study for the rise of ethnic societies. At the
time of the first census in 1790, Pennsylvania had the lowest percentage of individuals of English descent of any of the states, a mere 35
percent of the population. The state boasted sizable German, Irish,
and Scottish populations, and Philadelphia, the largest city of the colony, likewise, had a very diverse population. The Scots were the first
to organize ethnic friendly societies in Philadelphia and many other

11 Peter Clark, *British Clubs and Societies, 1580-1800: The Origins of an Associational World* (Oxford
University Press, 2000), 302.
12 Clark, *British Clubs and Societies*, 296-303.

cities in America. They had a long tradition of forming associations for mutual benefit in Britain, and the custom continued when they immigrated to the colonies. In Philadelphia, Scots formed the St. Andrew's Society in 1749 as a charitable association to help fellow Scots and a social institution to hold regular dinners to celebrate their common heritage. Germans also organized themselves into the Deutschen Gesellschaft von Pennsylvanien in 1764. The aim of this organization was to enact new laws for better treatment of immigrants on vessels crossing the Atlantic, and to collect food, clothing, and money for poor German immigrants in Philadelphia. The Irish followed suit, organizing several national associations. Irishmen first formed the Hibernian Club in 1759, primarily a social organization. In 1771, the Irish formed the Society of the Friendly Sons of St. Patrick of Philadelphia for the Relief of Immigrants from Ireland, which continued to celebrate Irish holidays, but focused more on alleviating the suffering of poor immigrants. The English in Philadelphia were the last to organize a formal society to help fellow compatriots with the creation of The Society of the Sons of St. George in 1772. The formation of ethnic societies in Philadelphia demonstrates that St. George's societies did not develop in isolation, but were part of a larger movement among different ethnic groups to form associations to aid recent immigrants from their homelands.[13]

The two most significant societies dedicated to St. George in the United States were in Philadelphia and New York. They also happen to be two of the oldest English societies, but the distinction of having the first St. George's society falls to Charleston. The first ethnic society founded in Charleston was St. Andrew's Society in 1729; the Scots again led in creating organizations in the colonies. The English formed a St. George's Society in 1733, making the Charleston group

---

[13] Carl, Bridenbaugh and Jessica Bridenbaugh, *Rebels and Gentleman; Philadelphia in the Age of Franklin.* (New York: Reynal & Hitchcock, 1942), 236-40; George David Rappaport, *Stability and Change in Revolutionary Pennsylvania: Banking, Politics, and Social Structure* (University Park: Pennsylvania State University Press, 1996), 72-73; Peter Clark, *British Clubs and Societies, 1580-1800: The Origins of an Associational World* (Oxford: Oxford University Press, 2002), 301-6.

the oldest society dedicated to St. George in North America. Charleston had many other national fraternities: German Friendly Society (1766), St. David's Society (1778), Friendly Sons of St. Patrick (1773), and Hebrew Orphan Society (1791).[14] The English society at Charleston never rose to the prominence of the societies in New York and Philadelphia, even though the latter two formed nearly forty years later.

The earliest meeting of Englishmen in Philadelphia took place at Tun Tavern, the site of the formations of the St. Andrew's Society, the first Masonic Lodge in North America, and the Marine Corps, among other organizations. An informal St. George's Society was created at the Tavern on April 23, 1729, and the feast of St. George was celebrated in the 1730s.[15] The English organized again under the title of the British Club (or the Gentlemen of British Society), and they met first in 1759 at Griffen's Tavern, primarily as a social institution.[16]

Two years prior to the founding of a formal society in 1772, no organization associated with St. George held celebrations for the patron of England in Philadelphia. Alexander Mackraby, a resident of Philadelphia, wrote in a letter to Sir Philip Francis, an English politician, complaining about the lack of celebration on St. George's Day in April 1770. He protested, "Would you think that in a city with twenty thousand inhabitants we should find difficulty in collecting twenty native Englishmen to celebrate St. George's Day yesterday?" A small celebration was hastily put together for the feast, and Mackraby provided a short description of the revelry: "We met at a tavern, stuffed

---

[14] James Raven, *London Booksellers and American Customers: Transatlantic Literary Community and the Charleston Library Society, 1748-1811* (Columbia: University of South Carolina Press, 2002), 50.

[15] Peter Thompson, *Rum Punch and Revolution: Taverngoing & Public Life in Eighteenth-Century Philadelphia* (Philadelphia: University of Pennsylvania Press, 1999), 84, 229; Douglas and Compton, *The American Book of Days*, 226.

[16] J. Thomas Scharf and Thompson Westcott, *History of Philadelphia, 1609-1884* (Philadelphia: L.H. Everts & Co, 1884), 1467; Carl Bridenbaugh and Jessica Bridenbaugh, *Rebels and Gentleman: Philadelphia in the Age of Franklin* (New York: Reynal & Hitchcock, 1942), 237.

roast beef and plum pudding, and got drunk, *pour I honneur de St. George;* wore crosses, and finished the evening at the play-house, where we made the people all chorus 'God save the king,' and 'Rule Britannia,' and 'Britains strike home' &c., and such like nonsense; and in short, conducted ourselves with all the decency and confusion usual on such occasions. My head aches plaguely!"[17]

The first formal institution called the Society of the Sons of Saint George (SSG) was founded in Philadelphia on April 23, 1772. They met at Patrick Byrne's Tavern on St. George's Day and adopted a constitution to govern the society. The extended title of the association reveals the main aim of the SSG: "For the advice and assistance of Englishmen in distress." The Introduction of the Constitution states that "numbers of Englishmen have arrived in this city, and being disappointed in their expectations have been reduced to the lowest ebb of distress; and not knowing where to apply for relief or advice, have sunk into ruin almost unnoticed." The society hoped to provide distressed Englishmen with "good counsel, or a small pecuniary assistance." [18]

The SSG was founded with eighty-five members in 1772. Robert Morris, signer of the Declaration of Independence and the Constitution and financier of the Revolution, was its most prominent member, and served as the first vice-president of the society. At the second meeting of the society, Thomas Penn, the governor of Pennsylvania, and Rev. William White, the future first Episcopal bishop in America, joined the Society.

The SSG's connection to St. George was evident in its celebration of St. George's Day and its symbols. The society met quarterly, on the 23 of April, July, October and January. The most important meeting occurred on St. George's Day; it was an occasion to deliberate on the business of the society and elect new officers: president, vice-

---

[17] Henrietta Ellery, "Diary of the Hon. William Ellery, of Rhode Island, June 28 – July 23, 1778," *The Pennsylvania Magazine of History and Biography* 11 (1877): 493.
[18] Theodore Christian Knauff, *A History of the Society of the Sons of Saint George, Established at Philadelphia, for the Advice and Assistance of Englishmen in Distress, on Saint George's Day, April 23, 1772* (Philadelphia: 1923), 15-17.

president, treasurer, secretary, the stewards, and messenger. April 23 was also a festive and social occasion to celebrate English nationalism. The society's symbols depicted the patron saint of England. Its seal consisted of the arms of England, St. George and the dragon, and the words "Libertas et Natale Solum"[19] on the top and "I was a stranger and ye took me in" on the bottom.[20]

The young institution was disturbed by the chaos of the Revolutionary War. The battles of Lexington and Concord occurred on April 19, 1775, and during the annual meeting on St. George's Day, Robert Morris announced news of the fighting. The society was torn between loyalists and supporters of independence. Some members left the meeting depressed by the report of hostilities, while others greeted the news with rejoicing. The following meeting on July 24, 1775, was poorly attended, and the society voted to suspend its activities temporarily. Tension between members escalated as the colonies moved closer to declaring independence. One member of the society, John Kearsley, an outspoken royalist, was arrested for his political activities. The SSG called an emergency meeting in March 1776, and among other business, expelled Kearsley from the society.[21]

The members also decided to hold the annual St. George's Day dinner, and the division of the society between loyalists and patriots was evident in the St. George's Day celebrations of 1776. John Adams wrote a letter to his wife on April 23, 1776, in which the renowned statesman described the festivities:

> This is St. George's day, a festival celebrated by the English, as St. Patrick's is by the Irish, St. David's by the Welsh, and St. Andrew's by the Scotch. The natives of Old England in this city heretofore formed a society which they called St.

---

19 "Freedom and Birth Land"
20 Knauff, *A History of the Society of the Sons of Saint George.*
21 Knauff, *A History of the Society of the Sons of Saint George,* 26-9; Scharf and Westcott, *History of Philadelphia,* 1467.

George's Club or St. George's Society. Upon the 23rd of April, annually, they had a great feast. But the Tories and politics have made a schism in the society, so that one part of them are to meet and dine at the City Tavern, and the other at the Bunch of Grapes, Israel Jacobs's, and a third party go out of town. One set are stanch Americans, another stanch Britons, and a third, half-way men, neutral beings, moderate men, prudent folks; for such is the division among men upon all occasions and every question.[22]

The chaotic celebration in 1776 marked the end of the society's activities for the rest of the revolutionary period.

The revolutionary era reveals a complex relationship between the English heritage of the colonists and their political views. Perhaps surprisingly, Americans insisted on celebrating St. George's Day, the national day of England, even as they prepared to break from the empire. Their push towards independence did not consist of a rejection of English culture. As with the case of St. George's Day, rebels saw the Revolutionary War as being consistent with English political traditions. In the future, St. George's societies continued the difficult act of balancing their pride in being English and loyalty to the American state.

The SSG reconvened on April 23, 1787, beginning a long period of growth and stability. The first matter of business was to amend the constitution to accommodate the changed political situation. A revised set of rules were approved on April 23, 1788. The new constitution removed the arms of England and "Libertas et Natale Solum" from the seal, and in their place added thirteen stars, the eye of providence, a wreath, a young phoenix, and the motto "add to brotherly love, charity." A shift from pounds to dollars and province to state was also required. The revived society grew in numbers; the most respected new member was Benjamin Franklin. The society won

---

[22] John Adams and Abigail Adams, *The Letters of John and Abigail Adams,* ed., Frank Shuffelton (New York: Penguin Books, 2004), 163.

recognition from the state of Pennsylvania, receiving a charter in 1813 from Governor Simon Snyder.[23]

The establishment of an English society in New York took place during the same era. The first celebration of St. George's Day in New York occurred in 1762, and a newspaper description of the festivities reads: "Friday last, being the Anniversary of St. George his Excellency, Sir Jeffrey Amherst gave a ball to the ladies and gentlemen of this city at Crawley's New Assembly Room. The company consisted of 96 ladies and as many men all very richly dressed and 'tis said was the most elegant ever seen in America."[24] Through the 1760s, meetings were held sporadically, and in 1770, a formal institution, the Sons of St. George, began holding annual dinners with the leading men in politics and the military attending the early dinners. These included General Thomas Gage, commander in chief of the North American forces, and John Murray, 4th Earl of Dunmore, governor of New York. The celebration in 1771 was a particularly elaborate affair. Among the surviving records of the dinner are the first list of toasts, a mainstay of future celebrations, and a song, "The Song for St. George's Society." Annual dinners continued for most of the Revolutionary period, and evidence for the event from 1778 to 1783 exists. The society had a distinctly loyalist element, with toasts from 1781 dedicated to the king and queen and a score of English generals and admirals. The celebrations ended in 1783, the year the British abandoned New York.[25]

The modern St. George's Society of New York (SGNY), which continues to the present day, formed in 1786. The English who remained in New York wanted to revive the society that ceased to exist in 1783 and to restore the social activities and charitable work of the earlier institution. The early history of the society is difficult to ascer-

---

[23] Knauff, *A History of the Society of the Sons of Saint George.*
[24] Charles W. Bowring et al., *A History of St. George's Society of New York from 1770 to 1913* (New York: Federal Printing Company, 1913), 22, 26.
[25] Bowring, *A History of St. George's Society of New York*, 28-31.

tain due to a lack of documents. The original records, including the book of minutes starting in 1786, were lost in the chaos of the yellow fever epidemic of 1822. The constitution of the society was also lost during the same period, but J. H. V. Cockcroft found a copy of the constitution in his possessions soon after the epidemic ended. His grandfather, James Cockcroft, was a member of the society in 1787.[26] According to the constitution, the organization was named "The St. George Society," and the motto was "Let mercy be our boast and shame our only fear." Members had to be born in England or be a descendant of one born in England; potential members had to be nominated by a present member and then approved by a three-fourths majority. The society met quarterly on the 23 of January, April, July, and October, and an annual dinner was held on St. George's Day. Membership requirements included an annual fee and attendance at the quarterly meetings and annual dinner. In 1787, the society had eighty-one members.[27] The constitution underwent changes over time. In 1824, the name changed to "St. George's Society of New York," and the quarterly meetings were moved from the 23 to the 10 of the month. In 1836, eligibility for membership was extended to grandsons of English natives. The society received official recognition on March 23, 1838, when incorporated by the state of New York.[28]

The societies of St. George in Philadelphia and New York were two of the oldest and most significant societies in North America. From the roots in these two cities, St. George's societies spread to other locations on the continent. Canadians formed numerous societies, and the oldest society started in Halifax, Nova Scotia, on February 25, 1786, when sixty-two members initiated a St. George's

---

[26] Bowring, *A History of St. George's Society of New York*, 35-36.
[27] St. George's Society (New York, N.Y.), *Rules of the Society of St. George Established at New-York, for the Purpose of Relieving Their Brethren in Distress* (New York: J. M'Lean, & Co., 1787), 1-15.
[28] Bowring, *A History of St. George's Society of New York*, 36, 37, 40, 46, 72.

society for fellowship and to aid those in need.[29] A society was formed in St. John in 1802.[30] English settlers in Toronto first celebrated St. George's Day on April 23, 1834. During the gathering, participants resolved to found a society dedicated to St. George, and regular meetings commenced the following year. The purpose of the society was for "mutual and friendly intercourse" and to provide advice, counsel, and assistance to English and Welsh in need.[31] In the same year, a society was founded in Montreal, and the following year, English in Quebec started a society. The first meeting in Quebec was on October 16, 1835, but rules and regulations were not approved until November.[32] Other societies of St. George were founded in Ottawa in 1844, London, Ontario in 1867, Barrie in 1875, Hamilton, and Trenton.[33]

In addition to New York, Philadelphia, and Charleston, Americans started St. George's societies in cities across the United States. Some groups modeled their organizations directly on early societies. In Providence, Rhode Island, a group of English men founded a St. George's Society on St. George's Day in 1841. Members of the society based it on the constitution of the SGNY and held similar celebrations on April 23.[34] The St. George's Society of Utica, New York was organized on February 4, 1858.[35] In 1860, groups in Cincin-

---

[29] The Royal Society of Halifax, "How we began," The Royal Society of Halifax, http://www.royalstgeorgessocietyhalifax.org/pages/How-we-began.aspx (accessed February 12, 2010).
[30] Paul R. Magocsi, *Encyclopedia of Canada's Peoples* (Toronto: University of Toronto Press, 1999), 483.
[31] Anne Storey, *The St. George's Society of Toronto: A History and List of Members, 1834-1967* (Agincourt, Ontario: Generation Press, 1987), 1.
[32] Arthur G. Doughty and N. E. Dionne, *Quebec Under Two Flags* (Quebec: Quebec News Company, 1903), xxix- xxx.
[33] Magocsi, *Encyclopedia of Canada's Peoples*, 483.
[34] "St. George's Society Providence, R. I.," *The Albion*, May 15, 1841, 20.
[35] Daniel E. Wager, *Our County and Its People, Oneida County* (Boston: Boston History Co, 1896), 146-48.

nati and Albany requested copies of the constitution of the SGNY to form their own society.[36] Baltimore founded a society in 1867.[37]

The societies were local organizations but remained in contact with other branches. Often the major societies—New York, Philadelphia, Toronto—sent telegraphs to other societies to be read during St. George's Day celebrations. The societies strengthened their connections with the formation of the North American St. George's Union in 1873, bringing together societies from Canada and the United States. A survey conducted for the fifth annual convention of 1877 in Philadelphia requested sixty-two societies to respond, but received information from only thirty-four: eighteen from the United States and sixteen from Canada. These thirty-four societies had 5,000 members and funds of $115,794.[38] Yearly meetings of the Union alternated between locations in Canada and the United States: 1876 in Hamilton, 1877 in Philadelphia, 1878 in Guelph, 1879 in Bridgeport, 1880 in Ottawa, 1881 in Washington, 1883 in Toronto, 1886 in London, Ontario, 1891 in Oswego, New York, and 1899 in Hamilton.[39] These meetings took place for four decades before the Union dissolved. According to the constitution of the Union, the purposes of the organization were "to promote social intercourse, benevolence, and mutual assistance among the members of the affiliated Societies; to encourage the formation of new St. George's Societies; for the advancement of friendship between the English-speaking nations; and for the preservation of Anglo-Saxon Institutions."[40] J. Herbert Mason, president of the Union, addressed the collection of societies at Toronto and remarked that the Union primarily aimed to help immigrants in need. In his words, the Union sought to do this more effectively by "the formation of St. George's Societies in every city and town where

---

[36] "St. George's Day," *The Albion*, April 26, 1860, 17.

[37] J. Thomas Scharf, *History of Baltimore City and County, from the Earliest Period to the Present Day: Including Biographical Sketches of Their Representative Men* (Philadelphia: L. H. Everts, 1881), 667.

[38] "St. George's Societies," *New York Times*, September 13, 1877, 1.

[39] "St. George's Union Officers," *New York Times*, August 27, 1886, 4; "St. George's Union," *Oswego Daily Times*, August 29, 1891, 5.

[40] The Royal Society of St. George, *Annual Report and Year Book 1904* (London: 1904), 64.

Englishmen exist," and "to increase the number and usefulness and enlarge the membership of such societies."[41] Philadelphia hosted a grand meeting of the Union in 1902. The gathering was well received, but it was also the last recorded meeting of the organization in the United States.[42]

The organization soon fell into decline, and by 1904, it had only nine societies, 2,300 members, and invested funds of $140,000. Many members left to join the Sons of England or the Sons of St. George, and thus, the societies of St. George decreased rapidly in number. The executive committee speculated that charitable organizations, such as the societies of St. George, were not as popular as new orders that paid benefits to the members. They reported soon after 1900: "Two powerful Beneficial Orders have sprung into existence within the past twenty years, and these, one in Canada and one in the United States, absorb the young blood. Benevolence alone is not sufficient, benefits must accrue also, hence not only are there no new St. George's Societies forming, but those already in existence in small towns are fast becoming extinct, only the more powerful Societies in the large centres of population are able to hold their own."[43] The Canadian societies, however, started a new conference to replace the Union directed by Halifax's St. George's Society in 1911.[44]

In 1871, the Order of the Sons of St. George emerged in Scranton, Pennsylvania. The Sons of St. George had many similarities to earlier groups dedicated to St. George, but it was a distinct organization formed in the coal regions of Pennsylvania as a response to the activities of the Molly Maguires. The Mollies, a secret Irish organization associated with mine laborers, carried out attacks against mine owners and their acquaintances. The Sons of St. George waged a suc-

---

[41] Samuel Thompson, *Reminiscences of a Canadian Pioneer for the Last Fifty Years. An Autobiography* (Toronto: Hunter, Rose & Co, 1884), 234-36.

[42] Knauff, *A History of the Society of the Sons of Saint George.*

[43] The Royal Society of St. George, *Annual Report and Year Book 1904,* 64-65.

[44] Magocsi, *Encyclopedia of Canada's Peoples,* 483.

cessful campaign against the Mollies, but the organization continued to exist in other capacities after the Mollies were subdued.[45] Like earlier societies, the Sons of St. George took an active role in the assistance of the needy. Members were required to pay an annual fee, and the money was used as a funeral benefit for widows, medical aid to sick members, and assistance to poor English individuals. The society limited membership to those born in England and their sons and grandsons; although many branches allowed the Welsh to join. Yet, the Sons of St. George differed from earlier societies dedicated to the saint. A secret organization with sacred rituals, passwords, and gestures, they bore more resemblance to the Freemasons than to earlier St. George's societies. Their rituals were based on the martyrdom of St. George, and their emblem was St. George and the dragon. The Sons of St. George was a collection of poor individuals who sought to help themselves or other poor individuals, rather than wealthy individuals helping their ethnic kin, which was the purpose of the St. George's societies. One further distinction was their loyalty to America. The Sons of St. George advocated loyalty to America in addition to loyalty to England and celebrated July 4 as much as April 23. The purpose of the institution, according to the lodge in Worcester, founded in 1873, was "to promote the interests and welfare of the Order of Sons of St. George through the attractive medium of public parades and military displays; to revive and adopt the ancient spirit of chivalry to the conditions of modern civilization; to develop physical grace and soldierly bearing by means of martial exercises to educate its members socially, morally and intellectually; to establish a fund for the relief of sick and distressed members and to give moral and material aid to its members and those dependent upon them."[46] A branch for women, called the Daughters of St. George, also existed. It origi-

---

[45] Albert Clark Stevens, *The Cyclopedia of Fraternities* (New York: E.B. Treat and Co., 1907), 279.

[46] Charles Nutt, *History of Worcester and Its People* (New York: Lewis Historical Pub. Co, 1919), 331; Abijah P. Marvin, *History of Worcester County, Massachusetts, Embracing a Comprehensive History of the County from Its First Settlement to the Present Time, with a History and Description of Its Cities and Towns* (Boston: C.F. Jewett, 1879), 656.

nated in Cleveland, Ohio in 1885, formed as a beneficial society for the wives, daughters, and mothers of the Sons of St. George. The wide appeal of the Sons of St. George contributed to its success, and by 1904, the order had spread across the United States and Canada consisting of 500 lodges and 35,000 members. Every state had a State Grand Lodge and the headquarters of the fraternity was the Supreme Lodge in Philadelphia.[47]

Another organization, the Sons of England Benefit Society was founded in 1874 and headquartered in Toronto. The structure and purpose of the Sons of England mirrored the Sons of St. George. It accepted all Englishmen and their descendants and provided mutual support in time of sickness or death. Besides welfare, the Sons of England promoted the "memories and ideals of the Motherland." The organization grew to 200 lodges and 20,000 members by 1904.[48]

In addition to providing mutual assistance, the many organizations associated with the patron saint of England celebrated St. George's Day as their main festival of the year. The primary function of the groups, as demonstrated above, entailed welfare. Some organizations provided aid and advice to English immigrants, and other groups provided sick and death benefits to their members. The secondary function of the associations was social; the societies provided opportunities for native English and their descendants to gather and celebrate their common heritage. While celebrations occurred throughout the year, they singled out April 23 as a special day to meet and hold festivities. Dozens of societies of St. George and hundreds of lodges of the Sons of St. George and Sons of England took part in the commemoration of St. George's Day. The feast was celebrated in

---

[47] Freemasonry and Fraternal Organizations, "Order Sons of St. George: Initiation Ritual," Argus Foundation, http://www.stichtingargus.nl/vrijmetselarij/songeorge_r.html (accessed February 16, 2010); The Royal Society of St. George, *Annual Report and Year Book 1904*, 67-69.

[48] The Royal Society of St. George, *Annual Report and Year Book 1904*, 66-67.

a variety of fashions. Many groups organized parades as a public sign of their presence. They commonly held church services on the feast, with a sermon preached by a notable cleric. Revelers also took to the outdoors for picnics, cricket matches, and other sporting events. The most common celebration was a public dinner to celebrate St. George's Day. Thousands of people associated with these groups partook in the annual festivities, and thus, April 23 became an important day in the celebratory calendar of nineteenth-century North America.

Countless records of the celebrations of St. George's Day exist in the form of newspaper articles and archival material. The most abundant records of St. George's Day in the nineteenth century come from the St. George's Society of New York. The weekly periodical *The Albion, A Journal of News, Politics, and Literature* (1822-1876) carried detailed descriptions of the annual festivities. *The Albion* was centered in New York and covered British news and politics. In the next several pages, a typical St. George's Day celebration in New York is described, based on a compilation of articles from *The Albion* and supplemented by information from St. George's Day celebration in other cities collected from other sources. In addition to the abundance of evidence, SGNY is a fitting case study because of its status as one of the oldest and most prominent societies dedicated to St. George; furthermore, the festivities consisted of a variety of events, including church services, sporting events, and public dinners.

Many St. George's Day celebrations began with a business meeting. The SGNY met quarterly, and in the early years, they held a business meeting on the morning of April 23. The meeting consisted of the election of officials, introduction of new members, and a review of charitable work. After meeting, society members frequently attended a religious service. The SGNY's practice of sponsoring an Episcopal service started in 1848 and continued sporadically to recent times. The immediate cause initiating the church services was a lack of funds for the charitable committee. By 1847, the committee had not only run out of funds, but also had overdrawn its account. A

committee of seven, selected to raise money, suggested a church service be held before the annual celebration as a means of collecting
donations. Trinity Church was selected for the first service, and Rev.
Wainwright delivered the sermon. After the sermon, a collection of
$111.60 was taken up for the charitable committee.[49] In the following
decades, services were held in many churches in the city: Trinity, St.
George Martyr, St. John the Evangelist, and St. Thomas. If the church
was close to the reception hall, members would proceed from the
business meeting to the church as a group on foot. Services over the
years included divine services, morning and evening prayers, choral
and organ arrangements, prayers for the royal family, collections, and
sermons. In 1850, the theme of the sermon was "Love the Brotherhood, fear God, honour the King."[50] The sermon in 1858 focused on
"the favoured condition of England, blessed in her Queen, her warriors dead and alive, and her children, scatter far and wide over the
world."[51] Sermons in New York City usually discussed the charitable
work of the society, English patriotism, the royal family, and St.
George as an exemplary Christian.[52]

The religious component was more pronounced in the Canadian
societies. Before SGNY instituted a religious service, a writer lamented in 1847: "No collection is made after dinner for the fund, as is
done at similar dinners at home; neither do the members assemble in
the morning, as in the cities of Canada, walk in procession to the cathedral, and listen to a sermon from the lips of a minister of God,
inculcating charity, benevolence, and brotherly love."[53] In Montreal,
the society marched in 1835 from the place of their meeting to
Christ's Church with a band playing patriotic music and members
carrying banners of St. George and the dragon, the red cross, and

---

49 Bowring, *A History of St. George's Society of New York*, 52-53.
50 "St. George's Day," *The Albion*, April 27, 1850, 17.
51 "St. George's Day in New York," *The Albion*, May 1, 1858, 18.
52 "Gleanings," *Christian Union*, May 4, 1882; 18; "St. George and Merrie England!" *The Albion*, April 17, 1858, 16; "St. George's Day." *The Albion*, April 29, 1876, 18.
53 *The Albion*, May 8, 1847, 19.

Britannia. Once they arrived at the church, the crowd heard a sermon and contributed to a collection for their charitable fund.[54] The celebration in Quebec featured a similar schedule in 1846. In the morning after a general meeting, a procession composed of a band, society members, and individuals with banners and insignia formed at the Place d'Armes and marched to the cathedral. Participants then participated in a divine service and listened to a sermon. The ceremony concluded with a collection for the charitable fund and a musical demonstration.[55] As chronicled, Canadian societies had a religious component central to their celebration from the very beginning, while societies in the United States, such as New York, incorporated a religious service into their annual festivities several decades after their founding.

The climax of the annual celebration was the public dinner attended by members of the SGNY and distinguished guests. In New York, attendance ranged from one hundred to two hundred guests throughout the nineteenth century, and only men partook in the meal, with women arriving for the toasts and speeches. Invited guests included representatives of the British government in the United States. The British minister in Washington, D.C. and the British consul in New York regularly attended the dinner; for instance, Lord Napier, British Minister to the United States, attended the festivities in 1858.[56] The presence of Britain's highest ranked diplomat demonstrates that New York had the premier St. George's society. Leading politicians also were guests at the dinner; Governor William Henry Seward, for instance, attended the dinner in 1841.[57] The mayor of New York, James Harper, was present at the meeting in 1845 and gave a speech to those congregated. In addition to civil leaders, distinguished members of the American and British military were frequent guests.

---

[54] "St. George's Day at Montreal," *The Albion*, May 2, 1835, 18.
[55] St. George's Society of Quebec, *St. George's Society, Quebec, Founded 1835, Officers and Members, with the Reports, Ending 5th January, 1847* (Quebec: J. C. Fisher: 1847), 5.
[56] "St. George's Day in New York," *The Albion*, May 1, 1858, 18.
[57] "The Anniversary of the St. St. George's Society of New York," *The Albion*, May 1, 1841, 18.

Clergymen were also present at the gatherings, led by the chaplains of the SGNY and other Episcopalian ministers in New York. Presidents of sister societies were also invited to the gathering, including the presidents of the St. Andrew's Society, Friendly Sons of St. Patrick, St. Nicholas Society, New England Society, and St. David's Society. The practice of inviting fellow presidents to the annual dinners started in the 1820s with invitations to the presidents of St. Andrew's Society (1827) and Sons of St. Patrick (1828), and from this starting point, the practice became a regular occurrence.[58]

Some of the most prominent buildings in New York City served as locations for the annual dinners. Early banquets were held in taverns such as Bolton's, Hull's Tavern, Mr. Strachan's Head Tavern, and Mr. Amory's Tavern. In the nineteenth and twentieth centuries, City Hotel, Astor House, Delmonico's, and Waldorf-Astoria Hotel hosted the society's banquets, and their grand dining rooms were lavishly decorated for the celebrations.[59] City Hotel in 1840 was adorned with flags, a new St. George's standard of "satin and emblazoned by a fine painting of our patron saint," a transparency of the saint, and a collection of silk national banners.[60] In 1843, the Astor House dining room was decorated with national emblems from England and America "indicative of the harmony existing between them." The walls also displayed banners of the society and famous works of art creating a scene that "has never been equaled... on this side of the Atlantic shores."[61] The 1859 celebration included the embellishments of flags, banners, and the portrait of the queen.[62] At Delmonico's in 1860, the dining room had the flags of England and America and the portrait of the queen by Winterhalter.[63] In 1869, American and Eng-

[58] Bowring, *A History of St. George's Society of New York,* 37.
[59] Bowring, *A History of St. George's Society of New York*, 322.
[60] "Dinner of the Society of St. George in the City of New York," *The Albion*, May 2, 1840, 18.
[61] "St. George's Day," *The Albion*, April 29, 1843, 17.
[62] "St. George's Day in New York," *The Albion*, April 30, 1859, 18.
[63] "St. George's Day," *The Albion*, April 26, 1860, 17.

lish flags, the portrait of Queen Victoria, and "cartoons, emblematical of England, Scotland, and Ireland" adorned Delmonico's.[64]

The dinner started with a blessing by one of the attending clerics, often the chaplain of the SGNY. In 1841, Chaplain Rev. Wainwright offered the following blessing:

> Almighty God, we humbly and devoutly implore Thy blessing upon the present occasion; and as we sit down to the table which thy rich bounty hath spread before us, may we remember, in deep gratitude, the manifold mercies which thou has showered upon our glorious father-land, and upon this our free and favoured home. Upon this auspicious day we would commend unto they Divine favour and protection, the youthful Queen of Great Britain with her Princely consort and their lovely offspring. May she and her posterity, in bright succession, reign over a free united and prosperous empire, until the kingdoms of this world shall have become the kingdoms of our Lord and of his Christ. All which we ask in his name, and to him with the Father and the Holy Spirit be ascribed eternal praises. – Amen.[65]

This blessing was analogous to religious statements made during other dinners. Framed with eloquent prose, the prayers conveyed patriotic sentiments towards the United States, Great Britain, the empire, and the royal family. Oddly, the blessing did not mention St. George, the religious symbol at the center of the celebration.

After the blessing, the assembled members enjoyed an elaborate meal. The 1846 meal consisted of "Soup, Fish, Flesh, Fowl, Game, Pastry, Preserves, &c."[66] In 1859, "Scotch salmon and English beef" were served.[67] The food was occasionally brought from England. The

---

[64] "The St. George's Society of New York," *The Albion*, May 1, 1869, 18.

[65] "The Anniversary of the St. George's Society of New York," *The Albion*, May 1, 1841, 3.

[66] "St. George's Society of New York," *The Anglo American, a Journal of Literature, News, Politics, the Drama, Fine Arts*, April 25, 1846, 1.

[67] "St. George's Day in New York," *The Albion*, April 30, 1859, 18.

captain of the royal mail steamboat, *Asia,* presented "a turbot, a baron of beef, and a saddle of Southdown mutton" in 1851 and "English turbot and mutton" in 1852.[68] Sophisticated desserts were distributed after the meal; the celebration in 1852 had confections in the shapes of "St. George and the dragon, temple of liberty, Roman helmet, Apollo's lyre, Gothic pavilion, national pyramid, statue of Britannia and tower of London."[69] Societies across North America had equally elaborate dinners. A dinner menu from the annual feast in Philadelphia detailed an intricate ten course meal, and the dinner also included a different wine with each course. The annual dinner by the end of the nineteenth century in New York, Philadelphia, and across North America had evolved into a refined, sophisticated celebration.

After dinner, servers removed the cloth from the tables, and the focus shifted to speeches and toasts. The speeches were preceded by the entrance of women into the hall. Traditionally, only men were allowed in the banquet hall, and women had to listen to the festivities in separate rooms. Starting in 1851, women attended the second half of the dinner in the main dining room. The ladies were introduced, and then they processed into the hall, escorted by stewards during dessert, while the band played "Then the toast be dear women." The women then sat at the end of the hall to hear the addresses. The innovation was hailed a success and became a precedent for future engagements.[70] Following dinner, the choir sang "Non Nobis Domine," a popular selection for formal dinners in Britain in the eighteenth and nineteenth centuries as grace after meals.

The president of the society gave the first address after dinner. The speech provided an opportunity to welcome distinguished guests. He also gave a short report on the charitable work of the society for those who did not attend the business meeting and to promote the

---

[68] "St. George's Day in New York," *Gleason's Pictorial Drawing - Room Companion,* May 22, 1852, 21; "St. George's Day," *The Albion,* April 26, 1851, 17.
[69] "St. George's Day in New York," *Gleason's Pictorial Drawing,* May 22, 1852, 21.
[70] "St. George's Day," *The Albion,* April 26, 1851, 17.

good work of the society. Lastly, the president's oration contained patriotic statements regarding such things as the closeness of the United States and England, the royal family, the greatness of the empire, and recent English achievements in technology, exploration, or the military.

A round of toasts followed the president's address. The toasts were a central part of all the annual dinners, and many commentators remarked that they were the highlight of the evening. Participants first announced a number of preplanned, formal toasts; each toast was followed by a response or series of responses and a song. At the end of the set toasts, individuals could propose volunteer, or spontaneous, toasts. The list of formal toasts fluctuated from year to year, but the standard subjects were as follows:

1. The day and all who honor it – "Britons strike home"
2. The Queen (or King) and royal family – "God save the Queen"
3. The President of the United States – "Hail Columbia"
4. British Navy and Army – "Rule Britannia"
5. Her Majesty's Ministers – "Oh Albion"
6. Our Native Land – "Isle of Beauty"
7. The Land we live in – "Yankee Doodle"
8. American Navy and Army – "Star Spangled Banner"
9. Our Sister Societies – "Friendship, Love and Truth"
10. English Ministers serving in the United States – "The Englishman"
11. The Mayor, the City and Municipal Authorities – "Mynheer van Dunk"
12. Women – "Here's a health to all young lasses"

Other formal toasts, though used less frequently, included the press, charity, commerce, the fair of America and Britain, the British colonies, and the British constitution. After a toast, the band performed a musical piece with typical songs listed after the toasts above. Selected individuals had an opportunity to respond. Military leaders from Britain and America responded to toasts concerning the military, as political leaders responded to toasts directed towards them. Presidents of the other ethnic societies—Irish, Scottish, Welsh, German, and Dutch—offered lengthy speeches after the toast to the sister societies. Finally, telegraphs or letters sent by the monarch, English political leaders, and presidents of other St. George societies, were read to those assembled.

Volunteer toasts followed the formal list of toasts, voiced spontaneously by members present at the occasion. Some of the most popular toasts acclaimed great men in English history, and the three most common recipients were Wellington, Nelson, and Shakespeare. Individuals involved in the celebration were often toasted, including the president of the SGNY, the stewards for planning the festivities, the musicians, the chaplains, elderly members of the society, and distinguished individuals in attendance. Other volunteer toasts included Canada, the commercial navy, benevolent institutions, language, charity, prosperity, the flag, and colonization of Africa.

The routine of toasts and speeches formed part of the annual dinner across North America. Other societies included many of the same toasts mentioned in New York, but added some locally inspired comments. In Philadelphia, additional toasts to Pennsylvania, George Washington, and Joseph Pilmore, an early benefactor of the society, were regular parts of the ceremony. The society in Quebec had the traditional toast of "England and Canada: May the Atlantic which rolls between them be always a Pacific Ocean."[71]

These toasts and replies articulated significant attention to American and English identity among participants. The English monarch, navy, army, empire, and great men figured prominently in the evening's discourses. Allegiance to two countries caused controversies at times. The Philadelphia society, which from its founding was more

---

[71] "Epitome of the Times." *Atkinson's Saturday Evening Post*, May 18, 1833, 2.

independent than the New York society, omitted the toast to the queen in 1855. This omission caused a minor disagreement when the British consul, George Mathew, refused to attend the St. George's Day dinner. He wrote to Richard Smethurst, the president of the SSG, "In consequence of the repudiation of the toast of 'The Queen,'... I was obliged to decline the invitation with which I was favoured." He found it strange that during a national feast, the leader of a nation was not honored, and noted that it would be odd for the president not to be honored on July 4. Smethurst responded, "I submit, also, that public opinion ought to condemn American citizens of British birth, who place in the first honor the incumbent of a foreign throne."[72] This controversy, the exception more than the rule, shows that the delicate balance between English and American allegiance was difficult to maintain.

The omission of St. George from the toasts reveals that the saint was not the focal point of the ceremony. In the early years, the first toast included St. George using the following formula: "The Day and all who honor it—St. George and Merry England." By the 1840s, the toast omitted "St. George and Merry England." The patron saint only received passing mention in a few of the speeches. The emphasis of St. George's Day as shown by the list of toasts was no longer St. George, but England.

Throughout the history of the SGNY, political events unfolding in the world influenced the celebrations of St. George's Day. Sometimes, the relationship between England and the United States was strained, and the circumstances negatively impacted the tone of the celebrations. As previously mentioned, festivities were suspended because of the Revolutionary War. During the War of 1812, the SGNY similarly adjourned meetings. The last meeting took place in 1812 until eventually resuming with its next meeting on April 3, 1815. Records from 1815 state that "during the war no annual meetings

---

[72] "Correspondence," The Albion, May 5, 1855, 18.

were called," and a resolution was passed making it optional for members to pay their dues that year. Regular activities for the society and annual dinners were restored the following year.[73] Tension also flared during the Oregon border dispute of the 1840s. The American and British government both claimed territory in the Pacific Northwest, and in American politics, ambitious Democrats campaigned in the 1844 election under a radical expansionist platform. When the Democrat James K. Polk won the election, it appeared that another war might flare up between the two countries. The issue figured prominently in the 1846 annual dinner. After the toast to the British representatives in America, the British counsel in New York, Anthony Barclay, addressed the assembly. He declared his views on the Oregon question, including opposition to war between the two countries, a belief that the territory was not worth fighting over, and a hope that the British government was working to prevent war. Unity between the two nations was mentioned several times in his speech: "Are the hands of Brother to be raised against Brother? ... Are the land and the sea to be stained with blood shed by kindred? ... May the Almightily dispose the hearts of the rulers in both countries to the consideration of their consanguinity and identical interest, and to the preservation of family peace."[74] The Oregon Treaty of 1846 resolved the dispute without war, but in the 1850s, relations between the two countries cooled again over the issue of the Crimean War, when the British staged a recruiting effort in America for volunteers to serve in the war. American prosecutors brought a case against the British Foreign Office, and Caleb Cushing, the attorney general, expelled the British minister and three consuls involved in the recruiting effort from the United States. The mood at the 1856 dinner was subdued because of the "disturbed nature of the political relations existing between Great Britain and the United States." An attendee of the

---

[73] Bowring, *A History of St. George's Society of New York*, 36
[74] "St. George's Society in New York," *The Albion*, April 25, 1846, 17.

dinner from *The Albion* berated "Mr. Cushing's malice and scheming."[75] The Chinese question was yet another point of tension between the two nations. Britain defeated China in the First Opium War (1839–42), after which they were granted favored trading rights. The United States, which also desired access to Chinese markets, negotiated a trading treaty with similar rights. At the annual meeting in 1858, Lord Napier addressed the crowd, stating that a universal trade agreement with China was one of the "last impediments to a perfect understanding" between the two countries.[76] Such periods of disagreement between America and England altered the celebration of St. George's Day. In the cases of war, celebrations were suspended, and during periods of political controversy, festivities were held, but in a muted fashion. Yet, the dinners always reappeared in traditional fashion after the disagreements were resolved and the Anglo-American alliance restored.

Similarly, events unfolding in the British Empire also influenced the commemoration of St. George's Day. The annual dinner in New York was cancelled in 1847 because of the great famine in Ireland. Successive years of failed potato crops in Ireland had left the country starving, and many members felt that a public feast would be inappropriate given the great suffering in Ireland. Other members disagreed and were upset over the short notice cancelling the dinner. At least four private dinners were held that year in New York on St. George's Day. The stewards who organized the dinner were particularly displeased by the cancellation of the dinner and held a semi-official dinner at City Hotel. The toasts reflected the disdain: "Toast 3rd. The Prince of Wales, Prince Albert and the Royal Family; may the distress of Ireland or any other land never prevent them from celebrating St. George's Day," and St. George "destroyed the monster Dragon. So we have destroyed the monster Hunger, by our own

---

[75] "The St. George's Banquet," *The Albion*, April 26, 1856, 17; Howard Jones, *Crucible of Power: A History of American Foreign Relations to 1913* (Lanham, Md.: Rowman & Littlefield Publishers, 2009), 186.

[76] "St. George's Day in New York," *The Albion*, May 1, 1858, 18.

feasts at the board."[77] The society later apologized to the stewards for postponing the dinner at the last minute. The press, however, was not as kind to the stewards for hosting a semi-official dinner. *The Albion* questioned, "How would our toasts, shouts, and huzzas after dinner have sounded in contrast with the woe and lamentations wafted to us at the same moment from suffering Ireland?" The society was scolded as well for not organizing any relief for the starving Irish.[78] The dinners also reflected conflicts unfolding in the world. During the Crimean War, the hall was decorated with Turkish and French flags in addition to American and British flags, and praise was delivered to the former English enemy, France, and the Turks in the war effort against the Russians.[79] In the years that followed, the Indian Rebellion of 1857 was a main topic in the toasts and replies. The president addressed the assembly in 1858 with a discourse on the events that took place in India: "All England was struck with horror... at the dreadful news from India, which told us of the massacre of our brave countrymen... But, here, in comparatively a few months, owing to the indomitable valour and courage of Great Britain's sons... those years collapsed into days, and this evening we have received the news of the conquest of Lucknow. [Immense enthusiasm, the gentlemen rising, cheering, and waving their handkerchiefs.]"[80]

St. George's Day festivities attracted celebrated individuals of the day. St. George's Day in 1838 marked the arrival of the first transatlantic steamboat, which crossed the Atlantic in record time. The SS *Great Western* launched in 1838, traveling between the English port of Bristol and New York as the first regular transatlantic line. A rival company leased the SS *Sirius*, a boat operating between Cork and London, to compete for the first transatlantic steamboat crossing.

---

77 *The Albion*, May 8, 1847, 19.
78 *The Albion*, May 8, 1847, 19; "The Anniversary of St. George's Day," *The Anglo American*, May 1, 1847, 2.
79 "Annual Festival of St. George," *The Albion*, April 29, 1854, 17.
80 "St. George's Day in New York," *The Albion*, May 1, 1858, 18.

The SS *Sirius* left first on April 4, and the SS *Great Western* left four days later. The SS *Sirius* arrived first on April 22, but it needed to burn cabin furniture, a mast, and other spare wood in order to complete the voyage. The SS *Great Western* arrived the next day, having completed the journey in a much faster time with coal to spare, but still losing to the SS *Sirius*. A newspaper commented, "The anniversary of St. George's Day was... a day of jubilee and good feeling between Johnny Bulls and the Yankee Doodles, who shook hands more cordially than ever, and congratulated one another on the triumph of steam, and the safe arrival of the first steam-ships that had ever reached this city from the British Islands."[81] The stewards in charge of the annual festival in 1838 formed part of the welcoming committee for the SS *Sirius*, and in the evening of St. George's Day, the two commanders of the steamboats joined the SGNY for their annual dinner. They were esteemed guests and the subjects of toasts and accolades.[82] The following year, the commander of the SS *Great Western*, Captain Hosken, could not attend the dinner because of the early departure of his ship, but he presented the society with his ship's flag "to commemorate the important event, and as a memento of the *Great Western*'s auspicious arrival here on St. George's Day, 1838."[83]

The SGNY had a relationship with the famous British actress Frances Anne Kemble, and she was a guest at numerous events hosted by the society. She performed a reading in 1849 to raise money for the charitable trust successfully enough that the members of the society voted to commission a gold medal for her services. She completed another reading of Hamlet in 1858, contributing $800 to a charitable fund.[84] Kemble recorded in her letters that she "valued it [the medal] extremely," and "it was very precious" to her. She also revealed that

---

[81] *The New - York Mirror: a Weekly Gazette of Literature and the Fine Arts*, May 5, 1838, 45.
[82] "St. George's Day in New York," *The Albion*, April 28, 1838, 17.
[83] "St. George's Day in New York," *The Albion*, April 27, 1839, 17.
[84] Bowring, *A History of St. George's Society of New York*, 55-56, 64-65.

the society wanted to make her an honorary member, but they could not because the constitution limited membership to males.[85]

Furthermore, St. George's Day was intertwined with the sport of cricket. The club team in New York was named after St. George, and many players on the cricket team were members of the SGNY. The season commenced in New York on St. George's Day. According to a newspaper report for April 23, 1844, the men gathered at noon to play cricket, took a break at 2:00 PM for lunch, restarted the game at 3:00 PM, and then headed to the city in the evening for the annual dinner. The English in New York promoted cricket as a "manly British sport," and cricket reached a high point in the United States during the 1850s.[86] When baseball eclipsed cricket in popularity in the second half of the nineteenth century, cricket fell from the St. George's Day festivities.

St. George's Day was a significant day for English-Americans; conceivably, it was the most important English holiday in America. What did these festivities celebrate? One symbol that was not central to the celebrations was St. George. Pictures, medals, and banners depicted him, and his name was attached to the day and the societies that celebrated the day. Yet, St. George was hardly ever mentioned in the celebrations; even the religious ceremonies rarely brought up St. George. As mentioned above, the first toast of the SGNY included "St. George, the Day and all who honour it," but later, St. George was completely absent from the toasts, the highlight of the dinners.

Participants in these celebrations neglected St. George for numerous reasons. The religious attack on St. George during the Reformation and the scholarly attack on St. George in the Enlightenment had a lasting impact on popular conceptions of St. George. By the nineteenth century, most individuals did not know who St.

---

[85] Fanny Kemble, *Further Records, 1848-1883; A Series of Letters* (New York: H. Holt and Company, 1891), 295, 299-300.

[86] "St. George's Cricket Club of New York," *The Anglo American*, April 27, 1844, 1.

George was, or thought he was a purely mythical creation. One commenter in America wrote, "An Englishman's notions of his tutelary saint are undeniably nebulous and anything but reverential. To the question, 'Who was St. George?' the reply is usually, 'O, he was a knight of old, a sort of Guy of Warwick, or Bevis of Hampton.' We were never fortunate enough to meet with anyone who got much farther than this or the story from the Golden Legend."[87] And, "Who was St. George? Is he a myth or was he a real personage? I have known many excellent Englishmen awfully stumped when asked for an answer to this question."[88] English-Americans' lack of knowledge about St. George and their disinterest in the patron saint demonstrates that very few desired to find out more about the saint or to include him in the celebrations.

In nineteenth-century America, St. George's Day celebrated English heritage. The holiday focused on England, the monarch and royal family, great Englishmen, and the achievements of England. For one day, English-Americans focused on their connection to the English race over their present nation. Devotion to England was evident in the speeches, the toasts, and the sermons. The president of the SGNY in 1841 remarked that St. George's Day was "the Englishman's Sabbath of the year; on that day he placed an offering on the altar of his country."[89] In 1858, the president declared the day was for "expressing our love, loyalty, and devotion to our country's [England's] cause."[90] Some members thought the toast, "'The Queen, God bless her'... should come *before* 'The Day and all who honour it,'" and thus, the first toast of the day be directed to the monarch, and not St. George's Day.[91] The emphasis on England over St. George demonstrates the difference between the religious holy day of the medieval period and the secular, nationalistic festival of the modern period.

---

[87] "St. George's Day," *The Albion*, April 23, 1870, 17.
[88] "Saint George," *The Albion*, April 28, 1866, 17.
[89] "The Anniversary of the St. George's Society of New York," *The Albion*, May 1, 1841, 18.
[90] "St. George and Merrie England!" *The Albion*, April 17, 1858, 16.
[91] "St. George's Day," *The Albion*, April 28, 1866, 17.

Nineteenth-century America witnessed a revival in the discussion of saints, but these new "saints" were of a different mold from traditional saints. Sir Henry Bulwer, British Minister, spoke in 1851 about "St. George, St. Jonathan, and St. Knickerbocker, because this good city of New York, may, I believe, be said to have been built by these three Great *Free* Masons!" The three saints were the patrons of the three prominent ethnicities in New York: English, American, and Dutch. He introduced St. George as an "illustrious emigrant" who was present by the "side of Wolfe" and "shoulder to shoulder with Nelson" and "looked down with Wellington from the heights of Waterloo." St. Jonathan was "a Virginia Planter...Western Farmer...New England Pilgrim... New York Merchant... [and] American Statesman." St. Knickerbocker was an alias of St. Nicolas, patron saint of Holland and the Dutch in Manhattan. The three saints were not described as holy individuals who had lived in the past, but rather as ideal representations of the three nations. These sentiments were first mentioned in the literature of the early modern period, in *The Seven Champions of Christendom* and the *Faerie Queen*, but in the nineteenth century, the mythical St. George played a more prominent role than the real St. George.

St. George had many rival saints in America, including St. Jonathan, as proclaimed by the opening stanza of a poem by John Godfrey Saxe:

There's many an excellent Saint, -
St. George, with his dragon and lance;
St. Patrick, so jolly and quaint;
St. Vitus, the saint of the dance;
St. Denis, the saint of the Gaul;
St. Andrew, the saint of the Scot;
But JONATHAN, youngest of all,

Is the mightiest saint of the lot![92]

The origins of St. Jonathan, also formulated as Brother Jonathan, dates from the Revolutionary War, when the British and loyalists referred to the revolutionaries collectively as Jonathans. The most accepted legend explains that "Jonathans" originated from Jonathan Trumbull, governor of Connecticut, friend of George Washington, and supporter of the revolutionary effort. Immediately after the war, Jonathan symbolized a typical country person, but by mid-nineteenth century, Jonathan came to represent all Americans. In 1855, an anonymous author wrote, "But, we sons of Columbia, descendants of the Pilgrims, the true votaries of Liberty, will invoke no saint but St. Jonathan, and our children and our children's children to the latest generation, shall revere his name, resolving that henceforth and for ever St. Jonathan shall be the patron saint of the universal Yankee nation - and the Fourth of July, St. Jonathan's Day."[93]

In addition to St. Jonathan, St. Tammany developed as another mythical American saint. By the 1770s, Americans were seeking an alternative to the patron saints of the British Isles with their corresponding feast days and societies. The process of canonization for St. Tammany was slow and evolutionary. Tammany (also Tamanend) was based on a seventeenth-century Native American chief. A social club was formed in 1772 in Philadelphia called the Sons of King Tammany. By the next year, he was referred to as St. Tammany and recognized as the tutelary saint of Pennsylvania. During the Revolutionary War, he became the guide and protector of the Continental Army; after the war, he was elevated to the national saint of the United States. The society associated with St. Tammany spread from Philadelphia throughout the country, with the most well-known branch in New York. St. Tammany had his feast day on May 1, and an elaborate ceremony developed for the occasion. William Eddis, in a letter from 1771, described an early celebration:

---

[92] John Godfrey Saxe, *Poems* (Boston: Ticknor and Fields, 1866), 283.
[93] Albert Matthews, *Brother Jonathan* (Cambridge: J. Wilson and Son, 1902), 27.

Besides our regular assemblies, every mark of attention is paid to the Patron Saint of each parent dominion; and St. George, St. Andrew, St. Patrick, and St. David are celebrated with every partial mark of national attachment. General invitations are given, and the appearance is always numerous and splendid. The Americans on this part of the continent have likewise a Saint, whose history, like those of the above venerable characters, is lost in fable and uncertainty. The first of May is, however, set apart to the memory of Saint Tamina, on which occasion the natives wear a piece of buck's tail in their hats, or in some conspicuous situation. During the course of the evening, and generally in the midst of the dance, the company are interrupted by the sudden intrusion of a number of persons habited like Indians who, rush violently into the room, singing the war song, giving the whoop, and dancing in the style of those people; after which ceremony a collection is made, and they retire well satisfied with their reception and entertainment.

A popular song performed on St. Tammany's feast also mentions his challenge to the old patron saints: "Of St. George, or St. Bute, let the poet Laureat sing, Of Pharaoh or Pluto of old, While he rhimes forth their praise, in false, flattering lays, I'll sing of St. Tamm'ny the bold, my brave boys. Let Hibernia's sons boast, make Patrick their toast, And Scots Andrew's fame spread abroad, Potatoes and oats, and Welch leeks for Welch goats, Was never St. Tammany's food, my brave boys." [94]

---

[94] Edwin P. Kilroe, *Saint Tammany and the Origin of the Society of Tammany, Or Columbian Order in the City of New York* (New York: 1913), 33, 85-86.

St. George's cult in America also had to contend with another George, George Washington. After the Revolutionary War, devotion to Washington reached a level typically reserved for gods. The *Pennsylvania Journal* reported in 1777, "Had he lived in the days of idolatry, he would have been worshipped like a god," and a nineteenth-century tourist in the United States remarked, "Every American considers it his sacred duty to have a likeness of Washington in his home, just as we have images of God's saints."[95] In a 1907 address at Dickenson College, the Revolutionary War was described as "Saint George Washington spearing a George Third dragon," which drew directly from the imagery of the patron saint of England.[96]

St. Jonathan, St. Tammany, and St. George Washington rivaled St. George in nineteenth-century North America. St. George and other ethnic saints were popular enough that Americans felt obligated to create their own saints. American saints, similar to St. George, had feast days with detailed celebrations, and St. Tammany had a society dedicated to him. St. Tammany was a particularly apt replacement for St. George because he battled evil spirits, similar to St. George and the dragon. Additionally, both St. Jonathan and St. Tammany were loosely based on real individuals, but honored primarily as mythical figures. American saints in the eighteenth and nineteenth centuries differed from medieval, Catholic saints, who were historical individuals that lived a life of prayer and penance in service to God. The new, secularized St. George and his fellow American saints were mythical figures and representatives of the nation.

The creation of separate American saints in opposition to St. George revealed that the relationship between America and England was at times strained in these years. The Revolutionary War and the War of 1812 were periods of direct conflict. English-Americans also had to deal with mixed loyalties. They sought to balance devotion to

---

[95] Stanley Weintraub, *General Washington's Christmas Farewell: A Mount Vernon Homecoming, 1783* (New York: Free Press, 2003), 66.
[96] Moncure Daniel Conway, *Addresses and Reprints, 1850-1907: Published and Unpublished Work Representing the Literary and Philosophical Life of the Author* (Boston: Houghton Mifflin, 1909), 415.

their home country and honor to the nation of their origins. In spite of this conflict of interests, St. George's Day flourished in America under the auspices of the societies dedicated to the patron saint of England.

The eighteenth and nineteenth centuries were a period of resurgence for St. George's Day in North America, but the revived holiday was different from earlier manifestations of the day as a religious, royal, and popular feast in the medieval period, though earlier festivities influenced the modern celebration. The empire and its former colonies added to the tradition in a new and unique fashion. The celebrations outside of England helped St. George's Day regain some of its popularity, and subsequently resulted in a rebirth of the holiday in England. Cultural events, therefore, transferred two-ways in the empire. Not only did English culture flow from the metropole to the periphery, and local culture flow in the opposite direction, but English culture developed in North America transferred back to England as well. As this study argues, the revival of St. George's Day, the Englishman's Sabbath, was first a product of the periphery and then slowly was restored in the home country.

Chapter Six

An English Celebration:
St. George as an Ideal

The Royal Society of St. George (RSSG) was founded in 1894 as a patriotic society. Its earliest known pamphlet, from 1905, stated the two-fold purpose of the society as "reviving the observance, at Home and throughout the Empire, of St. George's Day, April 23rd: and for strengthening and maintaining that spirit of nationality and sentiment of Race."[1] The pamphlet acknowledged that the majority of the English did not know the day of their patron saint and that his feast day had been neglected. After summarizing the life of the saint and the history of his cult in English, it contained an interesting admission: "We are not, however, concerned with St. George, beyond the fact of his being the Patron Saint of England— the National figure head: we seek to rehabilitate him in the affectionate regard of our countrymen, and revive his festival, only so far as it may stimulate the patriotism of Englishmen."[2] The revival of St. George and St. George's Day, in other words, was not due to devotion to the saint, but was solely to increase English patriotism. This patriotic sentiment was also found in an article of *The Daily Telegraph* from the year the RSSG was founded: "So, if it be feasible, let this day be more and more every year cultivated and celebrated as the name-day and festival of England... and hold in mind to-day, not the Empire, not the United Kingdom, not this or that outlying corner or

---

[1] The Royal Society of St. George, *The Royal Society of St. George* (London: 1905), 1.
[2] The Royal Society of St. George, *The Royal Society of St. George*, 4.

fringe of the Realm, but England herself—the 'predominant part-
ner'—the immensely powerful, important, and patient part of these
islands, which really makes the rest of them rich, safe, and respected,
and from her vast capital, the City of London, rules the World of
Commerce, the Ocean, and the Dominions of the Queen."[3]

The RSSG successfully revived the celebration of St. George's
Day in England, with the rebirth of interest beginning in the 1890s
and continuing until World War II, at which point it fell into a long
period of decline. The festivities in North America, recounted in the
last chapter, partially inspired the revival, but the renewed celebrations in England were grander in scope. The English celebrated April
23 throughout their country and empire with dinners, parades, concerts, and church services, but celebrations were limited by the fact
that the holiday never received official recognition from the government as a bank holiday. As alluded to by the RSSG's pamphlet, the
holiday focused on English nationalism. Celebrations were nostalgic,
with participants often regretting the abandonment of a traditional
English way of life and lamenting the lost festivals of Merry England.
They also commemorated recent accomplishments in British history—victories   in   the   World   Wars,   imperialistic   conquests,
technological achievements—but highlighted the role of England in
these successes. St. George's Day became more exclusive with time,
and by the 1970s, racists and extreme nationalists had usurped the
holiday. Noticeably absent from the celebration, St. George did not
play a significant role in the modern festival. The holiday, therefore,
was not a revival of the medieval holy day in honor of St. George, and
had minimal veneration of St. George as a martyr, an element that
featured prominently in earlier festivities.

---

[3] *The Daily Telegraph*, April 23, 1896, quoted from, The Royal Society of St. George, *The Royal
Society of St. George*, 9-10.

Celebration of St. George's Day reached a low point at the end of the eighteenth century, but April 23 still remained a significant day in the national calendar. In 1789, George III selected St. George's Day for a service of thanksgiving for his recovery from a mental illness. One year before, he had suffered a severe mental breakdown, and he appeared unfit to rule. The king, however, recovered from his illness, and organized a four-hour service to express his gratitude to God. It was held at St. Paul's and was attended by the royal family and leading members of the House of Commons and the House of Lords. One of the focal points of the service was the performance of a choir composed by 6,000 children from local charities.[4] The service was the solitary event on April 23 under George III, demonstrating that his devotion to St. George was limited. Under his son, George IV, however, a small revival of the holiday occurred.

George IV (r. 1820-1830) was born on August 12, but celebrated his birthday on April 23, St. George's Day. He selected the date because it was his name day and August was "too late for the fashionable season."[5] The birthday celebrations entailed military parades, greeting of guests, and grand dinners. In 1828, the celebration began, for instance, with three regiments parading in the park near St. James's Palace, and the regimental bands playing "God Save the King" and the "Coronation Anthem" of Handel, among other selections.[6] Public festivities continued with the Park and Tower Guns firing a double royal salute, the flag of England being flown from public buildings, and bells ringing from parish churches throughout all of England. The climax of the festivities was the greeting of guests in the levée and drawing room and the elaborate dinners held to commemorate the day. During the Regency, Queen Charlotte on several occasions received guests in her drawing room. In 1818, the queen arranged an elaborate drawing room for the prince's birthday, accompanied by the Prince Regent and members of the royal family.

---

[4] E. A. Smith, *George IV* (New Haven: Yale University Press, 1999), 58.
[5] "The Prince Regent's Birth-day," *The Times,* April 24, 1818, 3.
[6] "The King's Birth-day & Drawing-Room," *The Times,* April 24, 1828, 6.

They received guests for three hours, including leading churchmen, politicians, foreign ministers, and nobility. After the drawing room gathering, the queen hosted a great dinner in honor of her son.[7] George continued the practice after his coronation. In 1829, he received 1,000 to 1,200 guests in his drawing room to celebrate. The elite of society attended the festivities, and numerous dinners were held in honor of the day.[8]

The royal celebration of St. George's Day included dinners held by the knightly orders associated with St. George. George IV, as the Prince of Wales, held dinners for the Order of the Garter on their annual feast, and William IV hosted yearly grand dinners for the Garter in the 1830s. In the early nineteenth century, another knightly fraternity was created under the patronage of St. George. As Prince Regent, George IV formed the Order of St. Michael and St. George in 1818. The Order honored those who served with distinction in the newly acquired territories of Malta and Ionian Islands. The importance of the Order increased later in the nineteenth century when membership was opened to anyone serving in the British Empire. The annual service of the Order on St. George's Day was instituted in the early part of the twentieth century and is examined in more detail below.

The most consistent celebrations on April 23 in the nineteenth century were not associated with St. George, but were those in Stratford-upon-Avon in honor of Shakespeare's birth and death on April 23 (presumed date of birth). An article in *The Times* on the anniversary in 1864 reveals a disconnect between the festivities in Stratford and St. George: "Englishmen do not keep the twenty-third of April—St. George's Day—as Irishmen keep St. Patrick's and Scotsmen keep St. Andrew's. The great champion who slew the dragon is not much cared for, but a large portion of the human race commemorates to-

---

7 "The Prince Regent's Birth-day," *The Times*, April 24, 1818, 3.
8 "The King's Birthday," *The Times*, May 1, 1829, 2.

day the birth of a Warwickshire boy 300 years ago."[9] Though neglected, St. George appeared in the pageant at Stratford, a central element
of the celebrations. The Shakespeare Club of Stratford, founded in
1824, organized the festivities to honor England's famous bard. The
revelry lasted for three days, with April 23 the culmination of the
event. The first commemorations directed by the Shakespeare Club
were held in 1827 and hailed as the greatest celebration of Shakespeare since the famous Jubilee of 1769 devised by the actor David
Garrick. Celebrations after 1827 were held every three years, and
commentators claimed the gala of 1830 surpassed even those in
1827.[10] In 1830, the day began with "guns firing, flags waving, bells
ringing." A procession followed composed of bands, individuals carrying banners, and one hundred fifty characters. The parade included
characters from the plays of Shakespeare as well as an individual representing St. George, "The tutelar saint of England, seated on a gray
horse, richly caparisoned, with a plume of feathers on his head." The
procession started at the house of Shakespeare, where a bust of the
bard was crowned with a laurel, and a member of the Stratford Theater gave an address. The pageant then moved to the parish church,
and Shakespeare's epitaph was sung. A banquet was held in the evening at the town hall, and the night ended with concerts, fireworks,
illuminations, and a dramatic performance.[11] Celebrations continued
at Stratford on future anniversaries with similar commemorations,
and the tercentenary of the birth of Shakespeare in 1864 produced a
particularly grand ceremony.

During the nineteenth century, several societies and the monarchy
occasionally held events on St. George's Day. The Society of Antiquaries held their annual meeting on April 23. The Grand Lodge of
Freemasonry in England conducted annual meetings on the Wednesday after St. George's Day. Concerts and balls also marked the

---

[9] "Shakespeare," *The Times*, April 23, 1864, 14.
[10] "Stratford-upon-Avon Tercentenary Festival," *The Times*, April 23, 1864, 14.
[11] "Shakespeare, Jubilees, Festivals, and Commemorations," *Chambers's journal of popular literature, science and arts*, February 1864, 126.

national day of England, but they were irregular occurrences. Queen Victoria routinely inspected the navy and army on St. George's Day. At the conclusion of the Crimean War for instance, she went to Spithead to review the fleet returning from the Baltic Sea and the Black Sea on St. George's Day. From her yacht, the *Victoria and Albert*, she inspected two hundred forty ships.[12] At Aldershot, a military camp constructed during the Crimean War, Victoria often inspected troops from the royal pavilion constructed on the site. On St. George's Day in 1858, she attended a military parade at Aldershot, reviewing 15,000 troops.[13]

While Victorians only sporadically celebrated St. George's Day, the saint was a popular subject in art. The Pre-Raphaelite Brotherhood, a group of English artists in the late nineteenth century, used medieval themes for many of their paintings, and several artists painted scenes from the legends of St. George. Edward Burne-Jones in the 1860s painted a series of seven canvases detailing the story of St. George. The same decade, Dante Gabriel Rossetti designed a sequence of six stained glass windows recounting the story of St. George. He also painted *The Wedding of St. George and the Princess Sabra* (1857) and *St. George and the Princess Sabra* (1861-2). The Pre-Raphaelites chose St. George as a subject because of their interest in medieval culture, but the depictions of St. George in their art focused on a post-medieval image of St. George. The most common theme was the relationship of St. George and Princess Sabra, and Burne-Jones and Rossetti painted numerous depictions of the marriage between St. George and Sabra. Medieval accounts of St. George, including the *Legenda Aurea*, claimed that the king offered St. George riches, not his daughter, but St. George refused the king's offer, departed the kingdom after slaying the dragon, and died a virgin and martyr. In the early modern period, Spenser and Johnson introduced

---

[12] W. Laird Clowes and Clements R. Markham, *The Royal Navy: A History from the Earliest Times to the Present* (London: Chatham Pub, 1996), 503.
[13] "Her Majesty at Adlershott," *The Times*, April 24, 1858, 12.

the marriage of St. George to the princess into their accounts, which became the focus of nineteenth-century works of art.[14]

John Ruskin, one of the few Victorians devoted to the patron saint of England, founded an organization dedicated to St. George in the 1870s, first called St. George's Fund, then the Company of St. George, and finally, the Guild of St. George. Ruskin created the Guild in reaction to what he saw as the deteriorating culture of the modern, industrial world, and to help members of the Guild, called companions, form communities based on subsistence farming and cottage industry manufacturing. He described his plans in a collection of letters he wrote to the laborers of England entitled *Fors Clavigera.* The Guild first met in 1879, and several attempts were made to start a small community, notably a farm in Bewdley and a museum in Sheffield. The Guild never became a national movement, to Ruskin's great disappointment.[15] The Guild did not officially celebrate St. George's Day, but one early companion, Rev. Richard Free, commemorated the day in his parish starting in 1903. He stated the festivities were inspired by the "spirit of the Guild" and included a procession of boys and girls, a Queen of the May, flying the banner of St. George, a Jack-in-the-Green, evensong in the church, and a concert.[16] The Guild belonged to a larger movement during the nineteenth century that held a romantic view of the past, and attempted to restore traditional values that were lost due to modernity and industrialization. In the case of Ireland, the Gaelic revival of the nineteenth century sought to restore a lost way of life by reviving Irish sports, music, literature, customs, and language.[17] Even though the Guild failed, a nostalgic view of the English countryside and the attempt to restore it formed a part of the ideology of the RSSG and influenced future celebrations of St. George's Day.

---

[14] Riches, *St. George*, 187-88.
[15] Michael Wheeler, *Ruskin's God* (Cambridge: Cambridge University Press, 1999), 222-34.
[16] "St. George's Day," *The Times*, April 26, 1932, 12.
[17] Timothy G. McMahon, *Grand Opportunity: The Gaelic Revival and Irish Society, 1893-1910* (Syracuse: Syracuse University Press, 2008).

George IV, the Shakespeare Club, the Pre-Raphaelites, and John
Ruskin brought attention to St. George and his day, but in the nineteenth century, the general public was apathetic toward St. George's
Day. It is difficult to prove that something did not happen, but several accounts exist from the era revealing a lack of interest in the feast
of St. George. An article on the history of St. George from 1868 began: "Patron saints are not now so indispensable as they once were,
and people are not curious about their lineage or history. Once upon
a time, knights were ready to fight to the death in honour of their
patron saints, and in vindication of every word of the amazing tales of
which they are the glorious heroes. But times have changed… and
with that and other fine practices of the good old times has passed
away the disposition to care much about patron saints."[18] An article
from 1882 was more direct about the lack of celebration on St.
George's Day. The author remarked that the English were once a very
patriotic nation, but recently had lost their sense of nationalism:

> We went to the opposite extreme, lost all pride in our individ-
> uality, forgot our patron saint, and allowed his festival to sink
> into oblivion, so that it is pleasant to look back at the senti-
> mental side of the subject in a day when so little sentiment
> about it exists. It is to be doubted if half-a-dozen educated
> Englishmen out of every hundred know the day of their pa-
> tron saint… When half-a-dozen Scotsmen are gathered
> together, no matter in what quarter of the world, on the last
> day of November the festival of St. Andrew is celebrated by a
> dinner, and in many places—notably in the United States—St.
> Patrick's Day is observed with equal enthusiasm; but who ever
> heard of a St. George's dinner?[19]

---

[18] "St. George for Merrie England!," *Chambers's journal of popular literature, science and arts*, April
18, 1868, 254.
[19] "St. George and His Day," *All the year round*, May 1882, 294.

Walter Besant, a writer and historian, issued a plea for a national holiday in 1897 to increase nationalism in the English-speaking world: "There is yet another method of creating sentiment which the Americans have practiced, also with the greatest success. It is to hold a day of nation—a holiday—a Day of feasting and of speech-making. They have instituted two such Days—the Day of Independence and the day of Thanksgiving. They are days... [that] move profoundly the many who love nothing so much as processions, flags, bands, of music, scarves and decorations, and perfervid orations... What Day of Celebration have we? None." He suggested April 23 for the new national day, not as St. George's Day, but due to its association with Shakespeare.[20] Lastly, a book review from 1898 on imperialism stated: "The Scot also, and the Irishman and the Welshman... have each a national day and a national idea wherein to find enlargement and escape. Not so your Englishman. For him St. George's Day, though it chances to Shakespeare's day too, is merely April 23, and England is but a geographical expression."[21] These commentators unanimously declared the absence of activities on St. George's Day, and they argued that it was a symptom of declining English nationalism, which was not the case with the Scottish, Welsh, Irish, and Americans.

The revival of St. George's Day occurred mainly due to the efforts of the RSSG. The RSSG's origins begin with earlier English societies dedicated to St. George. Previous societies met sporadically, and left behind minimal records of their existence. In 1879, one precursor formed in London, and its members included the Duke of Manchester, Lord Alfred Churchill, Sir Philip Cunliffe Owen; Messrs. Beresford-Hope and Puleston, of the House of Commons; Blanchard Jerrold, Hyde Clarke, W. Hepworth Dixon, and Walter Besant. The organization met to celebrate the feast of St. George and revive interest in St. George. It also promoted a new history of the saint written

---

[20] Walter Besant, "A Day of Celebration," *The Cornhill magazine,* April 1897, 442.
[21] "At Last – He Understands," *The Outlook,* July, 1898, 727.

by Rev. Dr. Barons.[22] The society held a dinner on April 23, 1883, at
the Pall Mall Restaurant in London with John Henry Puleston acting
as the chairman. He offered the keynote address and remarked on the
purpose of the society, "In England it might be admitted that it had
no *raison d'être*; here Englishmen were at home, and the society had
therefore but little work to perform. It was thought desirable however, that the society should be kept alive, in order to afford the means
of communication with the various Societies of Saint George which
existed abroad."[23] In other words, the chairman conceived the role of
the English organization as coordinating other St. George's societies
throughout the world.

The relationship between the American societies and the London
society was very strong, and evidence suggests that the Americans
inspired the formation of the English society. The second half of the
nineteenth century was the height of St. George's societies in America, and conversely, this period was a low point in the celebration of
St. George's Day in England. Several of the individuals who argued
for the revival of a national holiday, such as Walter Besant, looked to
the United States as an example. In addition, John Henry Puleston
provides a direct link between the American societies and the society
founded in England. Puleston, the chairman of the London society,
spent several years as a young adult in the United States before his
election to parliament. While in the United States, he presided over
the St. David's Society in New York; interestingly, he was Welsh, not
English.[24] He attended the annual dinner of the New York Society of
St. George as the president of an affiliated society, and he was listed
as a guest at the St. George's Day dinner in 1869.[25] Therefore, he was
familiar with the ethnic societies in the United States, and he brought

---

[22] Samuel Thompson, *Reminiscences of a Canadian Pioneer for the Last Fifty Years* (Toronto: Hunter, Rose, 1884), 238.
[23] "The Society of St. George," *Western Mail* (Cardiff, Wales), April 25, 1883.
[24] "The Society of St. George," *Western Mail* (Cardiff, Wales), April 25, 1883.
[25] "The St. George Society of New York," *The Albion*, May 1, 1869, 18.

that knowledge back to England. No document states that the founding of the Society of St. George in London was directly inspired by the societies in America, but a significant amount of circumstantial evidence suggests that the English were aware of the American societies and wanted to emulate the American institutions.

The society in London ceased to exist by the 1890s, but Howard Ruff, an agriculturist and sportsman from Wraysbury, and H. W. Christmas, former secretary of the previous organization, sought to establish a similar society but on a stronger and more permanent footing. In 1894, they founded the society that still exists today. Queen Victoria became the Royal Patron in 1896, which greatly added prestige to the society, and every monarch since has also served as patron. Edward VII in 1902 authorized the use of the prefix "Royal," and the Royal Charter of Incorporation was signed by Elizabeth II in 1963.[26] Ruff became the driving force behind the society after its founding. Concerned about the absence of English nationalism, he expected the RSSG to restore pride in being English. In 1900, Ruff retired from farming to focus on the society full-time.[27]

The RSSG was one of many patriotic associations founded at the turn of the century; such as the British Empire League (1895), the Victoria League (1903), the League of the Empire (1903), the Imperial Federalist Association (1905), and the Imperial Federation League (1905).[28] To promote its causes, the RSSG worked with these other organizations that focused primarily on imperialism, but the RSSG was unique in its emphasis on celebrating England and St. George's Day.

The objectives of the RSSG as stated in 1899 were "to encourage the spirit of patriotism among all classes of Englishmen; to revive the recognition and celebration in every part of the world, and especially throughout the Empire, of the old English national festival of St.

---

[26] The Royal Society of St. George, "The History of The Royal Society," http://www.royalsocietyofstgeorge.com/intro.htm (accessed February 22, 2010).
[27] "Mr Howard Ruff," *The Times*, October 31, 1928, 16.
[28] The Royal Society of St. George, *Annual Report and Year Book 1905* (London: 1905), 84-85.

George on St. George's Day."[29] The objectives are similar to those outlined in the 1963 Royal Charter: (1) to foster love for England and spread knowledge of English history, traditions, and ideals (2) to keep the memory of those who served England (3) to combat activities that undermine England (4) to ensure that St. George's Day is properly celebrated.[30] The celebration of St. George's Day was always a key component of the organization, and Howard Ruff in 1904 even declared the "primary objective" of the RSSG was "an all-English observance of St. George's Day."[31]

The RSSG held an annual dinner on St. George's Day, the principal gathering of the organization. *The Times* carried an article on the dinners every year for the first half of the twentieth century, and the annual ritual can be recreated in detail based on a compilation of these articles. The dinners took place in some of the finest establishments in London, including Cecil Hotel, Connaught Rooms, Mansion House, Guildhall, Criterion Restaurant, and Holborn Restaurant. The dining halls were decorated with the banner of St. George, depictions of St. George, red and white roses, and representations of famous Englishmen, of which a bust of Shakespeare was often mentioned. The dinners attracted several hundred of the elite of English society and were attended by members of the royal family, members of parliament, mayors of the leading municipalities, officials from the foreign service, military leaders, foreign ambassadors, presidents of other societies dedicated to St. George, and high-ranking clerics from the Church of England.

The dinner began with men in historic military dress carrying in the baron of beef, accompanied by the singing of the "The Roast Beef of Old England." The meal followed, with special attention given to serve native dishes using native ingredients. Following dinner,

---

29 "St. George's Day," *The Times*, April 24, 1899, 9.
30 The Royal Society of St. George, "What does the Society do?,"
http://www.royalsocietyofstgeorge.com/guide2.htm (accessed February 22, 2010).
31 The Royal Society of St. George, *Annual Report and Year Book 1904*, 1.

the presiding official read messages sent from societies of St. George in the United States and throughout the empire. The reigning monarch and other members of the royal family also sent messages to the society. The chairman then sent responses back to the societies and royal family. Toasts and responses to toasts constituted the next part of the evening; the most frequent toasts honored the monarch; royal family; Navy, Army, and Imperial Forces; empire; Society of St. George; memory of those that died for England; and kindred societies. Less common toasts were to Shakespeare and other great Englishmen, the chairman, the president, guests, and the Ladies. On some occasions, members toasted a particular colony due to the presence of a special guest from the colony, such as India, Australia, New Zealand, or Canada. The principal toast of the evening was to England, and the main speech followed it. Completion of the toasts marked the end of the dinner, but on some occasions, a ball followed the dinner.[32]

Some of the most famous individuals of the early twentieth century presided over the annual dinners: Duke of Marlborough, Winston Churchill, Lord Alverstone, Duke of Norfolk, Lord Redesdale, Lord Northcote, Lord Halsbury, Lord Willoughby de Broke, Lord Milner, Rudyard Kipling, Lord Selborne, Stanley Baldwin, Edward VIII (as the Prince of Wales), Lord Birkenhead, Prince George (Duke of Kent), Prince Arthur (Duke of Connaught), Lord Ampthill, and Austen Chamberlain. The presiding official typically responded to the toast to England with a lengthy oration, and by the 1930s, the BBC broadcasted the speeches on the radio, greatly increasing the audience.

The two most memorable speeches were by Kipling in 1920 and Churchill in 1933. The discourses shared several points in common,

---

[32] Some articles containing a description of the annual dinner are: "St. George's Day," *The Times*, April 25, 1904, 7; "St. George's Day," *The Times*, April 24, 1909, 10; "St. George's Day," *The Times*, April 25, 1910, 4; "St. George's Day," *The Times*, April 24, 1917, 5; "St. George's Day," *The Times*, April 24, 1918, 9; "Strengths of England," *The Times*, April 24, 1920, 15; "England's Ideals," *The Times*, April 25, 1922, 14; "The Prince on England," *The Times*, April 24, 1923, 16; "Royal Society of St. George," *The Times*, May 7, 1930, 18.

and these shared ideas exemplified many of the speeches delivered on St. George's Day. The central theme was the greatness of England and the English people. Kipling's speech was entitled, "The Strength of England." He claimed that the secret of England's unique vigor was its ability to overcome the persecution of outsiders and foreign ideas: "Roman, Dane, Norman, Papist, Cromwellian, Stuart, Holland-er, Hanoverian, Upper Class, Middle Class, Democracy... And herein, as I see it, lies the strength of the English—that they have behind them this continuity of immensely varied race-experience and race-memory, running equally through all classes back to the very dawn of our dawn." Churchill, likewise, praised the English for their great financial systems, legal structure, toleration, navy, loyalty, and service during World War I.

Both men remarked that the English were reluctant to praise themselves and that many individuals were hostile to English nation-alism. Kipling opened, "I think this is an occasion on which it behooves us all to walk rather circumspectly." He then related a story about how during the Roman Empire, the Picts and Scots had one day a year on which they could tell the Romans how they truly felt about them. Presently, the RSSG, he remarked, provides one day when the English can speak freely about their feelings about being English. Churchill, whose speech was broadcast by the BBC, warned that "we must be careful, however. You see these microphones? They have been placed on our tables by the British Broadcasting Corpora-tion... We can picture Sir John Reith, with the perspiration, mantling on his lofty brow, with his hand on the control switch, wondering, as I utter every word, whether it will not be his duty to protect his inno-cent subscribers from some irreverent thing I might say." They both voiced contempt for politicians and intellectuals who sought to un-dermine the greatness of England. Churchill attacked the government in power by retelling the story of St. George and the dragon. He claimed that a contemporary St. George would be:

Accompanied not by a horse, but a secretariat. He would be armed not with a lance, but with flexible formulas. He would, of course, be welcomed by the local branch of the League of Nations Union. He would propose a conference with the dragon – a Round Table Conference, no doubt – that would be more convenient for the dragon's tail. He would make a trade agreement with the dragon. He would lend the dragon a lot of money for the Cappadocian taxpayers. The maiden's release would be referenced to Geneva, the dragon reserving all his rights meanwhile. Finally St. George would be photographed with the dragon.

Churchill's version specifically targeted the pacifism of Prime Minister Ramsay MacDonald, and the growing threat of Hitler in Germany as a result of his seizure of power in January 1933. Churchill's speech also revealed his opposition to the Round Table Conferences (1930–32) that aimed to give India more political independence. The key elements of the speeches mirrored the objectives of the RSSG: to promote English nationalism in a society that was largely apathetic and to question those opposed to English nationalism.[33]

In addition to the annual dinner, the society sponsored a religious service on St. George's Day. Services took place in Westminster Abbey, St. Paul's Cathedral, and St. George's Church, Hanover Square. The annual national service developed into an elaborate affair, and many organizations joined the RSSG, including the Legion of Frontiersmen, Navy League, British Legion, Girls' Friendly Society, Girl Guides, Crusaders, Distinguished Conduct Medalists' League, Boy Scouts, and English County Societies.[34] The service entailed the reading of lessons and a sermon by a leading cleric. The primary focus of the service was to remember those who served England, especially

---

[33] Winston Churchill, *Never Give in!: The Best of Winston Churchill's Speeches* (New York: Hyperion, 2003), 103-5. Rudyard Kipling, *A Book of Words* (New York: Charles Scribner's Sons, 1928). 189-200.
[34] "St. George's Day," *The Times,* April 24, 1935, 7.

those who fought and died for their country. The society also re-membered fallen soldiers by placing chaplets of red and white roses and laurels on the Cenotaph in Whitehall, London, and the memorial at the Royal Exchange every St. George's Day. Inscriptions on the chaplets in 1921 read, respectively, "St. George's – England's day. In remembrance of our gallant countrymen who died that we might live," and "All honour to London men who fell on the Western front and in Palestine under Allenby, the last and greatest Crusader."[35]

The RSSG also promoted the use of traditional English symbols as part of St. George's Day. They specifically endorsed wearing a rose and flying St. George's banner, the traditional flag of England. The rose has been a symbol of England and the English monarchy for centuries. It became a national symbol in the fifteenth century during the War of Roses between the House of York, which used the white rose, and the House of Lancaster, which used the red rose. When Henry VII from the Tudor family seized power, he combined the two symbols to create the red and white Tudor Rose. The importance of the Tudor Rose as a symbol of the monarch and English nation con-tinued to grow through the reign of the Tudors and beyond. The association of the rose with St. George's Day is more difficult to re-construct. On one level, the relationship was natural since St. George's Day was the national day of England, and the rose was the national flower of England. An ancient tradition of wearing a rose on St. George's Day is unlikely, considering native roses do not bloom by April 23, which means the custom could not predate the advent of modern transportation or greenhouses. Furthermore, no references exist to wearing roses as part of the medieval feast day, or from the eighteenth and nineteenth-century celebrations in the United States and Canada.

An early twentieth-century source claimed the earliest instance of displaying a rose on St. George's Day was "from the time of George I

35 "St. George's Day," *The Times*, April 25, 1921, 7.

until the reign of the late Queen Victoria a golden rose decorated the royal dining table."[36] However, the custom of wearing a rose on St. George's Day started as a military tradition. The Royal Fusiliers and Royal Northumberland Fusiliers, regiments created in the seventeenth century, had representations of English symbols on their uniforms. The badge of the Royal Fusiliers was composed of a rose, garter, and crown, and the badge of the Royal Northumberland Fusiliers included St. George and the dragon, a crown, and a rose.[37] A tradition formed for the regiments to attach a real rose to their uniform on St. George's Day. On April 23, 1858, Victoria reviewed the troops, and a report of her inspection recounted, "The 5th [Royal Northumberland Fusiliers] and 7th Regiments [Royal Fusiliers] showed particularly well in marching. The former corps bloomed like a rosegay, for yesterday was St. George's Day, and according to the old custom, all the men and officers carried a red rose on their caps and breasts."[38] An article from 1892 remarked that on St. George's Day, "Those of Her Majesty's regiments who wear on their badge the device of St. George and the Dragon also don a rose in his honour."[39] The evidence does not provide an exact date when the tradition started, but wearing a rose had become an "old custom" by 1858.

Through the efforts of the RSSG, wearing a rose in one's buttonhole on April 23 became a common practice by the early twentieth century. The society was the first institution to encourage all English people to wear a rose, not just members of the military. Members of the society also purchased a large quantity of roses to distribute, and they sent roses to the queen on St. George's Day. In 1911, the society sent Queen Mary a basket of 100 Richmond (red) roses and 100 Frau

---

[36] Margaret H. Bulley, *St. George for Merrie England* (London: G. Allen, 1908), 30-31.

[37] John Percy Groves, Richard Cannon, and G. H. Waller, *Historical Records of the 7th or Royal Regiment of Fusiliers, Now Known As the Royal Fusiliers (the City of London Regiment), 1685-1903* (Guernsey: F.B. Guerin, 1903), 235; *A Short Narrative of the Fifth Regiment of Foot: or Northumberland Fusiliers, with a Chronological Table and Succession List of the Officers, from 1st January, 1754, to 1st May, 1873* (London: Howard, Jones and Parkes, 1873), 11.

[38] "Her Majesty at Aldershott," *The Times*, April 24, 1858, 12.

[39] Charlotte A. Price, "St. George and the Dragon," *Belgravia: a London magazine* 79 (September 1892): 23.

Karl Druschki (white) roses with ribbons, declaring "To England's Queen on England's Day... With the love, homage, and devotion of the members of the Royal Society of St. George and branches."[40] The gift of roses to the queen became a yearly tradition. The RSSG presented Queen Mary with a wagon of roses in 1916. The wagon, based on a historic Sussex hay cart, was made by the Rural Society, painted in red and white, and covered with roses. The gift was in honor of "St. George's – England's Day – the name day of our beloved King and the tercentenary of the death of Shakespeare."[41] The society also provided roses for the military serving abroad. After World War I, the society sent 20,000 to 30,000 roses to English soldiers stationed in the Rhine.[42] The custom of wearing a rose became fairly popular by 1919, and the scene on St. George's Day was described: "There will be countless real roses on sale too. Covent Garden market will receive tons of them grown chiefly under glass in the Thames valley and at Colchester. It has been found impossible to get enough."[43] Before World War II in 1936, the Society sent 90,000 roses "to battleships and regiments and the Royal Air Force all over the world, at home and abroad" to celebrate St. George's Day.[44] The National Rose Society, which was founded in 1876 to promote the showing of roses, also supported the display of roses on St. George's Day. The society held a spring show of roses on St. George's Day in 1914 and took the opportunity to send a basket of roses to the queen, patron of the society.[45]

The RSSG also advocated the flying of the flag on the national day of England, and in particular, the society wanted to revive the use of St. George's Cross, a red cross on a white background. St. George's Cross was the national flag of England, but merged with St.

---

[40] "St. George's Day," *The Times*, April 22, 1911, 10.
[41] "Wagon of Roses for the Queen," *The Times*, May 3, 1916, 5.
[42] "St. George's Day on the Rhine," *The Times*, April 9, 1919, 13.
[43] "St. George's Day," *The Times*, April 23, 1919, 12.
[44] "St. George's Day," *The Times*, April 21, 1936, 9.
[45] National Rose Society, *The Rose Annual* (Croydon: Jesse W. Ward, 1915), 161.

Andrew's Cross in 1606 and St. Patrick's Cross in 1801 to create the current form of the Union Flag. During the turmoil of World War I, the society organized flag days on April 23.[46] As a result of their efforts, the old English flag became a common sight on St. George's Day. In addition to roses, the society distributed thousands of miniature flags; for example, in 1919 they produced 200,000 silk flags and one million paper flags for sale on St. George's Day.[47] Two years later, the organization sent thousands of flags throughout the empire, including 50,000 to India.[48]

The RSSG successfully restored St. George's Day to prominence. The neglect that had marked St. George's Day throughout the nineteenth century disappeared in the decades after the founding of the society. Only six years after the creation of the society, a commentator remarked, "The efforts of the Society of St. George to resuscitate the observance of the ancient festival are, however, bearing fruit, for not only did more people wear the national emblem, but the bells of a larger number of churches were rung, and more flags were displayed, than on previous anniversaries. There were a plentiful supply of roses, considering the time of year, and a fairly brisk business was done throughout the day by flower-sellers, many of whom had been supplied by... the society with a large card on which were printed 'St. George's Day, wear the Red Rose.'"[49] By 1904, there was "a steadily growing movement in favour of the practical recognition of St. George's Day. The memory of the patron saint of England is said to have been more widely and conspicuously honoured on Saturday [April 23] then ever before, whether by church services, by dinners and other social gatherings, or by the wearing of roses in the street. Much is, no doubt, due in this connection to the efforts of the Royal Society of St. George."[50] By 1910, a news article stated, "The observance by Englishmen of the festival of St. George has been

---

[46] "England's Flag Day," *The Times*, March 21, 1917, 5.
[47] "St. George's Day," *The Times*, April 23, 1919, 12.
[48] "Rose of St. George," *The Times*, April 21, 1921, 8.
[49] "St. George's Day," *The Times*, April 24, 1900, 10.
[50] *The Times*, April 25, 1904, 9.

increasingly noticeable during recent years, and for this the Royal Society of St. George is largely responsible. Through the efforts of the society the wearing of the rose as the national emblem on this anniversary has become much more general, and it is now regarded as an appropriate thing to display the flag of St. George, with its red cross upon a white ground, upon St. George's Day."[51] In short, contemporaries saw the RSSG as the driving force behind the revival of St. George's Day through the promotion of attending church services and dinners, wearing roses, flying flags, and engaging in other forms of patriotic activities.

Annual reports of the RSSG documented their successful revival of the holiday. These yearly documents mostly contained summaries of St. George's Day celebrations, and the society sought to list every celebration of April 23 in the world. Howard Ruff wrote in the introduction of the 1905 annual report: "There are few people, rich or poor, throughout the Empire, who have not heard of St. George's— 'England's Day,' and who do not also comprehend its meaning."[52] The annual report from 1905, only eleven years after the society was founded, provided a summary of festivities in forty towns and cities throughout Britain and Ireland, and listed another forty-two celebrations without providing details. It also described eight celebrations in Africa, eleven in Australia and New Zealand, seven in Canada, three in the United States, and one each in India, China, and Japan. The list was far from exhaustive, but it shows how quickly the society spread the holiday around the world.[53]

Amidst the revival of St. George's Day, the RSSG continued to grow. From the original entity, the organization fostered many branches in England and throughout the world. The society counted 20,000 members in 1921.[54] By 1925, the Society had 100 branches

51 "St. George's Day," *The Times,* April 21, 1910, 13.
52 The Royal Society of St. George, *Annual Report and Year Book, 1905,* 3.
53 The Royal Society of St. George, *Annual Report and Year Book, 1905.*
54 "Rose of St. George," *The Times,* April 21, 1921, 8.

directly associated with it.[55] Two years later the society had grown to 30,000 members and 107 branches, and in 1939, overseas branches alone constituted 95 branches.[56] The society's size and impact climaxed in the 1930s, but after World War II, it entered a period of slow and constant decline. By 1971, membership hovered around 10,000, and the comptroller of the society described the mood of the public on St. George's Day as one of "apathy and indiscipline."[57]

During the revival of St. George's Day, repeated attempts occurred to make April 23 an official holiday in England. In the medieval period, the church designated holidays, but the state appropriated control of the calendar in the modern period. Days of restricted work in modern England are called bank holidays, based on the fact that financial transactions are postponed to the next day. In the early part of the nineteenth century, banks in England frequently closed, with the Bank of England, for instance, closing for thirty-three days.[58] A list compiled in 1811 of bank holidays in northern England contained sixteen days, and the list combined religious feasts and monarchical anniversaries: New Year's Day, Queen's Birthday, King Charles' Martyrdom, Ash Wednesday, Holy Thursday, Good Friday, Easter Monday and Tuesday, Restoration of Charles II, Whit Monday and Tuesday, King's Accession, Gunpowder Plot Day, Christmas Day, St. Stephen's Day, and St. John's Day.[59] In 1834, the Bank of England radically reduced the number of holidays to only four: Good Friday, May 1, November 1, and Christmas Day. The Factory Act of 1833 had stipulated that Good Friday and Christmas were mandatory holidays for young people covered by the act. The legislation behind the

[55] "Royal Society of St. George," *The Times*, April 21, 1925, 16.
[56] "St. George's Day," *The Times*, April 19, 1927, 13; "Royal Society of St. George," *The Times*, October 26, 1939, 11.
[57] Philip Howard, "Homage paid as usual to St. George," *The Times*, April 24, 1971, 2.
[58] *Encyclopaedia Britannica: A Dictionary of Arts, Sciences, Literature and General Information*, 11th ed., s.v. "Bank Holidays."
[59] John Hughes, *Liverpool Banks & Bankers, 1760-1837: A History of the Circumstances Which Gave Rise to the Industry, and of the Men Who Founded and Developed It* (Liverpool: H. Young & Sons, 1906), 41.

creation of the current system of holidays was the Bank Holidays Act, passed through the efforts of Sir John Lubbock in 1871. The act created four holidays in England: Easter Monday, Whit Monday, first Monday in August, and St. Stephen's Day (Boxing Day). These four days were in addition to Good Friday and Christmas, which prior to the act were considered days of no work, and thus not included. Bank holidays were implemented in financial sectors but quickly became universal in all industries. The slate of holidays was not the same throughout the United Kingdom, nor was the list permanent. In Scotland, bank holidays consisted of Good Friday, first Monday in May, first Monday in August, and Christmas. In 1903, St. Patrick's Day was added to the list of holidays in Ireland.[60] The Bank Holidays Act was superseded by the Banking and Financial Dealings Act of 1971, and in England, the Whit-Monday holiday moved to the last Monday in May, and the first Monday in August holiday moved to the last Monday in August.

Many have struggled to make St. George's Day a bank holiday, but thus far, it has been an unsuccessful effort. The RSSG passed numerous proposals supporting the movement to make St. George's Day a national holiday, and they lobbied successive governments on the cause. The issue reached the House of Commons several times. Colonel Burn asked to introduce legislation to make St. George's Day a public holiday in 1914. Liberal Prime Minister H. H. Asquith responded, "This matter has been considered by successive Governments, which have all decided in the same sense."[61] In the 1920s, Lt. Colonel Croft requested the government make St. George's Day a school holiday, and reserve April 22 to teach children about great events in English history. He implied that the Scottish celebrated the feast of St. Andrew in a similar fashion. The President of the School Board, E. Wood, responded that local authorities should de-

---

[60] *Encyclopaedia Britannica: A Dictionary of Arts, Sciences, Literature and General Information*, 11th ed., s.v. "Bank Holidays."
[61] "House of Commons," *The Times*, March 24, 1914, 13.

termine whether the practice was implemented. Mr. Lansbury, a Labour MP, replied that April 30 should be designated for international
history, and May 1 should be a national holiday. Lansbury's remark
prompted Croft to jest, "St. George is our national saint, not Karl
Marx."[62]

The government considered the matter several times in the 1950s,
and though St. George's Day did not become a bank holiday, authorities agreed to fly the flag on April 23. Brigadier Rayner, a
Conservative MP, brought the matter to the attention of Prime Minister Clement Attlee in 1951. He asked for the government to
participate more on St. George's Day by flying the flag from government buildings. He explained that the Scottish and Welsh fly their
national flag on their respective holidays. Attlee responded, "There is
no really great demand for celebrating St. George's Day, but there is
no objection whatever to the flag being flown... I have not up to the
present been told of any great demand and I do not think there is."[63]
The matter was debated again when Norman Pannell requested that
flags be flown on St. George's Day in 1959. Pannell's initiative was
supported by twenty-nine Conservative MPs, and Harold Macmillan,
then prime minister, supported the measure. Elizabeth II, later in the
year, approved the measure, mandating the flag of England to be
flown from public buildings on St. George's Day.[64]

A new bank holiday on May 1 was announced in 1976 and introduced in 1978. The Conservative Party resisted the holiday because of
its association with workers' celebrations in communist countries.
Robert Atkins, a Conservative MP, sought to replace May Day with a
more appropriate holiday, and St. George's Day was the leading proposed replacement in England. The introduction of the bill to find an
alternate holiday was defeated 148 votes to 124, and thus, the effort
to make April 23 a bank holiday failed again.[65]

---

[62] "House of Commons," *The Times,* March 15, 1923, 7.
[63] "House of Commons," *The Times,* May 31, 1951, 4.
[64] "St. George for England," *The Times,* August 20, 1959, 10.
[65] "May Day holiday date no to be changed," *The Times,* June 30, 1982, 4.

St. George's Day shared the patriotic calendar with Empire Day, another nationalistic holiday created at the end of the nineteenth century. Canadians, first to celebrate Empire Day in the 1890s, inspired Reginald Brabazon, 12th Earl of Meath, to bring Empire Day to England. He envisioned the day as a time to instruct children on the mermerits of the empire, and he helped create celebrations in schools consisting of ceremonies around the Union Flag, singing patriotic songs, and lessons on the "superiority of the Anglo-Saxon race and its civilizing mission, the empire story (replete with myths and heroes), and the vast geographical extent of the British Empire."[66] By 1919, 27,323 schools in Great Britain celebrated the holiday.[67] These celebrations in schools inspired other festivities in the community, and Empire Day activities soon consisted of public concerts, parades, church services, and lectures.[68] The success of the holiday was due to the tireless effort of Meath, and the organization which he founded, the Empire Day Movement. Empire Day was first celebrated in England on May 24, 1904, and continued as a mainstay of the celebratory calendar of England until it fell out of favor after World War II.

Empire Day in Canada took place on May 24, the birthday of Queen Victoria, and Meath continued the tradition when he introduced the holiday in England. The RSSG disagreed with the selection of May 24 to celebrate the empire. Howard Ruff wrote a letter to *The Times* explaining the undesirability of Meath's plan. He maintained that May 24 was too close to the Whit Monday holiday, and more importantly, a day already existed to celebrate the empire—St. George's Day. Foreseeing tension with non-English supporters, Ruff offered a compromise date of the August bank holiday.[69] Meath responded to Ruff in an editorial in *The Times* and argued that August

---

[66] Jim English, "Empire Day in Britain, 1904-1958," *The Historical Journal* 49, no. 1 (2006): 249

[67] Andrew S. Thompson, *The Empire Strikes Back?: The Impact of Imperialism on Britain from the Mid-Nineteenth Century* (New York: Pearson Longman, 2005), 118.

[68] Jim English, "Empire Day in Britain, 1904-1958," 254.

[69] Howard Ruff, "Empire Day," *The Times*, May 17, 1904, 3.

was the least desirable time for a holiday. He stated that the RSSG was free to celebrate Empire Day in August, but the colonies, government, and schools were celebrating the holiday on May 24.[70] Ruff's reply to Meath's assessment clarified that the RSSG supported Empire Day, but it added another public holiday to a period of six weeks which already had four: Good Friday, Easter Monday, Whit Monday, and St. George's Day.[71] Ruff was concerned that the many similarities between St. George's Day and Empire Day and their proximity in time might diminish the importance of the holiday he sought to restore. Ruff's fear was unfounded, for the two holidays thrived in the first part of the twentieth century. They both declined, however, in the second half of the century, not from competition, but from a change in the attitudes of the general population.

Military celebrations were essential to the renewal of St. George's Day. As noted above, the Fusiliers began the tradition of wearing a rose on April 23. The Northumberland Fusiliers were the military unit with the closest association to St. George. Started as an Irish division in Dutch service in 1674, the regiment moved to English service as part of the Glorious Revolution. The connection with Northumberland began when the Duke of Northumberland served as the commanding officer in the late eighteenth century.[72] The regiment's badge depicted St. George and the dragon, and the regiment holiday was St. George's Day. The regiment's activities on April 23 were described in 1905 as "trooping the Colours, wearing red and white roses in their busbies, and decorating the drums, and the drum major's staff, and practically everything that can be so decorated, with our national emblem. Dinners and dances are the order of the day—or rather of the night—sports are generally held for the men of the regiment, and the festival is celebrated with a generosity and fitness

---

[70] Lord Meath, *The Times*, May 24, 1904, 5.

[71] Howard Ruff, "Empire Day," *The Times*, May 26, 1904, 10.

[72] Walter Wood, *The Northumberland Fusiliers* (London: G. Richards, 1901), 211-14.

worthy of traditions of the 'Fighting Fifth.'"[73] An account from 1920 depicted the holiday as a time when "all ranks wear red and white roses in their headdresses from dawn until midnight, and festivities include the ceremony of Trooping the Colours, a luncheon given by the officers, and in the evening that time-honoured institution the sergeants' ball." The trooping of the colors by the Northumberland Fusiliers was well-known for the appearance of the famous third, or drummer's colors, which commemorated the capture of three thousand elite French grenadiers at the Battle of Wilhelmsthal in 1762. The drummer's colors were only displayed on St. George's Day, carried by the smallest drummer boy in the regiment.[74]

The Northumberland Fusiliers were also involved in a larger controversy over wearing national emblems. The House of Commons debated the issue of national emblems in 1913. Mr. Hunt MP questioned "whether in view of the fact that Irish soldiers were allowed to wear the shamrock on St. Patrick's Day, he [Colonel Seely] could say whether English soldiers were allowed to wear the rose on St. George's Day." The authorities at the War Department responded, "Emblems may be worn on the headdress on anniversaries provided authority has been obtained. The Northumberland Fusiliers are permitted to wear the rose on St. George's Day. No other regiments have asked for permission to do so."[75] The exchange reveals that all Irish soldiers regularly wore the shamrock on St. Patrick's Day, but only the Northumberland Fusiliers wore a rose. Thus, the Northumberland Fusiliers had a unique connection with St. George's Day in the English military.

The Honourable Artillery Company (HAC) and St. George's Volunteers were other military units associated with St. George that celebrated April 23. The HAC was created in 1537 by royal charter as

---

[73] Honora Twycross, "St. George for England," *The English Illustrated Magazine* 33 (April 1905): 3.
[74] "St. George's Regiment," *The Times*, April 23, 1920, 19.
[75] "The rose on St. George's Day," *The Times*, April 16, 1913, 12.

the Fraternity or Guild of St. George, and is the oldest regiment in the British Army. It was formed for the promotion of the science of artillery, longbows, crossbows, and handguns.[76] The company's title transitioned to Artillery Company, to which the prefix "Honourable" was later added. The annual feasts of the HAC did not occur on St. George's Day, but in the twentieth century, the company held dinners on April 23. At the dinner in 1953, Winston Churchill delivered the keynote address, lamenting the decline of England and dissolution of the empire, the evening before he was made a knight of the Garter.[77] The St. George's Volunteers were first organized in 1792 and revived several times during the Napoleonic Wars. After the conclusion of the wars, the St. George's Volunteers was the only volunteer unit that continued to exist. In 1835, the unit changed its name to Victoria's Rifles. A new unit, the St. George's Rifles, was raised, but it merged with Victoria's Rifles in 1892.[78] Under the patronage of St. George, the volunteer unit celebrated St. George's Day with an annual dinner during the nineteenth century.[79]

Throughout the history of England, the cult of St. George often grew as a result of wars. In the medieval period, the Hundred Year's War was instrumental in the popularization of St. George in England, and in modern times, World War I aided the revival of St. George. In the opening days of the war, the patron of England was said to have appeared at the Battle of Mons. The story originated from a fictional account of the battle written by Arthur Machen in *The Evening News*. The story proved popular, and Machen published it along with several other short stories in *The Bowmen, and Other Legends of the War* in 1915. In the introduction of the work, he mentioned that the story was fabricated and had no foundation in the facts of the battle. The story claimed that in the face of a German advance, an unnamed soldier

---

[76] G. A. Raikes, *The History of the Honourable Artillery Company* (London: R. Bentley & Son, 1878), 17; G. A. Raikes, *The Royal Charter of Incorporation Granted to the Honourable Artillery Company* (London: C.E. Roberts, 1889), 3-9.
[77] "Britain Must Have Faith," *The Times*, April 24, 1953, 3.
[78] "The Victoria and St. George's Rifles," *The Pall Mall Gazette*, February 6, 1897, 3.
[79] "St. George's Rifles, London," *The Aberdeen Journal*, May 8, 1861, 10.

cried, "Adsit Anglis Sanctus Georgius—May St. George be a present help to the English." After his prayer, he heard thousands of voices shouting "St. George" and saw "men who drew the bow, and with another shout, their cloud of arrows flew singing and tingling through the air towards the German host." Ten thousand Germans fell by the heavenly force, and the English knew "St. George had brought his Agincourt Bowmen to help the English."[80] The story did not generate much interest for about seven months, and then on April 24, 1915, the story reappeared. The date significantly followed St. George's Day by one day. The story of a strange cloud at the Battle of Mons appeared in the *Light*, a magazine associated with the supernatural, and within a week, *The Universe*, a Catholic newspaper, carried a story about an apparition of St. George at the battle.[81] In the spring and summer of 1915, numerous stories circulated attesting to the truth of the legends. Edward Begbie collected accounts of soldiers who saw the phantoms in *On the Side of the Angels*, and Ralph Shirley produced a similarly themed pamphlet, *The Angel Warriors at Mons*, both published in 1915. One of the most famous versions was based on the testimony of Phyllis Campbell, a nurse serving in France. According to her story, a Lancashire Fusilier asked her for a picture of St. George "because he had seen him on a white horse, leading the British at Vitry-le-François, when the Allies turned." Another soldier confirmed the story, claiming everyone had seen the apparition: "The next minute comes this funny cloud of light, and when it clears off there's a tall man with yellow hair in golden armour, on a white horse, holding his sword up, and his mouth open as if he was saying, 'Come on, boys, I'll put the kybosh on the devils.'"[82] Critics questioned Campbell's account because she never named the two soldiers who saw St.

---

[80] Arthur Machen, *The Bowmen, and Other Legends of the War* (New York: G.P. Putnam's Sons, 1915), 23-31.

[81] David Clarke, "Rumours of Angels: A Legend of the First World War," *Folklore* 113, no. 2 (October 2002): 151-73.

[82] Hereward Carrington, *Psychical Phenomena and the War* (New York: Dodd, Mead and Co, 1918), 345-51.

George, and no military figure at the battle confirmed her story. Even though Machen repeatedly stated that his story was a fictional story and none of the apparitions could be verified by firsthand accounts, the legend of St. George appearing to help the English at Mons, as with Agincourt and Jerusalem, became part of popular English culture.

On April 22, 1915, the eve of the feast, the Germans launched chlorine gas during the Second Battle of Ypres, initiating large-scale chemical warfare into human history. The chemical attack opened a four-mile gap in the Allies' (Entente's) frontline, and on St. George's Day, English and French soldiers launched a counterattack to close the line and clear the Germans. A poem by Henry Newbolt recounts the battle, and the stanza announces: "Let be! they bind a broken line: As men die, so die they. Land of the free! their life was thine, It is St. George's Day."[83] The Second Battle of Ypres, as the poem reveals, thus became permanently associated with St. George's Day. The East Surrey Regiment, which saw heavy action on April 23, took the day as a regimental anniversary under the name Ypres Day.[84] The Ypres League, formed after the war to commemorate the events that unfolded on the three battles of Ypres, celebrated April 23 with festivities and memorial services.[85] The Ypres League, however, selected October 31, the start of the First Battle of Ypres, as Ypres Day and the main day to remember the battles.

The event that forever connected St. George's Day with World War I, however, was the Zeebrugge Raid on April 23, 1918. This operation attempted to neutralize the ports of Zeebrugge and Ostend, which were connected by canals to Bruges, a base for German submarines. The plan called for the British Navy to sink obsolete cruisers, three in the canal connecting Bruges and Zeebrugge and two at the entrance of the port at Ostend. The attack at Zeebrugge also

---

[83] George Herbert Clarke, *A Treasury of War Poetry, British and American Poems of the World War, 1914-1919* (Boston: Houghton, Mifflin Co, 1919), 20-21.
[84] "Ypres Day Observed," *The Times*, April 25, 1955, 6.
[85] "Memories of Ypres," *The Times*, April 18, 1922, 21.

included the cruiser *HMS Vindictive*, which was to use its guns to bombard the shore batteries and land Royal Marines to take strategic positions on a mole protecting the harbor at Zeebrugge, and two submarines filled with explosives to blow up a viaduct connecting the mole to the mainland. The raid was launched on the night of April 22, the eve of St. George's Day. Vice-Admiral Roger Keyes, commander of the operation, commenced the attack with the message, "St. George for England," and Captain Carpenter of the *Vindictive* replied, "May we give the dragon's tail a damned good twist."[86] The expedition produced mixed results. The *Vindictive* and landing parties were ineffective in capturing the guns on the mole protecting the port, partially because of a failed smokescreen, but the submarines managed to destroy the viaduct. The three blocking ships, *Thetis, Intrepid,* and *Iphigenia,* faced heavy fire as they approached the canal entrance. The *Thetis* came to a halt five hundred meters from the canal, but the *Intrepid* and *Iphigenia* were successfully scuttled in the canal. The raid at Ostend failed completely with the two ships unable to reach their objective. According to the official reports, the *Sirius* and *Brilliant* did not find the entrance of the port and sank two thousand yards east of the harbor.[87] The impact of the engagement was minimal. The Germans at Zeebrugge later widened and deepened the canal and removed two piers. They claimed that two days after the battle small torpedo boats and submarines were able to use the port of Zeebrugge, and by the middle of May, destroyers were also using the port.[88]

The press and general public overlooked the strategic failure of the operation and hailed the raid as a great success. After the war,

---

[86] Roger Keyes and C. Sanford Terry, *Ostend and Zeebrugge, April 23-May 10 1918: The Dispatches of Vice-Admiral Sir Roger Keyes, and Other Narratives of the Operations* (London: Oxford University Press, 1919), 49.

[87] The official report on the raid by the British Admiralty can be found in Charles F. Horne and Walter F. Austin, *The Great Events of the Great War, A Comprehensive and Readable Source Record of the World's Great War* (New York: J. J. Little & Ives Co, 1920), 133-39; Keyes and Terry, *Ostend and Zeebrugge.*

[88] Paul G. Halpern, *Naval History of World War I* (Pasadena: Theosophical University Press, 1995), 415.

Keyes was made a baron because of his war service, and numerous honors were awarded to those who had participated in the raid, including eight Victoria Crosses. Admiral Sir Walter Cowan said Zeebrugge had done "more for the honour and reputation of the Navy than anything in the war." Winston Churchill claimed the raid "has given them back the 'panache' that was lost at Jutland."[89] George V and Queen Mary visited those injured during the raid, and the king spoke of the "gallantry of all who took part in the exploit."[90]

The immense public interest in the raid helped raise the prominence of St. George's Day. April 23 became Zeebrugge Day, and the raid was often referred to as the St. George's Day Raid. Anniversaries of the attack were marked with several memorial events. St. George's Church in Canterbury on April 23, 1919, received one of the flags used to signal "St. George for England" during the raid and a special tablet. The tablet depicted St. George slaying a dragon, and had an inscription remembering those who died at Zeebrugge and an explanation of the flag. Keyes and the Kent branch of the RSSG, of which Keyes was the vice-president, presented the flag and tablet to the church.[91] Memorial services were held at the Church of St. George in Canterbury every April 23 throughout the interwar years, but ended when the church was destroyed in World War II. Memorial services for those who died during the raid also took place at St. Mary's Church in Dover. After a service, the congregation processed to the Cemetery of St. James, where servicemen killed in the raid were buried. Keyes was also buried in the cemetery after his death in 1945. King Albert of Belgium presented Dover with the bell that the Germans rang to announce the coming invasion, and the bell is rung every year as part of the memorial service to commemorate the attack.[92] In addition, a memorial was constructed to Keyes in St. Paul's Cathedral. The fund to construct the memorial was announced on St.

---

[89] Quotes from John Toland, *No Man's Land: 1918, the Last Year of the Great War* (Lincoln: University of Nebraska Press, 2002), 198.

[90] "Heroes of the St. George's Day Raid," *The Times*, May 1, 1918, 8.

[91] "Zeebrugge Fight," *The Times*, February 4, 1919, 7.

[92] "Anniversary of Zeebrugge," *The Times*, April 23, 1920, 16.

George's Day in 1947 by Winston Churchill, and Churchill unveiled
the tablet monument on April 27, 1950. The feast of St. George was
also remembered at the site of the battle in Belgium. A memorial fund
was started in 1920 to raise money for a monument, with a special
effort to raise money on April 23. The cornerstone of the memorial in
Zeebrugge was laid on April 22, 1923, and many of those involved in
the raid, including Keyes, attended the ceremony.[93] Two years later on
April 23, 1925, King Albert unveiled the memorial, and Keyes and
nearly two hundred eighty survivors of the raid attended the ceremony. The memorial consisted of a large marble column topped with a
bronze statue of St. George.[94] The Germans destroyed the monument
at Zeebrugge during World War II, but a new memorial was constructed in the years following the war. Veterans of the raid celebrated
St. George's Day every year by attending memorial services and reun-
ion dinners. The last congregation of survivors occurred in 1983
when six veterans, all in their eighties, met at Zeebrugge.[95]

As well as remembering Zeebrugge, St. George's Day was a day of
general mourning after World War I. An organization called The Cir-
cle of Hope was founded on St. George's Day in 1916, with the
purpose of remembering the dead of the war by placing wreaths and
flowers on their tombs. Church leaders selected the Sunday before St.
George's Day as a national day of remembrance in 1918.[96] In addition, memorial services took place throughout England on St.
George's Day after the war. In 1919, an elaborate memorial service
took place in a packed Chichester Cathedral. The service commemorated all the men of Sussex who fell during the war, and it consisted
of a procession composed of every mayor in Sussex, a military escort,
religious leaders, and other local politicians. Those processing presented to the Bishop a list of every individual from Sussex who died

93 "The Zeebrugge Memorial," *The Times,* April 23, 1923, 13.
94 "The Zeebrugge Memorial," *The Times,* April 23, 1925, 12.
95 "Veterans mark Zeebrugge raid," *The Times,* April 23, 1983, 4.
96 "St. George's Day," *The Times,* April 6, 1918, 3.

in the war, whereupon he laid the list on the altar.[97] Ultimately, Armistice Day, November 11, became the official day to mourn the dead of World War I, but St. George's Day also served for much of the interwar years as a day of reflection and remembering.

World War II had a different impact on the celebration of St. George's Day. The years after World War I experienced a great increase in the celebration of April 23, but after World War II, St. George's Day entered a period of long decline. During the war itself, many of the celebrations—dinners, balls, parades—were cancelled due to the stress of the conflict. The main activities that remained on St. George's Day were church related. The RSSG cancelled its annual dinners, but it continued to hold its national church services. Their national services were held in the crypt of St. Paul's Cathedral, and in 1941, it took place shortly after the church was targeted by German bombers. Church leaders also promoted St. George's Day as a day of prayer. William Temple, archbishop of Canterbury, was enthroned in 1942 on St. George's Day, and he called for prayers for the war effort on that day. He wrote in *The Times* asking everyone "to join me at some time during the day in an act of dedication of ourselves, our nation, our Church, to God and His service." He called St. George a model to "serve our country to the utmost, both now in the time of war and in the days of peace which follow."[98] Two years later on April 23, 1944, the archbishop called for another national day of prayer. He asked, "The Feast of St. George… should be observed as a special day of prayer and dedication in all parishes in England, with special reference to the critical phase in the war which has now been reached and the testing experiences through which we must expect to pass," and he added prayers focused on St. George and the war to all church services.[99] The Warriors' Chapel (formerly the Chapel of the Holy Cross) in Westminster Abbey changed in 1944 to the Chapel of St. George in recognition of the patron saint's association with the Eng-

---

[97] "St. George's Day," *The Times*, April 24, 1919, 7.
[98] "St. George: The Archbishop's Appeal," *The Times*, April 23, 1942, 5.
[99] "Archbishops' Call to Prayer," *The Times*, April 12, 1944, 7.

lish military. The RSSG requested the rededication, and the society
paid to redecorate the chapel.[100]

St. George and his feast day came to symbolize resistance during
the war. George VI created the George Cross and George Medal to
honor civilians and soldiers not engaged in battle for heroic deeds.
The distinctions were created in September 1940 as a way to reward
the heroic actions of civilians during the London Blitz. The George
Cross was of equal rank to the Victoria Cross, while the George Medal was designated for more general distribution. They both featured
St. George killing the dragon as the central image. In addition to the
new awards, St. George's Day was a day of defiance against the German onslaught. Winston Churchill gave a speech during a secret
session of the House of Commons on St. George's Day to address
the fall of Singapore in 1942. The same year a pageant was organized
for St. George's Day in Royal Albert Hall called "Battle for Freedom." The stage was decorated with a large backdrop of St. George,
and the hall was filled with flags of the allied nations. The pageant
reenacted scenes from British history, including the Crusades, growth
of the empire, and the First World War; these reenactments were
accompanied by musical presentations, historical narratives, military
demonstrations, and orations. Churchill and many military personnel
attended the pageant, and the performers intended to "express in
spectacle and song the nation's pride in its past, tenacity and courage
in the present struggle, and faith in the future."[101] The interest in St.
George's Day during World War II quickly came to an end after the
war, and evidence for festivities on April 23 in the post-war era con-
siderably declined. Possibly the festivities, which had celebrated
imperialism, masculinity, militarism, and nationalism, seemed out of
place in a world trying to grasp the atrocities of Nazi Germany.

---

[100] "St. George's Day," *The Times*, April 22, 1944, 6.
[101] "St. George's Day Pageant," *The Times*, April 24, 1942, 2.

In addition to World War I and the military, the cult of St. George grew due to the scouting movement. The Boy Scouts used St. George as a symbol to instruct young English boys, and St. George's Day was the principal holiday of the scouting movement. Robert Baden-Powell, a veteran of the South African Wars, started the scouts around the turn of the century. He wrote a series of texts that served as the founding documents for the movement, including the first edition of *Aids to Scouting for N.-C.Os and Men* in 1899, and a revised edition, *Scouting for Boys*, an international best-seller, in 1908. Baden-Powell thought chivalrous ideals were essential to the formation of young boys, and he saw St. George as a model for young scouts. He wrote in *Scouting for Boys*, St. George is "the patron saint of cavalry and scouts all over Europe... St. George's Day is 23rd April, and on that day all good scouts wear a rose in his honour and fly their flags. Don't forget it on the next 23rd."[102] Baden-Powell also mentioned St. George several times in *Rovering to Success*, his 1922 work for older scouts. He used St. George as an example of determination: "He is tackling the dragon with a smile, cheerily, and means to win. And that is the way to tackle any difficulty however ugly it may look."[103] The Boy Scouts often worked with a less successful group, the League of St. George, which campaigned against pornography and masturbation among young boys. Baden-Powell agreed with the League and maintained the opinion that such sexual impurities weakened men and their ability to fight.[104]

Scouts everywhere, but primarily in England and the empire, celebrated April 23 as Scout's Day with parades and church services. During church services on St. George's Day, scouts reaffirmed their Scout Promise: "To do my duty to God and the King; to help other people at all times; to obey the Scout Law." Parades of scouts took

---

[102] Robert Baden-Powell and Elleke Boehmer, *Scouting for Boys: A Handbook for Instruction in Good Citizenship* (Oxford: Oxford University Press, 2004), 214.
[103] Robert Baden-Powell, *Rovering to Success; A Book of Life-Sport for Young Men* (London: H. Jenkins, 1922), 26.
[104] Lawrence James, *The Rise and Fall of the British Empire* (New York: St. Martin's Griffin, 1995), 330.

place around the world, but some of the more notable ceremonies occurred in English cities. The scouts paraded annually on April 23 in London. Around 650 scouts, for instance, marched in 1927 on the Royal Mews, Buckingham Palace; they were inspected by Lt. General Sir Alfred Codrington, whose address reminded them that the patron of the scouts and England was St. George.[105] In 1935, two thousand Catholic scouts marched from the Mall to Westminster Cathedral. They attended a service presided over by Bishop Meyers, and then assembled on the Cathedral grounds for inspection by the bishop.[106] The scouts in Canterbury likewise held annual parades. Three thousand scouts from the county of Kent processed to the Canterbury Cathedral on St. George's Day in 1937. After the church service, the scouts marched by the Cathedral, and Lord Camden, president of the Kent Scouts, took the salute.[107]

The eminent annual event was the scouts' yearly gathering at Windsor, where the scouts held a national service on St. George's Day at St. George's Chapel. Contingents of scouts came from every county in England and throughout the empire. The scouts selected to attend the service were King's Scouts (upon the ascension of Elizabeth II, Queen's Scouts), the highest distinction for youth scouts. The reigning monarch or a member of the royal family inspected the scouts as part of the festivities. The national service started in the 1930s, though the scouts had attended services at Windsor since the 1910s, and in 1937, Baden-Powell attended the national service for the first time. That year, the ceremony began with a thousand scouts marching in the Great Quadrangle of Windsor Castle past George VI, Queen Elizabeth, Queen Mary, and Princesses Elizabeth and Margaret, and 30,000 spectators watched the parade. The scouts then attended a service in the chapel, and at the end, Baden-Powell led them in renewing their promise. After the service, he addressed the

---

[105] "Scouts' Commemoration," *The Times*, April 25, 1927, 9.

[106] "2,000 Roman Catholic Scouts on Parade," *The Times*, April 29, 1935, 11.

[107] "Scouts in Canterbury Cathedral," *The Times*, April 26, 1937, 21.

gathering again and cited St. George as a model: "They carried out the idea of St. George overcoming the dragon… by the way they fought temptation to be slack and by working to make themselves good Scouts."[108] After the death of George VI, Elizabeth II continued the tradition of greeting the scouts on St. George's Day, and Prince Charles greeted the scouts, in place of the queen, for the first time in 2010.[109] St. George's Day was also a day to remember Baden-Powell after his death, and a memorial to the founder of the scouts was unveiled in Westminster Abbey on April 23, 1947.[110]

St. George's Day was also revived as a royal and knightly celebration in the twentieth century. As mentioned above, celebrations of the Order of the Garter were sporadic in the nineteenth century, and another institution dedicated to St. George, the Order of St. Michael and St. George, was founded in the early part of the nineteenth century. Both fraternities greatly increased activities on April 23 in modern times. The only installation service of the Garter during the nineteenth century was on April 23, 1805; prior to 1805, the last two occurred in 1771 and 1762.[111] George V revived the rite of installation in 1911, but the ceremony took place in June, not on St. George's Day. The meeting of the Garter in 1911 included the investiture of the Prince of Wales and the first chapter meeting of the order in over a hundred years. The Garter continued to hold annual gatherings for the next three years in mid-June, until the outbreak of war disrupted the revival. No chapter meetings took place in 1912 or 1914; there were only processions in those years.[112] After a twenty-three year absence, the ceremony was revived for one year in 1937, and it took place in the middle of June. On St. George's Day in 1948, the Garter

---

[108] "Scouts Greet the King," *The Times*, April 26, 1937, 14.
[109] The Prince of Wales, "The Prince of Wales reviews The Queen's Scouts at Windsor Castle,"
http://www.princeofwales.gov.uk/newsandgallery/news/the_prince_of_wales_reviews_the_queen_s_scouts_at_windsor_ca_1826952181.html (accessed May 26. 2010).
[110] "Memorial Tablet to Lord Baden-Powell," *The Times*, April 24, 1947, 7.
[111] "An Account of the Installation of the Knights of the Garter, on Tuesday, April 23, 1805," *Weekly Entertainer* 45 (May 1805), 349.
[112] "Garter Services," *The Times*, June 14, 1937, 17.

met once again. The gathering marked the six hundred year anniversary of the founding of the Garter, and it was also the first time since 1805 that new knights were formally installed into the order in their stalls.[113] Annual celebrations continued for the remainder of the reign of George VI, approximately around St. George's Day. In the reign of Elizabeth II, the tradition developed that the queen announced the new knights of the Garter on St. George's Day, and the investing of the knights, procession in state, and church service were in June, on a day called Garter Day. Though early in her reign, Elizabeth II invested Winston Churchill as a knight of the Garter on April 24, 1953, in a private ceremony. Interestingly, Churchill was offered the distinction in 1945 after he was voted out of office, but he turned down the honor.[114]

The chapel of the order, St. George's Chapel in Windsor, celebrated its five hundred year anniversary on St. George's Day in 1975. Edward IV commissioned the chapel in 1475, but it was not completed until the reign of Henry VIII. The anniversary celebration opened with a service in the chapel attended by the queen. Events continued throughout the summer of 1975, including a concert series and an exhibition (called "Chapel of the Kings") on the history of the important church.[115]

The Order of the Garter once again regularly gathered by the end of the twentieth century, but its devotion to the patron saint of England changed from the Late Middle Ages. The feast of the order was no longer on St. George's Day; only the sexcentennial of the founding of the order and the quincentennial of the commissioning of the chapel were celebrated on April 23. Moreover, the intercessory role of St. George disappeared. The patron saint was only mentioned once in

---

113 "Garter Service at Windsor," *The Times*, April 20, 1948, 7.

114 "Sir Winston Churchill K.G.," *The Times*, April 25, 1953, 6.

115 "For England and St. George," *The Times*, April 23, 1975, 16; Maurice Bond, *The Saint George's Chapel Quincentenary Handbook: Programme of Events and Catalogue of the Exhibition* (Windsor: Oxley and Son Ltd, 1975); Begent and Chesshyre, *The Most Noble Order of the Garter*.

the Installation Service. The formula from 1983 contains the prayer: "O Lord who didst give to thy servant Saint George grace to lay aside the fear of man and to be faithful even unto death. Grant that we unmindful of worldly honour may fight the wrong, uphold thy rule, and serve thee to our lives' end; through Jesus Christ our Lord. Amen."[116] The traditional practices of veneration to the saint during the chapter meetings, church services, and installation were mostly eliminated.

The Order of St. Michael and St. George helped revive the celebration of St. George's Day in the early part of the twentieth century. The Prince Regent, later George IV, created the Order in 1818 to reward the loyalty of natives of Malta and the Ionian Islands, territories acquired during the Napoleonic Wars, and British citizens who served on those islands. The Order was divided into three ranks with limited membership: eight Knights Grand Cross, twelve Knights Commander, and twenty-four Companions. Through the course of the nineteenth century, the number of members increased, and membership was opened to all serving in the British colonies or in foreign service. The Order originally did not commemorate the feast of its patron in an elaborate fashion. It held a dinner on St. George's Day in 1895 for the Duke of Cambridge, Prince George, on the fiftieth anniversary of his appointment as a knight of the Order; he served as Grand Master from 1850 to 1904.[117] In the first decade of the twentieth century, the fraternity began to hold an annual service in St. Paul's Cathedral. The archdeacon-canon of St. Paul's, William Sinclair, first voiced the idea of a new spiritual home for the Order in the 1890s, and the project started after the conclusion of the Second Anglo-Boer War. Somers Clarke designed the new chapel, and members of the Order financed its construction. Edward VII inaugurated the chapel in June 1906, and an annual service was held there every St. George's

---

[116] Ilse Hayden, *Symbol and Privilege: The Ritual Context of British Royalty* (Tucson: University of Arizona Press, 1987), 178.

[117] George, *George, Duke of Cambridge: A Memoir of His Private Life Based on the Journals and Correspondence of His Royal Highness*, ed., Edgar Sheppard (London: Longmans, Green, 1906), 2:240.

Day.[118] The service became an elaborate affair as a report from 1908 reveals. In that year, the service began with the reading of Psalm 72 and a selection from Deuteronomy; a sermon followed the readings. The most moving part of the ceremony was the commemoration of the deceased members of the Order. The officer of arms read a list of all the knights who had died in the past year. As the reading took place, the banners of the deceased Knights Grand Cross hanging in the chapel were removed, and the banners of the new Knights Grand Cross were hung. The reading of the dead was followed by the hymn, "The Saints of God! Their conflict past," the Apostles Creed, the Collects for St. George and St. Michael, and prayers for the monarch, British subjects, the Grand Master, and all the members of the Order. The service ended with the singing of the National Anthem.[119] George V, as the Prince of Wales, and Edward VIII, as the Prince of Wales, both served as Grand Masters, and they attended the annual service. In a 1909 review of St. George's Day, *The Times* stated, "The service of the Order of St. Michael and St. George will be the most important event of St. George's Day in this country."[120]

The celebration of St. George's Day remained an important event for the monarchy. Monarchs began marking the feast day with public appearances in the twentieth century. Queen Mary during World War I celebrated St. George's Day with a carriage ride in state through the town of Windsor. She was accompanied by her children, and the procession stopped at Edward VII Hospital to visit soldiers wounded in the war.[121] In the 1920s, George V and Queen Mary attended church services at St. George's Chapel in Windsor on St. George's Day. The simple services were also attended by the mayor and corporation of Windsor, the military knights of Windsor, and members of the Wind-

---

118 Derek Keene, Arthur Burns, and Andrew Saint, *St. Paul's: The Cathedral Church of London, 604-2004* (New Haven: Yale University Press, 2004), 259.
119 "The Order of St. Michael and St. George," *The Times*, May 1, 1908, 19.
120 "St. George's Day," *The Times*, April 22, 1909, 4.
121 Between 1916 and 1919; "St. George's Day," *The Times*, April 23, 1917, 5.

sor branch of the RSSG.[122] George VI celebrated St. George's Day in a variety of ways. He unveiled a memorial to his father, George V, on April 23, 1937, and the ceremony in Windsor was attended by the royal family.[123] He revived the Order of Garter celebrations later in his reign, and he also was the first reigning monarch to attend the services of the Order of St. Michael and St. George in 1938.[124] He frequently took the salute of the King's Scouts as they marched through the Quadrangle at Windsor Castle; Elizabeth II continued his tradition of celebrating St. George's Day by inspecting the Queen's Scouts at Windsor.

The revived celebrations of St. George's Day attempted to recreate some of the activities of Merry England. Rev. J. Cartmel-Robinson at Holy Trinity Church in Hoxton initiated a pageant on St. George's Day. For several years around the turn of the century, the pageant consisted of "a May Queen and morris dancers, Knights Crusaders in shining armour, 'grandes dames and famous persouns of historie,' to say nothing of 'cunninge players on reed and brazen instruments,' [who] paraded the dingy streets, just as they did when those same streets were flowery lanes in the spacious days of Good Queen Bess."[125] In 1902, the production at Hoxton included a performance of the old street play "St. George of Merrie England" by the Lads' Brigade and an "Empire song" composed by Cartmel-Robinson, sung for the first time.[126] In Bermondsey, an elaborate show composed of three hundred children was produced to celebrate the feast of St. George in 1910. Children dressed in traditional costumes, performed dances, and sang songs. Three saints—St. Martin, St. Nicholas, and St. George—were part of the pageantry. In the tradition of the medieval ridings, St. George entered with a captive dragon and a company

---

[122] Services were held in 1922, 1924, 1926, and 1927; "St. George's Day," *The Times*, April 24, 1922, 12; "St. George's Day at Windsor," *The Times*, April 26, 1926, 17.
[123] "Memorial George V," *The Times*, April 24, 1937, 9.
[124] "The King at St. Paul's," *The Times*, April 25, 1938, 9.
[125] The Royal Society of St. George, *Annual Report and Year Book, 1904*, 21.
[126] "St. George's Day," *The Times*, April 24, 1902, 10.

of attendants to the lines: "May way O. Awake, St. George, an English Knight, O. For summer is a-come O, and winter is ago."[127] In
Lichfield, St. George's Court, officially called "the court of view of
frankpledge and court baron of the burgesses within the manor and
city of Lichfield," meets every April 23 at noon, continuing to the
present day. It was a manorial court based on a charter from 1547,
but in modern times, the proceedings are purely for entertainment
and serves as a reminder of ancient customs.[128]

Parades were another form of celebration throughout England on
St. George's Day. The Boy Scouts and the military regiments associated with St. George organized most of the parades, but records
document several independent processions. In Liverpool, a collection
of 2,000 students from charitable and industrial schools processed
from Town Hall to St. George's Hall around the turn of the century.
The Lord Mayor led the procession in a state carriage accompanied by
bands playing patriotic songs.[129] In the 1920s, the Royal Marines at
Plymouth marched to celebrate Zeebrugge Day and St. George's
Day.[130] The Conservative Party organized a procession through East
London in 1929 in honor of St. George's Day. The demonstration
included 5,000 marchers and was more than a mile in length. The
procession contained "several bands and a number of tableaux on
lorries." The marchers carried banners with representations of empire
fruit and animals of the Dominions. The march ended with an open-
air rally at Victoria Park.[131] St. George's Day was selected as a day of
parading in Hastings on the eve of World War II. The mustering at
Hastings, a location strongly associated with invasion from the sea,
was to demonstrate the preparedness of the population. The parade

---

[127] "St. George and the Guild of Play," *Practical Teacher* 30, no. 12 (June 1910): 712-14.
[128] Margaret Gascoigne, *Discovering English Customs and Traditions* (Princes Risborough: Shire, 1980), 53-54.
[129] "St. George's Day," *The Times*, April 24, 1901, 10.
[130] "St. George's Day," *The Times*, April 25, 1921, 7.
[131] "East London Demonstration," *The Times*, Apr 24, 1929, 11.

of 1,500 was composed of a variety of groups from military regiments to air-raid wardens to ambulance drivers.

Concerts were a common feature of St. George's Day, and a popular venue was the Royal Albert Hall. A National Festival took place at the Hall on April 23, 1879, and at the celebration a new song, "St. George for Merrie England," was sung. The lyrics supported the militaristic expansion of the New Imperialism and soldiers fighting across the empire. The song proclaimed: "They love the cry, 'To arms! To arms! 'Tis music in their ear! God speed them, both by land and sea, Sustain their spirit brave and free, And let their watchword ever be 'St. George and merrie England!'"[132] During World War II, concerts were held at the Royal Albert Hall, and as mentioned previously, the musical performance "Battle for Freedom" took place on St. George's Day in 1942. The RSSG organized a concert, "mainly of English music," at Royal Albert Hall in 1944 with performances of Purcell, Elgar, and Butterworth.[133]

Large cultural gatherings frequently occurred on St. George's Day, and many exhibitions opened on April 23. The Lord Mayor opened the London International and Universal Exhibition at the Crystal Palace on April 23, 1884. The opening of the exhibition was accompanied by an elaborate musical performance in celebration of St. George's Day, and composer G. A. Macfarren premiered a St. George's *Te Deum* for the occasion.[134] The Lord Mayor of London hosted a colonial banquet at Mansion House on St. George's Day in 1894, and the imperial celebration was attended by representatives from throughout the empire.[135] George V opened the British Empire Exhibition at Wembley on April 23, 1924. The exhibition spread over 216 acres and included displays from all but two of the fifty-eight colonies and dominions, a sports arena, a forty-acre amusement place, and palaces of engineering, industry, and art. The exhibition promised

[132] Sarah Anne Matson, *St. George and the Dragon* (London: T. Fisher Unwin, 1893), 52-53.
[133] "St. George's Day," *The Times,* April 22, 1944, 6.
[134] "The Crystal Palace Exhibition," *The Times* April 24, 1884, 7.
[135] *The Times,* April 24, 1894, 9.

to display all the sights of the empire but in miniature. It was a major success with 17.4 million visitors in 1924 and 9.7 million in 1925.[136] The opening of the exhibit on St. George's Day was attended by 110,000 people in the stadium. April 23 was purposely selected for the opening because it was St. George's Day. The Prince of Wales, president of the committee organizing the exhibition, remarked in his speech to declare the exhibition open, "It is a particular satisfaction to all who have been engaged in its preparation that we can ask you to do this [opening the Exhibition] on St. George's Day."[137]

Church services continued to be an important element of St. George's Day. The Boy Scouts typically followed their parades with a church service, and the RSSG sponsored a national church service. The Order of St. Michael and St. George held an annual church service on the feast day of the Order. Churches dedicated to St. George, in particular St. George's Chapel in Windsor, held special services to commemorate their patron saint. In the Catholic Church, the celebration of the feast of St. George was commemorated with special attention at St. George's Cathedral in Southwark.

The feast of St. George was eventually altered in the Church of England. The attempt to produce a more conservative *Book of Common Prayer* (BCP) failed when a revised edition, which received church approval in 1928, was blocked by parliament. In recent years, several new liturgical works have been authorized for liturgical use along with the BCP from 1662. *The Alternative Service Book 1980* did not change the rank of the feast of St. George and lists it as a lesser festival. In 1996, a General Synod of the church elevated the feast of St. George to one of the twenty-eight major festivals. The newest liturgical work,

---

[136] John Mackenzie, "The Popular Culture of Empire in Britain," in *The Twentieth Century*, ed. Judith M. Brown, (Oxford: Oxford University Press, 2001), 213-15.

[137] "The Prince's Speech," *The Times*, April 24, 1924, 14.

Common Worship (2000), has separate liturgical provision for St. George's Day, including a Collect and Post Communion.[138]

The status of the feast day was also altered by the Catholic Church. In the Catholic calendar, the feast was first downgraded as part of the reforms that occurred after the Second Vatican Council. The traditional calendar was saturated with feasts by the twentieth century. After the Council of Trent, the calendar had 149 feasts, but by the reign of Pius X in 1912, there were 280. Pius XII initiated minor changes to the Roman Calendar in 1954, but the feast of St. George remained a semi-double feast.[139] John XXIII, in the reforms of 1962, altered the ranking of the feast days, and the feast of St. George changed to a commemoration. Substantial changes in the calendar took place as a result of the Second Vatican Council. The Council wanted to reduce the number of saints by removing some of the saints known only locally and those of questionable existence.[140] The new calendar was promulgated in 1969 based on the reforms outlined in the Council. St. George's feast, as with many other saints, was reduced to an optional memorial. He was not however included with other saints, such as Barbara and Christopher, who posed a serious historical problem and were removed from the calendar.[141] It is sometimes falsely alleged that St. George was dropped from the calendar, or that he was no longer a saint. In an article from *The Times* entitled, "No embarrassment over Vatican's ruling," a member of the RSSG, for example, commented on the ruling, "I do not care if he is a saint or not."[142] St. George remained a saint in the Catholic Church, and he remained on the calendar as an optional feast, which means the local priest has the option to celebrate the feast during the Mass.

---

[138] *The Alternative Service Book 1980* (Cambridge: Cambridge University Press, 1980), 19; *Common Worship: Services and Prayers for the Church of England* (London: Church Publishing House, 2000), 8, 430, 503, 529.

[139] Semi-double feasts were suppressed in 1955.

[140] Irenée Henri Dalmais, Pierre Jounel, and Aimé Georges Martimort, *The Liturgy and Time* (Collegeville, Minn.: Liturgical Press, 1986), 126-27.

[141] *The Roman Calendar: Text and Commentary* (Washington D.C.: United States Catholic Conference, 1976), 30-31.

[142] "No embarrassment over Vatican's ruling," *The Times,* April 24, 1971, 2.

The demotion of the feast of St. George in England was not permanent. The feast was elevated by Pope John Paul II in 2000 to a
solemnity for English Catholics in recognition of the importance of
St. George in England and his role as patron of the nation. A solemnity is the highest feast in the Catholic Church, and it shares many of
the liturgical elements of a Sunday celebration. In both the Church of
England and the Catholic Church, the elevation of the feast followed,
and perhaps was inspired by, the revival of the holiday in the general
population.

The revival of St. George's Day at the end of the nineteenth century was accompanied by a resurgence of works on St. George in
England. Some of the works were academic and helped determine the
historical development of the cult of St. George. E. A. Wallis Budge,
keeper of the Egyptian and Assyrian Antiquities at the British Museum, published translations of ancient texts on St. George along with
commentaries. He published Coptic texts in *The Martyrdom and Miracles
of St. George of Cappadocia* in 1888 and Ethiopian texts in *George of Lydda, the Patron Saint of England: a Study of the Cultus of St. George in Ethiopia*
in 1930. John Matzke, a linguist at Stanford University, in three articles published in the *Publication of the Modern Language Association*
between 1902 and 1904 analyzed the development of the medieval
legends of St. George. During the same period, many popular accounts on the history of St. George appeared in England.[143] The
RSSG facilitated the distribution of some of these works, publishing
Alice Brewster's book. The works of C. W. B. Clarke, Edward Clap-

---

[143] Sabine Baring-Gould's *Curious Myths of the Middle Ages* (1868), C. W. B. Clarke's *The True
History of Saint George the Martyr* (1900), William Fleming's *The Life of Saint George: Martyr, Patron
of England* (1901), Edward Clapton's *The Life of St. George* (second edition, 1903), Elizabeth
Oke Gordon's *Saint George: Champion of Christendom and Patron Saint of England* (1907), Margret
Bulley's *St. George for Merrie England* (1908), Cornelia Steketee Hulst's *St. George of Cappadocia in
Legend and History* (1909), H. O. F.'s *Saint George for England: The life, legends, and lore, of our
glorious patron* (1911), G. J. Marcus' *Saint George of England* (1929), Alice Brewster's *The Life of
St. George, the Patron Soldier-Saint of England* (1913) and Isabel Hill Elder's *George of Lydda: soldier,
saint and martyr* (1949).

ton and H. O. F. were also dedicated to the society.[144] These books attest to the popularity of St. George and growth of English patriotism during this period.

The meaning of the twentieth-century St. George had changed dramatically from the medieval version of the saint. In order to deconstruct the new symbolism of the patron saint of England, it would be fitting to examine the play *Where the Rainbow Ends,* one of the most prominent representations of the saint from the modern period. The play ran every Christmas season in London from 1911 to 1959, except 1947, and it toured the country during World War II. It was seen by millions of children and their parents during its long run and played a role in forming multiple generations' image of the saint. The play was not part of the St. George's Day celebration, but it came from the same cultural milieu that aided the revival of the holiday. St. George in the play embodied the same values found in the St. George of the Boy Scouts, the RSSG, Zeebrugge Day, and other modern representations of the saint. The play, therefore, provides a window into the meaning of the modern St. George.

The success of the play was a surprise, considering that the author, Clifford Mills, was virtually unknown. Fortunately from the onset, she collaborated with many talented and established individuals in the theatrical world. Reginald Owen, a young actor in 1911 who became one of Hollywood's most prolific actors, coauthored the play, listed under the penname John Ramsey, and he starred as St. George in several of the first productions. The success of the play was also due to the skilled producer, Charles Hawtrey; talented composer, Roger Quilter; and world-renowned instructor of acting, Italia Conti. Many children involved in the production as students of Conti became famous actors and actresses, including Noel Peirce Coward, Gertrude Lawrence, Jack Hawkins, and Richard Todd.

---

[144] Good, *The Cult of St. George,* 141.

The play begins with two children, Crispin and Rosamund, presumed orphans, living with their evil Aunt Matilda and Uncle Joseph. Rosamund finds a book, *Where the Rainbow Ends*, which describes a place where all lost ones are found in a land beyond the Dragon King's realm. Rosamund assumes that they will find their parents there. They need Faith's Magic Carpet to get to the land, which happens to be located in the house's library. The Carpet's Genie then appears and offers the children two wishes each before he takes them to the land where the rainbow ends. Crispin wishes for his friend Jim Blunders and Blunders' sister, Betty. Rosamund wishes for the adults to start dinner over, so they have more time, and for the aid of St. George. St. George then appears to the children as an old and forgotten ideal, but upon the request of Rosamund, he is transformed into a glorious knight. They are transported to a magical world by the carpet. Uncle Joseph and Aunt Matilda then find a piece of the carpet, which they use to summon the Dragon King, who promises to bring back the children. The children arrive at a safe spot in the Dragon's Wood because it is protected by St. George's banner. Betty is enticed by the Dragon King's dancing elves to leave the area protected by St. George, and the other children separate to look for Betty. Before they find her, Uncle Joseph and Aunt Matilda capture Rosamund and tie her up, leaving her for the hyenas. Meanwhile the boys meet the Slacker, an Englishman under the protection of the Dragon King who lives an idyllic life but is doomed to the fate of becoming a human-headed worm. Rosamund is rescued by the other children before the hyenas get her; Aunt Matilda is not so lucky. Uncle Joseph meets a similar fate at the hands of a black bear. Next, the children are captured by flying dragons and brought to the Dragon King's castle. They are given the death penalty for placing themselves under the patronage of an ideal, St. George. The children are saved by constructing a banner of St. George out of a white handkerchief and red ribbon, and flying it in place of the Dragon King's flag. Once the banner is in place, St. George appears and slays the Dragon King. The children are then led on a path to the golden beach where they are reunited with their parents who were not dead, but shipwrecked. St. George accompanies the children and their parents to England where he is restored to his rightful position as patron saint. The play ends with a short speech by St. George and the singing of the National Anthem.

The basic elements of the legend of St. George remain the same in the play. St. George as a knight comes to the aid of a young female and kills a dragon. The play, however, differs substantially in its depiction of St. George from older versions of the legend. Most significantly, he is not the martyr-saint of the Early Middle Ages, and the play fails to mention St. George's faith or his death for refusing to worship Roman gods. The St. George in *Rainbow* even states that he is not the martyr of earlier legends, and he blames his lack of popularity on being associated with a saint: "I am oft forgot… Sometime I think it's that word 'Saint' that's it—it doesn't give a chap a chance. I just try to do my duty like any ordinary fellow and they go and stick a halo on me—and a halo is such a misty unsoldierly sort of decoration."[145] St. George continues, "'Tis true you find me still in dim cathedrals, lifeless and cold, fashioned in marble, or pictured in musty unread books." He claims this is not his true home, "My home [is] the living hearts of my country's people."[146] In other words, St. George in the play is not the saint found in cathedrals and books, but he resides as a belief in the hearts of the English.

Furthermore, St. George is not granted the status of being a person; rather, he is portrayed as an ideal. The Dragon King describes the crime of the children as "having dared to place yourselves under the protection of an ideal—one George of England—Saint and Patron." He continues, "Know then that ideals are the Dragon's greatest enemy. Where ideals are honoured, our power is unknown; and this one in particular is here the most hated for he alone can build about

---

[145] Clifford Mills and John Ramsey, *Where the Rainbow Ends: acting edition* (London: Samuel French Limited, 1951), 12.
[146] Mills, *Rainbow*, 12.

your country, England, which I covet, a sure impregnable defense—
the wall of patriotism."[147] An ideal is something perfect, and it is the
end towards which one aims. Presenting St. George as an ideal, the
authors attempt to show that he is the perfect Englishman, and therefore, he is the goal for which Englishmen should aim. St. George is
presented as an archetype, rather than a real person.

St. George possesses several characteristics as an archetype. The
most prominent is a warrior. As a knight, he represents a militaristic
figure, and he further emphasizes the theme throughout the play. In
his first appearance to the children, he recounts the battle of Agincourt. He was "summoned by king…his unseen aid-de-camp, did I
ride from rank to rank," inspiring the men to cry "God for Harry—
England and St. George."[148] He continues to state that his goal presently is to "fight aggression and foul tyranny… till peace and justice
through the earth shall reign."[149] When St. George encounters Uncle
Joseph, he declares, "The fate of tyrants is—St. George's sword."[150]
At the climax of the play, St. George meets the dragon king and ex-
claims, "We meet arch-enemy, to fight the everlasting fight of good
and evil. Foul temper of my country, I challenge thee to mortal combat." The Dragon in turn vows "eternal war and destruction."[151] The
battle between the Dragon King and St. George is depicted as a battle
between good and evil. The encounter is described in language that
emphasizes battle: "mortal combat" and "eternal war," and the play
reinforces the notion that the triumph of good over evil is only accomplished with a fight.

St. George also represents patriotism. He promotes love for England and a belief in the supremacy of England. The play refers to him
as "St. George of England" and cheers him as "St. George for Merry

---

[147] Mills, *Rainbow*, 39.
[148] Mills, *Rainbow*, 12.
[149] Mills, *Rainbow*, 12.
[150] Mills, *Rainbow*, 22.
[151] Mills, *Rainbow*, 48.

England." Another cheer throughout the play is "God for England—freedom and the Right." St. George's ground, a piece of territory in the Dragon King's realm protected by St. George, is described as beautiful and as a typical English landscape, and Rosamund is portrayed as an "English maiden." The Dragon King argues that "patriotism" forms an "impregnable defense" around England.[152] England is referred to throughout the play, but a few references are made to other parts of the British Isles and the empire as well. In one instance, Cubs, the pet baby lion, drinks "Commonwealth Mixture for British Lion. Equal Parts of Canadian, Australian and New Zealand iron, mixed with South African steel."[153] A statement referring to England and Britain ends the play: "Rise, Youth of England, let your voices ring. For God, for Britain, and for Britain's King."[154]

The play also has a lengthy discourse on the banner of St. George. St. George's ground was won by St. George in battle, and in the play is protected by his banner. The Genie of the carpet instructs the children that under the banner "no ill can befall you."[155] Uncle Joseph is informed that the Dragon King's power is useless because "the children have placed themselves outside His Majesty's territory—there—under the protection of that flag." Uncle Joseph laughingly responds, "That! To think that his Majesty should be afraid of that—of its—its power—its protection. What's its protection worth? That children's plaything! That little bit of bumptious bunting." Bertrand, the French salesman (before World War I, a German), reprimands Uncle Joseph, "What? You mock at your own flag, you an Englishman... Insult no more your flag. That flag waved with mine. Beneath them our countrymen have fought side by side."[156] He continues to recount past battles the French fought with the British. When St. George appears later, he declares, "Unworthy son of your great country, behold the power at which you scoff. That banner emblem of a nation's pride, is

---

[152] Mills, *Rainbow*, 39.
[153] Mills, *Rainbow*, 2.
[154] Mills, *Rainbow*, 45.
[155] Mills, *Rainbow*, 16.
[156] Mills, *Rainbow*, 20.

also a sacred trust. You have defied the spirit of the flag by threatening those beneath its guardianship."[157] The banner is an essential element at the end of the play. When the children are captured and brought to the Dragon King's castle, St. George cannot help them because it is not his territory. The children plan to escape by taking "the castle for St. George." They accomplish the feat "by pulling down the Dragon's flag and putting up St. George's banner in its place. His flag once there, St. George can help us."[158] As the plan is enacted, the Dragon King realizes: "Ah, the English flag! The Red Cross of St. George. They seize the castle for mine enemy...err the flag is hoisted and my power is gone."[159] The use of the flag in the play highlights patriotism and English imperialism, implying anywhere the English flag is flown, subjects of England are safe and protected. That is, neither Dragon King nor any of his cohorts can attack anyone under the banner.

The play has a distinct goal pertaining to the cult of St. George. The authors did not merely present a version of the legend of St. George and hope that children would remember it. Rather, one of the central themes of the play is to keep St. George in mind. When St. George first appears after Rosamund wishes for him, he is "clad in a gray cloak."[160] Rosamund does not recognize St. George, and he responds, "Thus humbly clad, unnoted and unsung, do I lie in the hearts of men...Yet at my country's call quick as in days of old, shall I this same sword leap from its scabbard to defend the right."[161] He continues a little later, "I've not been in fashion much in England lately... I am often forgot."[162] The Dragon King affirms his efforts to ignore St. George: "It has been my plan to deaden in the hearts of Englishmen. Almost had I worked the downfall of his land—I flung

---

157 Mills, *Rainbow*, 22.
158 Mills, *Rainbow*, 41.
159 Mills, *Rainbow*, 48.
160 Mills, *Rainbow*, 10.
161 Mills, *Rainbow*, 11.
162 Mills, *Rainbow*, 12.

my gold dust in the people's eyes and lulled them into false security. Yes I had won—but… at her [Rosamund's] call, England awoke, and hailing my enemy as her champion."[163] One of the central lessons of the play is for children to remember and believe in St. George. On the one hand, failure to believe in St. George, as the Dragon King states, results in the end of his existence, for he lives only in the hearts of men. On the other hand, those who believe are rewarded, as the children in the play are saved by St. George and led to their parents. The hope of the author is that children will learn from their example. As one reviewer commented, "Where Peter Pan asks us to believe in fairies, Treasure Island in pirates, and Aladdin in magic caves, this play [*Where the Rainbow Ends*] asks us to believe in our own country and our own patron saint."[164]

The play initially was a resounding success in the view of critics and in terms of attendance. The initial reviews were all positive. The *Evening Standard* declared that "this is the children's play that we have been waiting for… It is a triumph for everyone concerned." "The most fascinating children's play we have ever seen," announced the *Daily News.*[165] On the twenty-fifth anniversary of the play in 1935, Princesses Elizabeth and Margaret attended a performance with their mother, and in 1938, the Lord Mayor and Lady Mayoress of London attended the play. These endorsements testify to the success of the play and its influence on English culture. As with St. George's Day, the play fell out of favor after World War II. In 1957, *The Illustrated London News* stated that it "has lost even its period quality…The play, I am afraid, is among the battered old lamps."[166] Two years later, *The Times* remarked, it was "not a real classic. And…never seemed genuine… with its outdated jingoistic Edwardian patriotism wrapped up thickly in pseudo-Shakespearean."[167] The harshest remarks came from

---

[163] Mills, *Rainbow, Rainbow,* 18.
[164] "The Holbron Empire: Where the Rainbow Ends," *The Times,* December 28, 1925, 14.
[165] Joan Selby-Lowndes, *The Conti Story* (London: Collins, 1954), 142.
[166] J. C. Trewin, "New Lamps and Old," *The Illustrated London News,* January 5, 1957.
[167] "Where the Rainbow Ends: A Sturdy Tradition Continues," *The Times,* December 27, 1958, 9.

The Stage and Television Today in a review for the last production: "Most of the children old enough to appreciate the plot are mentally wide-awake enough to dislike the chocolate box saintliness of the children in the story as much as their parents do and to realize that the sickly patriotism is downright embarrassing. Two world wars have been fought, endured and won by the people of this country since 'Where the Rainbow Ends' was written. To infer they lack feeling for home and country is as unfair as it is laughable."[168] Amid the many other changes of the post-war era, *Where the Rainbow Ends* and the imperialistic and nationalistic St. George fell out of favor.

After World War II, the celebration of St. George's Day went into decline. The association of St. George with imperialism, militarism, and racial superiority in the first half of the twentieth century seemed out of place after the war. The situation was further complicated by the extreme right's promotion of St. George and St. George's Day in the 1970s and 1980s. The National Front, a far-right political party, selected April 23 to hold parades and rallies. In 1976, the party marched through immigrant neighborhoods on St. George's Day, and the contentious march led to the arrests of twenty-six individuals.[169] In Trafalgar Square, an anti-immigration rally was held on St. George's Day of the same year. Charles Collett, a Conservative councilor from Birmingham, addressed the crowd about his twenty-year struggle to halt the tide of immigration.[170] The most publicized St. George's Day rally was in 1979, when the National Front organized a meeting at the Southall Town Hall in West London. The community had a sizable Asian population and minimal local support for the National Front. The location was selected because of the large immigrant population and meant to elicit a response. Local minority groups and

---

168 "Sutton: Where the Rainbow Ends," *The Stage and Television Today*, January 7, 1960.
169 "Calls for ban on National Front marches in city," *The Times*, April 26, 1976, 3.
170 "Pioneer campaigner against immigration says it is now too late," *The Times*, July 26, 1976, 3.

the Anti-Nazi League organized a demonstration to halt the National Front meeting. Only fifty National Front supporters attended the St. George's Day rally, but thousands of people protested the gathering. Clashes erupted between the anti-fascist protestors and the police protecting members of the National Front. In the mayhem that followed, one protestor, Blair Peach, was killed by the police, and count-countless injuries and hundreds of arrests occurred. [171]

The English National Party, founded in 1974 by Frank Hansford-Miller held numerous St. George's Day rallies in the late 1970s and early 1980s. The party shared many views with the National Front, but it focused on England more than Britain. The high point of the party occurred in 1976, when a member of parliament, John Stonehouse, left the Labour Party and joined the English National Party at the invitation of Hansford-Miller. The party held a St. George's Day rally in Trafalgar Square attended by Stonehouse, Hansford-Miller, and party faithful in 1976. The motto of the rally was "1776 – American Independence, 1976 – English Independence."[172] The party went defunct by the early 1980s, but Hansford-Miller continued to hold St. George's Day rallies at Trafalgar Square as part of his "Save England Crusade." He described his 1983 address in an editorial in *The Times*: "I made a stirring call for St. George's Day to be made a public holiday in England, with national celebrations in which, for one day at least, our political, racial and other differences could be forgotten and we could all celebrate together as one community, as in days of old of 'Merrie England.'"[173] The League of St. George, a neo-Nazi party, was founded in 1974 based on the principles of British fascist Oswald Mosley. The League's connection to St. George and England was minimal because it advocated for a pan-European fascist state, practiced Nordic paganism, and did not commemorate St. George's Day. The League's use of the name St. George

---

[171] Benjamin Bowling, *Violent Racism: Victimization, Policing, and Social Context* (Oxford: Oxford University Press, 1999), 49-50; Gerd Baumann, *Contesting Culture: Discourses of Identity in Multi-Ethnic London* (Cambridge: Cambridge Univ. Press, 1996), 58-59.

[172] "No, by George, just good fun," *The Sydney Morning Herald*, April 21, 1976.

[173] Frank Hansford-Miller, "Patriots of the air," *The Times*, April 30, 1983, 7.

and St. George's Cross as an emblem, however, further tarnished the image of the patron of England.[174]

As St. George's Day in the 1970s and 1980s became associated with far-right politics, violence, and racism, numerous attempts were made by political and religious leaders to stop the controversial marches and rallies, with particular focus on the National Front. The British Council of Churches signed a petition against the National Front in November of 1976, and the bishops of the Catholic Church in England and Wales agreed to support the measure. The Catholic Church sent the declaration to all its congregations and asked parishioners to sign it on St. George's Day in 1977. The timing of the signature drive against racism was a blatant attempt to retake the feast day from radical groups.[175] The government also moved to stop the parades and rallies of the National Front following the deadly riots of 1979. Home Secretary, William Whitelaw, banned all marches and processions in the London Metropolitan Police district for 28 days in April 1981. The action targeted the annual St. George's Day parade of the National Front. Organizers stated that 1,500 marchers planned to process through a racially diverse area of West Ham under the theme "British jobs for British workers." A counter-march of 4,000 was planned by a collection of Asian organizations.[176] The success of the radical groups in the late 1970s was short lived. Much of the impetus of the movement was squashed by the resounding victory of the Conservatives in 1979 and the change in politics under Margaret Thatcher. After the 1979 election, the National Front divided into splinter groups and fell into decline. The English National Party continued to

---

[174] Peter Barberis, John McHugh, and Mike Tyldesley, *Encyclopedia of British and Irish Political Organizations: Parties, Groups and Movements of the 20th Century* (New York: Continuum, 2001), 185.

[175] Clifford Longley. "Catholic bishops agree to join fight against racialism," *The Times*, April 7, 1978, 2.

[176] Geoffrey Browning, "Political marches in London banned to avoid disorders," *The Times*, April 24, 1981, 2.

exist for a few more years, but never fielded another political candidate.

The revival of St. George's Day in modern England occurred during the first half of the twentieth century. Many historians assumed that renewed interest in the day took place during the Victorian period in association with romanticism, the Pre-Raphaelites, the Neo-Gothic movement, and the Victorians' interest in chivalry and knights, but as argued above, the rebirth of April 23 as a major holiday in England only began in the 1890s. Furthermore, it reached its climax in the 1920s and 1930s, and steadily declined in the years after World War II. The connection between wars and the national day of England varied. On the one hand, the feast initially grew during the Second Anglo-Boer War, and World War I was instrumental to the rise of St. George's Day as a major holiday. On the other hand, World War II and the struggle of decolonization contributed to the decline of celebrations on April 23.

The revival was led by a few associations. The societies of St. George were the principal institutions that celebrated St. George's Day in North America. The revival of St. George's Day in England was primarily due to the RSSG. The society with its numerous branches throughout England and the world was the key component in the promotion of the holiday. Other organizations, such as the Order of the Garter, the Order of St. Michael and St. George, the Boy Scouts, and the Church of England were important, but secondary, to the RSSG.

In the modern celebrations, St. George represented the ideal Englishman. Correspondingly, twentieth-century festivities built on concepts outlined in popular legends of the post-Reformation period and in the celebrations of nineteenth-century America. As represented in *Where the Rainbow Ends*, St. George embodied the perfect ideal of Englishness. Even more, St. George represented the model soldier. A poem from World War I entitled "St. George of England" recounted the presence of St. George at every major battle in English history.

After relating the battle with the dragon, it reads, "Saint George he was a fighting man, as all the tales do tell... From Crecy field to Neuve Chapelle he's there with hand and sword, And he sailed with Drake from Devon to the glory of the Lord. His arm is strong to smite the wrong and break the tyrant's pride, He was there when Nelson triumphed, he was there when Gordon died... And faith! He's finding work this day to suit his war-worn sword, For he's strafing Huns in Flanders to the glory of the Lord."[177] In another example, after General Charles Gordon was killed in Africa in 1885, he was portrayed in the media as St. George, a British martyr fighting the dragon of slavery, barbarism, and oriental despotism.[178] To most English in the modern period, St. George was not a saint or Roman martyr or even a real person. He was a representation of the nation. Moreover, even those who believed in St. George and advocated for a "real" St. George did not hold the saint to be significant. In the documents of the RSSG, St. George was often mentioned only as the patron or representation of England, and not as a saint or intercessor. The society also frequently referred to April 23 as England's Day, and not as St. George's Day. They promoted St. George's Day to increase English nationalism, not to increase devotion to St. George.

Festivities on St. George's Day focused on English patriotism, imperialism, militarism, and masculinity. Besides St. George, other English symbols were promoted, such as St. George's Cross and the rose. Celebrations included English music and dances, English food, and English traditions and customs. They also commemorated the actions of great English individuals from Shakespeare to modern military heroes. Festivities were associated with achievements in the empire, and numerous empire-themed banquets, parades, and exhibitions took place on St. George's Day. Closely related to imperialism, the holiday was tied to militarism and the memory of those who died

---

[177] Clarke, *A Treasury of War Poetry*, 22-23.
[178] Patrick Brantlinger, *Rule of Darkness: British Literature and Imperialism, 1830-1914* (Ithaca: Cornell University Press, 1988), 170.

fighting for England. The emphasis on the military was most evident in the years following World War I. St. George and the festival were also connected to the cult of masculinity. From the Boy Scouts to the knightly orders, the movement to reinvigorate the men of England to be strong and morally pure used St. George as a model.[179] Unfortunately, some of the more radical movements connected St. George's Day with racism and belief in the superiority of the English people. From a political perspective, the political right promoted St. George's Day. Conservatives led the movement for the majority of the twentieth century, but later in the century, radical right-wing parties joined the effort. In opposition, the Labour Party was reluctant to elevate St. George's Day to a national holiday, and instead endorsed the international celebration of May Day.

The calendar as a whole changed in the modern period. The era after the Reformation saw the creation of a secular, national calendar, but alterations in the nineteenth century went even further. The creation of bank holidays reduced the number of holidays to four, and as a result, dozens of traditional holidays were eliminated. Instead of retaining two traditional holidays, legislation created the ambiguous and invented summer holiday, and the secular spring holiday replaced Whit Monday. In the 1970s, the international holiday May Day became a bank holiday, over the suggestions that St. George's Day be introduced as a new holiday. In short, introduction of bank holidays reduced the number of traditional, religious holidays on the English calendar, and replacement holidays were either days devoid of religious meaning, nationalistic holidays or international celebrations.

The success and failure of St. George's Day was based on the rise and fall of English nationalism. St. George's Day was an English, not British, holiday. The English often lamented that the Irish celebrate St. Patrick's Day, the Scottish celebrate St. Andrew's Day, and the Welsh celebrate St. David's Day, but the English forget St. George's Day. One reason for the lack of English nationalism was that many

---

[179] Joseph Kestner, "The Return of St. George 1815-1951," in *King Arthur's Modern Return*, ed. Debra N. Mancoff (New York: Garland Pub., 1998). 83-98.

English identified themselves as British. Great Britain was created by
the union of Scotland and England in 1707, and the United Kingdom
was created in 1801 with the union of Great Britain and Ireland. As a
new British identity was formed in the eighteenth and nineteenth centuries, English nationalism went into decline. English symbols were
replaced by new British ones, and St. George was superseded by Britannia. Originally a Latin term used by the Romans for the island of
Great Britain, Britannia was later also used as the female personifica-
tion of the nation. Rarely used during the medieval period, she rose in
prominence after the Union of 1707, and developed into the standard
image of a woman clad in classical dress with a sword or lance, Roman helmet, shield with the arms of Britain, and Phrygian cap of
liberty. She became the most prominent national symbol and appeared on coins, artwork, and cartoons.[180] British nationalism was
cemented in the century of wars fought mainly against the French—
War of the Spanish Succession, War of the Austrian Succession, Sev-
en Years' War, American Revolutionary War, and Napoleonic Wars.
Unusually, the cult of St. George, which was often associated with
war, declined in an era of almost constant conflict.

Conversely, the revival of St. George's Day was marked by an increased interest in English nationalism. The fragile British identity
started to splinter in the nineteenth century. The Irish, who were the
most reluctant participants in the union, developed a strong sense of
cultural nationalism, manifested in the Gaelic revival of the nineteenth
century. Irish nationalists eventually fought and won a separate
state.[181] Throughout the course of the twentieth century, the Scottish
and Welsh organized to gain separate legislative bodies, and each
gained a level of political and cultural independence. The English, as
the majority, were often equated with being British, and therefore,
remained without a separate legislative body. Today, the currents of

---

180 Hunt, *Defining John Bull*, 271.
181 John Hutchinson, *The Dynamics of Cultural Nationalism: The Gaelic Revival and the Creation of the Irish Nation State* (London: Allen & Unwin, 1987).

English nationalism are beginning to flow. St. George's Day's association with empire, war, and race relegated the holiday to the periphery
for the last sixty years, but the process of devolution and the resurgence of English nationalism in the last decade have brought the hol-
holiday back to the mainstream and poised for another revival.

Epilogue:
St. George's Day in Contemporary England

As part of the celebrations on April 23, 1971, "A chain of public houses named after the saint distributed 5,000 free pints of beer and delivered 6 lbs. of old English 'Epping' sausages to the Prime Minister at Downing Street in a stage coach. Fifty girls in 'hot pants' and patriotic tee shirts handed out cardboard reproductions of medieval pennies to stimulate patriotism and thirst for beer."[1] The commemoration of St. George's Day as a patriotic and nationalistic holiday declined after World War II, but is another revival possible through beer, sausages, and girls in hot pants? The commercialization of holidays from Christmas to St. Patrick's Day represents the latest controversy surrounding public celebrations, yet the revival of St. George's Day, the process of which is still underway, depends in part on corporations realizing that money can be made by celebrating the national day of England.

The current resurgence of interest in St. George's Day is not due to one particular institution, but is a diverse, and sometimes conflicting, movement. The process of detaching St. George from a "real" person, which began with the Reformation, has reached its natural conclusion resulting in St. George having no clear meaning at all. Unlike early nationalistic celebrations that focused on a specific ideal Englishman, current festivities honor a symbol that reflects the diverse values of the celebrants. In the past two decades, numerous

---

[1] "Homage paid as usual to St. George," *The Times*, April 24, 1971, 2.

factors and institutions promoted St. George's Day. Commercialization of the holiday by pubs and breweries greatly increased the visibil-visibility of April 23. The process of devolution and the rise of St. Andrew's Day, St. David's Day, and St. Patrick's Day led the English to promote St. George's Day, and increasing connections between national sports and St. George's Cross also benefitted the revival of St. George. Furthermore, negative reactions against European Union federalism helped increase English nationalism. Lastly, some argued that English symbols, such as St. George, must be mainstreamed in order to prevent radicals from using them to gain support. This potent mixture has allowed for a slow but steady increase in the celebration of April 23.

St. George's Day also currently faces numerous obstacles in contemporary England. The most pressing concern is the association of the holiday with radical right-wing movements. Many individuals in England and abroad still associate the English flag and St. George with racism. The second concern English have with their national day, closely related with the first, is guilt over the history of England. The history of the empire, and thereby England, is remembered as a story of violence and oppression. Many English are embarrassed by their history, and therefore, do not want a holiday to celebrate it. In the current politically sensitive world, a former victim or minority is easier to celebrate than a former conqueror; triumphalism is not popular. Lastly, larger and smaller communities rival English identity. A large number of English continue to identify themselves as British, while others associate with their county or local town more than with England.

Before any of these obstacles can be addressed, the lack of knowledge about St. George and his day needs to be resolved. Like their counterparts at the end of the nineteenth century, current commentators once again state that St. George's Day passes without observance, and evidence from surveys verifies their claims. *The Sun* reported in 2002 that a survey by Microsoft Encarta found one in three English people had never heard of St. George slaying a dragon, and one in ten people between eighteen and twenty-four only recognized St. George from the name of a local pub.[2] According to a 2008 poll conducted by *The Daily Telegraph*, only 48 percent of eighteen to thirty-four years olds could pick St. George's Day from a list of dates, and 70 percent were unaware of any events on April 23 in their neighborhood.[3] In 2009, *This England* magazine conducted a survey that revealed seven out of ten young people did not know when St. George's Day is, 40 percent did not know why St. George was the patron of England, and one in eight found it embarrassing to see St. George's Cross flying because of its connection to extremists.[4] *This England* commissioned another study in 2010 and discovered only a third of the respondents were aware of the date of St. George's Day, and 40 percent did not know why St. George was the patron of England. The study also revealed that the English were the least patriotic nation in Europe.[5] The results of these surveys prove that many English, in particular the young, not only neglect to celebrate St. George's Day, but they are also unaware of it.

Pubs and breweries in large part helped revive St. George's Day. St. George was traditionally associated with drinking because George was a popular name for inns and taverns. English breweries were also inspired by the efforts of Guinness to popularize St. Patrick's Day, and the profits which followed. Recently, Guinness started Proposi-

---

[2] "George: Saint, not a pub," *The Sun*, April 23, 2003, http://www.thesun.co.uk/sol/homepage/news/148222/George-Saint-not-a-pub.html#ixzz0aWygPVTu (accessed December 23, 2009).

[3] Philip Johnston, "St. George's Day: Britishness no longer enough," *The Daily Telegraph*, April 24, 2008.

[4] Sofia Petkar, "George Who? England's Patron Saint Forgotten," Sky News, April 23, 2009, http://news.sky.com/skynews/Home/UK-News/St-Georges-Day-New-Survey-Reveals-Majority-Of-English-People-Have-Forgotten-Englands-Patron-Saint/Article/200904415267361?lpos=UK_News_Third_Home_Page_Article_Teaser_Region__2&lid=ARTICLE_15267361_St_Georges_Day%3A_New_Survey_Reveals_Majority_Of_English_People_Have_Forgotten_Englands_Patron_Saint (accessed December 23, 2009).

[5] Nick Collins, "England 'least patriotic' country," *The Daily Telegraph*, April 12, 2010, http://www.telegraph.co.uk/news/uknews/7608125/England-least-patriotic-country.html (accessed May 26, 2010).

tion 3-17, a movement to collect signatures to make March 17 a holiday in the United States. Charles Wells Brewery[6] was the first to promote St. George's Day and its Wells Bombardier English Premium Bitter as the official drink of April 23. Nigel McNally, sales and marketing director, commented in 2005:

> Wells Bombardier began this campaign back in 1997 when no other company or brand had ever dreamed of looking at focusing time and energy into a patriotic campaign which uses St. George's day at its heart. Through sheer tenaciousness and hard work not only have we grown the sales of Wells Bombardier to high levels, we have solely established a must participate day on the pub calendar. St. George's Day is now in the top 3 days of celebration for our pub industry. This is a remarkable achievement over the course of 8 years, given back in 1997 the day was not even recognised by the industry or the population of the country.[7]

Wells Bombardier associated itself with St. George's Day through a series of advertising campaigns around April 23 each year. The company launched a national promotion with television commercials, advertisements in printed material, and a poster campaign. Wells Bombardier labeled itself the "patron pint of England," "drink of England," and "official drink of St. George's Day." One commercial ran the witty tagline, "St. George's Day – Make a Knight of it," and a poster featured the armored hand of St. George holding a pint of Wells Bombardier. In the last decade, Wells Bombardier also launched a website, www.thevalueofstgeorge.com, which listed events for St. George's Day and collected signatures to make St. George's Day a bank holiday. Charles Wells' deputy chairmen, Tom Wells, de-

---

[6] As of 2006, Wells and Young's Brewing Company.

[7] "Wells Bombardier English Premium Bitter officially takes ownership of St. George's Day," http://www.thevalueofstgeorge.com/index.php?oURL=home%2FNews%2FWells+Bombardier+closely+linked+with+St+Georges+Day (accessed December 23, 2009)

livered the petition with 62,000 signatures to 10 Downing Street.[8] Wells Bombardier also joined forces with the "Celebrate St. George's Day Campaign" organized by Bruno Peek, who stage managed the Queen's Golden Jubilee and the Trafalgar Weekend of 2005. Peek traveled to fifty cities with a loving cup dedicated to St. George, campaigning to make April 23 as prominent a celebration as March 17. The final toast of the loving cup occurred at 10:45 PM on St. George's Day in 2007 at a grand banquet in Mansion House. Peek selected Paul Wells, chairman of Wells and Young's Brewing Company, to give the final toast and Wells Bombardier to be the official drink of the toast.[9] The company also promoted the idea of a national toast on St. George's Day, and it suggested that "no St. George's Day celebration would be complete without joining the rest of the nation at 10:45 PM, by raising a pint of Wells Bombardier to England and St. George. People should herald the toast with: 'I have the honour of undertaking the following toast. Ladies & gentlemen, I give you England & St. George.'"[10] The campaign was a success for Wells Bombardier and St. George's Day. Between 1997 and 2005, Wells Bombardier saw a growth of 216 percent and was recognized as the beer most associated with St. George's Day.[11]

---

[8] "St. George's Day Petition," http://www.charleswells.co.uk/bombardier/promotions/petition/photos (accessed December 23, 2009).

[9] Amy Iggulden, "Have one for the road to help St. George," *The Daily Telegraph*, February 5, 2007, http://www.telegraph.co.uk/news/uknews/1541602/Have-one-for-the-road-to-help-St-George.html (accessed December 23, 2009).

[10] "Top tips for St. George's Day celebrations," http://www.charleswells.co.uk/bombardier/promotions/toptips (accessed December 23, 2009).

[11] "Wells Bombardier English Premium Bitter officially takes ownership of St. George's Day," http://www.thevalueofstgeorge.com/index.php?oURL=home%2FNews%2FWells+Bombardier+closely+linked+with+St+Georges+Day (accessed December 23, 2009); "Wells Bombardier English Premium Bitter nationally launches a 'really rather English' advertising campaign," http://www.wellsandyoungs.co.uk/wellsandyoungs/news/bombardier-english-premium-bitter (accessed December 23, 2009).

Widespread celebration of St. George's Day could generate a substantial amount of money for many industries. According to one study from 2007, if St. George's Day was celebrated in the same way as St. Patrick's Day, English companies could earn a potential £38.8 million, and pubs alone would gross an extra £14.1 million.[12] To increase revenue, pubs attracted consumers on St. George's Day with an array of English flags and decorations, and one way to gauge increased activity on April 23 in pubs is the rising demand for St. George's Day party packs. Peeks, a leading supplier of party packages, claimed demand in 2008 was increasing for its St. George's Day pack—a collection of English themed supplies from red and white plastic bowlers hats to red and white loo signs. From the year before, sales were up 50 percent, and for the first time in the sixty-year history of the company, St. George's Day packs surpassed those produced for St. Patrick's Day.[13] In addition to decorations, pubs and restaurants around England introduced menus with traditional English fare. The George and Dragon Pub in Swallowfield was one of many institutions serving English asparagus, beef and ale pie, and bread and butter pudding.[14] In addition to pubs, Clinton Cards introduced St. George's Day greeting cards in 1995, and within several years, it was selling 50,000 every April.[15] Local organizations led the promotion and celebration of St. George's Day, continuing the tradition of the guilds and societies of St. George. A small organization, St. George Unofficial Bank Holiday, tracks events for April 23 on its website, www.stgeorgesholiday.com. In 2007, they contacted every English Council, and found 80 percent were not planning any events. In 2009, they received the same response from the English Councils; however,

---

[12] Rosie Davenport, "For England and St. George," *Morning Advertiser*, February 22, 2007, http://www.morningadvertiser.co.uk/news.ma/article/28435?N=598267&Ne=598327%2B 598327&PagingData=Po_0~Ps_10~Psd_Asc (accessed December 23, 2009).

[13] Steven Morris and Nicholas Watt, "Here comes the knight: on April 23 Englishness is bursting out all over," *The Guardian*, April 23, 2008, http://www.guardian.co.uk/uk/2008/apr/23/britishidentity1 (accessed December 23, 2009).

[14] Richard Alleyne, "St. George's Day: Let's drink to a national celebration," *The Daily Telegraph*, April 23, 2008.

[15] Ian Bradley, *Believing in Britain: The Spiritual Identity of "Britishness"* (London: Tauris, 2007), 3-4.

the number of celebrations organized by pubs, clubs, and other organizations had increased by 300 percent during the same time
period.[16]

The current revival of St. George's Day is also associated with national sports. In particular, English sports fans are credited with reviving
the use of the English flag. During the post-war period, radical groups
hijacked St. George's cross and turned the flag into a controversial
symbol. At international matches, English fans displayed the Union
Flag and wore red, white, and blue, the colors associated with the flag.
The 1996 European Football Championship, held in England, was
the turning point in the use of the English flag. The opening ceremony featured a mock battle between St. George and the dragon similar
to the medieval ridings, and for the first time, fans displayed St.
George's cross and painted their faces red and white.[17] English supporters were partially motivated by England's placement in the same
group as Scotland. The Scottish, apparently, had no love for the English national team; 75 percent of Scottish football fans did not
support the English team and 40 percent preferred any other team to
win.[18] In light of the discord dividing Britain, many English felt better
represented by the English flag than the British flag. The high visibil-
ity of the cross of St. George at the matches brought respectability.
One reporter commented, "One of the greatest things about Euro
'96… is that it made it quite comfortable going to watch England
sitting in the crowd wearing an England shirt. It's almost like the de-
cent fans have reclaimed the England shirt. Before if you're in an
England shirt you automatically thought, 'steer clear, a bit dodgy.'"[19]

---

[16] "Does your Council support St. George?,"
http://www.stgeorgesholiday.com/events/events_council.asp (accessed December 23,
2009).
[17] Riches, *St. George*, 209.
[18] Thomas Hylland Eriksen and Richard Jenkins, *Flag, Nation and Symbolism in Europe and
America* (London: Routledge, 2007), 83.
[19] Scott Lash and Celia Lury, *Global Culture Industry* (Cambridge: Polity, 2006), 50.

Not everyone comfortably transitioned to the use of the English flag. In the 1998 World Cup match between Argentina and England, an injured Ian Wright was shown on television wrapped in an English flag. After the game, Lez Henry, a black fan, commented: "I thought 'What the fuck is he doing – has he lost his mind completely!' I mean the St. George Cross! That's the worst thing for a black person because according to them people you can't be black and English. May-Maybe Britishness would be something else because you can be 'black British' but English? Never."[20] Even in the face of opposition, the use of the cross of St. George has only grown in recent years. In preparation for Euro 2004, *The Daily Telegraph* declared a "flag crisis." One importer claimed, "We sold three million and, if we had the stock we would sell more."[21] Giles Morgan in his 2006 book on St. George went beyond the connection between football and the flag, and argued that David Beckham was the new representation of St. George. Kings and military leaders were portrayed as St. George in the past, but today a footballer best represents the modern St. George.[22] The popularity of the English flag reached a climax during the 2006 World Cup. The future mayor of London, Boris Johnston, wrote an editorial describing the flag's rise in respectability and the political left's reluctant acceptance of it. He called the movement a cultural revolution: "A revolution that was born among the scaffolders and the taxi drivers and the pub owners, and then spread to the bourgeoisie to the point where the Labour elite knew they could no longer contain it; they had to co-opt it."[23] The connection between sports and St. George is also evident in the 2012 gangster film, St. George's Day,

---

[20] Ben Carrington and Ian McDonald, *'Race', Sport and British Society* (London: Routledge, 2002), 99.
[21] David Sapsted, "St. George supplies flagging," August 9, 2004, *The Daily Telegraph*, http://www.telegraph.co.uk/news/uknews/1463990/St-George-supplies-flagging.html (accessed December 23, 2009).
[22] Morgan, *St. George*, 126-27.
[23] Boris Johnson, "C'mon Gordon, join the rest of us and fly the flag for England," *The Daily Telegraph*, June 8, 2006, http://www.telegraph.co.uk/comment/personal-view/3625544/Cmon-Gordon-join-the-rest-of-us-and-fly-the-flag-for-England.html#comments (accessed January 4, 2010).

which climaxes around a football match between England and Germany played on April 23.

The growth of a separate English identity, apart from British, has increased as part of the process of devolution. Northern Ireland, Wales, and Scotland have had their own assemblies since 1998, and a growing movement in Cornwall is demanding a separate assembly. English nationalists, disturbed by the absence of an English parliament, argue that members of parliament from Wales, Northern Ireland, and Scotland can vote on issues pertaining only to England, but representatives from England cannot participate in the Welsh, Irish, or Scottish assemblies. The disparity of political authority has fueled the English demand for a separate parliament. Soon after the creation of devolved assemblies in 1998, the "Campaign for an English Parliament" started, and aptly the campaign used the cross of St. George as an emblem. A 2008 poll by *The Daily Telegraph* found that a third of English people wanted an English parliament along Scottish lines, and 20 percent wanted English independence; therefore only a minority was content with the current political situation.[24]

Other national groups in the United Kingdom have been celebrating the feast of their patrons with increasing enthusiasm. St. Patrick's Day has been a bank holiday in Northern Ireland since 1903, and the Scottish parliament created a bank holiday for St. Andrew's Day in 2007. In Cornwall, many workers are off from work on St. Piran's Day as an unofficial holiday.[25] The Welsh and Cornish are petitioning to make their national days official bank holidays. Growing support for national days in Scotland, Wales, and Cornwall mobilized advocates of St. George's Day. The call for a bank holiday on April 23 has intensified in the last decade, with numerous petitions being delivered

---

[24] Philip Johnston, "St. George's Day: Britishness no longer enough," *The Daily Telegraph*, April 24, 2008.
[25] Ruth Gledhill, "Cornwall workers given an unofficial day off for St. Piran's Day," *The Times*, March 5, 2009, http://www.timesonline.co.uk/tol/news/uk/article5850736.ece (accessed December 23, 2009).

to the prime minister. In 2005, cricketing legend Ian Botham presented a petition signed by more than a half-million people to 10
Downing Street, demanding greater recognition for April 23.[26] Wells
Bombardier, as mentioned previously gathered 62,000 signatures for a
St. George's Day petition. Supporters of making St. George's Day a
public holiday collected signatures on several websites including
www.stgeorgesday.com and www.stgeorgesholiday.com. The popular
networking site Facebook has dozens of groups dedicated to celebrating St. George's Day, and one group "Let's ALL Celebrate St.
George's Day on 23rd April 2010" has several hundred thousand
members.[27] *The Sun* also supported the petition drive for a bank holiday by launching their "Let's Have It Off" campaign. The official site
of the prime minister allows individuals to create e-petitions, collect
signatures, and submit them to the government. The site has received
numerous petitions asking to create a April 23 bank holiday. The response from the government to one such petition reads: "At present,
we have no plans to change the current pattern of Bank Holidays, but
we are nevertheless considering all these suggestions carefully. Your
suggestion of a Bank Holiday to celebrate St. George's Day on April
23rd, which is also traditionally remembered as the birthday of William Shakespeare, has been one of the popular suggestions we have
received."[28] Numerous petitions and the popularization of St.
George's Day on the internet reveal the growing interest in the holiday and that more young people are becoming involved in the
movement.

Conservative MP Andrew Rosindell has led the movement in parliament to make St. George's Day a holiday. Rosindell is the chairman

---

[26] "England Celebrates St. George's Day," Sky News, April 23, 2005,
http://news.sky.com/skynews/Home/Sky-News-Archive/Article/200806413334778 (accessed December 24, 2009).
[27] 243,432 members, "Let's ALL Celebrate St. George's Day on 23rd April 2010!!!," Facebook,
http://www.facebook.com/group.php?gid=62468968108&ref=search&sid=21204402.50488
6535..1 (accessed February 20, 2010).
[28] "supportstgeorge - epetiton response," February 25, 2008,
http://www.number10.gov.uk/Page14640 (accessed January 2, 2010).

of The St. George's Day All Party Parliamentary Group, a collection
of members of parliament and peers that celebrate and support St.
George's Day.[29] He tabled a Private Member's Bill to make St.
George's Day a holiday, and also submitted an Early Day Motion for
the same cause with support from forty-six MPs.[30] With the exception
of a few politicians, the government has not been a leading supporter
of the modern revival of St. George's Day, and has provided very
little financial support for the celebration of April 23. *The Sun* reported in 2006 that the Government only spent £230 on St. George's Day
in the last five years.[31] Rosindell investigated the sum spent by the
Department for Culture, Media and Sport for St. George's Day. Upon
his request, it was revealed that the Department spent £114 in 2007,
and £116 in 2008. The funds were spent to fly St. George's flag, and
the Department had no other plans to celebrate the holiday in 2009.[32]
Rosindell maintained the problem was that no government department was taking responsibility for St. George's Day. Comparatively,
the Scottish government spent £440,000 on St. Andrew's Day in
2008.[33] London has hosted a St. Patrick's Day parade and festival
since 2002, and the city spent hundreds of thousands of pounds on
the celebrations. However, no equivalent St. George's Day festival
takes place in London. The only official support of the government

---

[29] "St. George's Day All Party Parliamentary Group," http://www.stgeorgesdayappg.co.uk/
(accessed January 2, 2010).

[30] Andrew Rosindell, "Early Day Motion: Celebration of St. George's Day," March 25, 2008,
http://edmi.parliament.uk/EDMi/EDMDetails.aspx?EDMID=35487&SESSION=891
(accessed January 2, 2010).

[31] Jon Gaunt, "NO money for the English, there's a surprise!," *The Sun*, June 13, 2006,
http://www.thesun.co.uk/sol/homepage/news/columnists/john_gaunt/1315172/Jon-
Gaunt-When-I-need-tips-on-being-English.html#ixzz0bVeygL4M (accessed January 2,
2010).

[32] Daily Hansard - Written Answers, "St. George's Day," January 27, 2009,
http://www.parliament.the-stationery-
office.co.uk/pa/cm200809/cmhansrd/cm090127/text/90127w0021.htm (accessed January
2, 2010).

[33] Christopher Hope and Simon Johnson, "Whitehall department spends just £116 on flag to
k St. George's Day," *The Daily Telegraph*, April 23, 2009,
/www.telegraph.co.uk/news/newstopics/politics/5200639/Whitehall-department-
ust-116-on-flag-to-mark-St-Georges-Day.html (accessed January 2, 2010).

has been to fly the flag of St. George, and Gordon Brown, a Scot, flew the flag of England over 10 Downing Street for the first time on April 23, 2008.

St. George's Day played a role in the 2010 General Election. The British National Party, for instance, launched their election manifesto on April 23.[34] The Conservatives also used the holiday to campaign for their cause. David Cameron and Boris Johnson attended a celebration in London, and they acknowledged that they were examining plans to make St. George's Day a bank holiday if they won the general election. Cameron argued the English "are reclaiming St. George's Day as an important day," and "from this point on, we should always properly celebrate St. George's Day."[35] The Conservatives' victory in 2010 moved St. George's Day closer to becoming a bank holiday, but substantial hurdles remain.

The celebration of St. George's Day and the display of the flag of England remain controversial undertakings. Legal disputes mark every April 23, battling over the appropriateness of symbols associated with the patron of England. For instance, a parade in Ilkeston organized by the St. George's Day Association was cancelled in 2007 after organizers were presented with a £20,000 bill for police presence.[36] A St. George's Day parade in Bradford was also postponed, later cancelled, for "health and safety reasons" on police advice in 2008. The fear of violence was ironic, considering 1,500 school children composed the majority of the parade, and planners proposed the event as

---

[34] Jonathan Brown, "BNP launch is politics with a hint of Python," *The Independent*, April 24, 2010, http://www.independent.co.uk/news/uk/politics/bnp-launch-is-politics-with-a-hint-of-python-1952966.html (accessed May 24, 2010).

[35] Christopher Hope, "General Election 2010: David Cameron wants English to reclaim St. George's Cross from BNP," *The Daily Telegraph*, April 23, 2010, http://www.telegraph.co.uk/news/election-2010/7624342/General-Election-2010-David-Cameron-wants-English-to-reclaim-St-Georges-Cross-from-BNP.html (accessed May 26, 2010).

[36] Laura Clout, "St. George's Day parade 'stopped by police bill,'" *The Daily Telegraph*, April 21 2007, http://www.telegraph.co.uk/news/uknews/1549237/St-Georges-Day-parade-stopped-by-police-bill.html (accessed January 3, 2010).

a multicultural event to bring the community together.[37] Flying the English flag has continued to be a contentious practice. *The Sun,* one of the promoters of the English flag, reported that a Labour communications officer stated his opposition to the English flag: "England, as opposed to Britain, has an unfortunate history around the world and within the British Isles and please do not say that it is all past. It is a fact that the right and extreme right in Britain cloak themselves in the English flag, the cross of St. George and claim to be the true representatives of the English."[38] Islamic radical, Anjem Choudary, claimed the flag represented a bloodthirsty past: "The cross does represent Christianity and for Muslims it also represents a crusader history of occupation and murder."[39] The newspaper collected a list of places and corporations that banned the display of the English flag, which included the cable company NTL, construction workers at Heathrow, taxi drivers in Blackpool, cabbies in Cheltenham, firemen in Barking East London, and Tesco lorry drivers. In one further example, the Liverpool City Council ordered the St. George's flags hoisted on lamp-posts to be taken down in 2009 for "health and safety grounds as they could cause harm to pedestrians and motorists." Local residents protested that flags were posted on the same lamp-posts on St. Patrick's Day.[40]

Religious institutions across England promoted the celebration of St. George's Day. The Church of England elevated the feast day in 1996, and the Catholic Church promoted April 23 to a solemnity in

---

[37] Nicole Martin, "St. George's parade through riot route stopped," *The Daily Telegraph,* April 21 2008, http://www.telegraph.co.uk/news/uknews/1896215/St-Georges-parade-through-riot-route-stopped.html (accessed January 3, 2010).

[38] Michael Lea, "Labour attack on England," *The Sun,* November 30, 2005, http://www.thesun.co.uk/sol/homepage/news/192182/Labour-attack-on-English.html (accessed January 3, 2010).

[39] Martin Phillips, "England Expects Flags," *The Sun,* June 2, 2006, http://www.thesun.co.uk/sol/homepage/news/50503/England-expects-flags.html (accessed January 3, 2010).

[40] Martin Thomas, "Liverpool Council tear down St. George flags," Click Liverpool, April 23, 2009, http://www.clickliverpool.com/news/local-news/124040-liverpool-council-tear-down-st-george-flags.html (accessed January 3, 2010).

England in 2000. Besides these liturgical alterations, church leaders voiced their support for the revival of a national celebration. John Sentamu, archbishop of York, in a speech before his enthronement, called for the English to reclaim their national identity and to celebrate St. George's Day in proper fashion. The Ugandan-born cleric remarked, "I speak as a foreigner really. The English are somehow embarrassed about some of the good things they have done. They have done some terrible things but not all the Empire was a bad idea."[41] Sentamu also expressed the idea of reviving St. George at *The Sunday Times* Literary Festival in 2009 when discussing the use of the flag of St. George during football tournaments: "Previously an icon of extreme nationalists, a sign of exclusion tinged with racism, the flag of St. George instead became a unifying symbol for a nation caught up in the hopes of eleven men kicking a ball around a field." He wondered, "Has the time come to make the Feast of St. George, the Patron Saint of England, a Public Holiday? A day to celebrate Englishness."[42] The former bishop of Rochester, Michael Nazir-Ali, encouraged the revival of St. George's Day and called for churches to ring their bells, fly the English flag, and hold church services. The Pakistani bishop stated that it was important to use the symbol of St. George: "George is a Christian saint and these are characteristically Christian values and virtues. In reclaiming St. George we are making sure that his name is not abandoned to a narrow nationalistic chauvinism."[43] The support of foreign-born bishops led to more widespread support of St. George's Day in the Church of England. Other church leaders, however, opposed St. George's role as patron of England. Philip Chester, vicar of St. Matthew's, Westminster, began a petition to replace St. George with St. Alban as patron of England. Chester

---

[41] Ruth Gledhill, "Multiculturalism has betrayed the English, Archbishop says," *The Times*, November 22, 2005, http://www.timesonline.co.uk/tol/news/uk/article592693.ece (accessed January 4, 2010).

[42] John Sentamu, "Archbishop's speech on 'Englishness,'" April 4, 2009, http://www.archbishopofyork.org/2369 (accessed January 4, 2010).

[43] Ruth Gledhill, "It's time we reclaimed our patron saint, says Dr Michael Nazir-Ali," *The Times*, April 23, 2009, http://www.timesonline.co.uk/tol/comment/faith/article6150614.ece (accessed January 4, 2010).

justified his effort to replace the patron saint on the lack of evidence for St. George and that he never lived in England. The measure had the support of some senior clerics and was considered at the General Synod in 2006, but ultimately, the motion failed.[44]

The new forces of commercialization, devolution, and sports renewed interest in St. George, but traditional institutions still encouraged the celebration of St. George's Day. The Boy Scouts and the RSSG continued to mark April 23 with festivities. The RSSG marked 1999 as a turning point in the apathy directed towards the holiday. The *English Standard*, the society's newsletter, announced: "By George, we've done it. 23rd April saw more people than ever celebrate St. George's Day." The society attributed the success to the media, which was the "touchpaper for this revival of English patriotism and pride. After years of completely ignoring the significance of St. George's Day, editors this time were only too eager to publicise our Society and its activities."[45] The British National Party saw a steady increase in support in the first decade of the twenty-first century, and the party continued to stir controversy on the feast of St. George. Other institutions also increased their support for St. George's Day. English Heritage, previously known as the Historic Building and Monuments Commission for England, started a campaign to celebrate St. George's Day. The institution hosted a St. George's Day Festival at the historic Wrest Park, the biggest celebration in the country, and several other events at historic venues.[46] Wells Bombardier, the official beer of English Heritage, sponsored English Heritage's St. George's Day events. In 2009, the department commissioned a poem in honor of St. George by Brian Patten, provided a free St. George's Day e-card, and published a guide on how to cele-

---

[44] Steve Doughty, "Will George be slayed as England's patron saint?," *Daily Mail,* July 2, 2006, http://www.dailymail.co.uk/news/article-393651/Will-George-slayed-Englands-patron-saint.html#ixzz0bfmFe5A1 (accessed January 4, 2010).
[45] Royal Society of St. George, *English Standard*, Autumn 1999, 1.
[46] English Heritage, http://www.english-heritage.org.uk/server/show/nav.20218 (accessed January 4, 2010).

brate St. George's Day. [47] The guide included "facts" about St. George, holiday games for children, a list of the sixteen events sponsored by English Heritage, festive drinks for the holiday, and recipes for festive dishes, including traditional beer battered fish and modern chicken tikka masala. In 2010, the Worshipful Company of Armourers & Brasiers held its first St. George's Day parade in London since 1585. The procession included the Band of the Parachute Regiment, the Regimental Colour Party, St. George on a horse, some knights, and a lamb in a crib on wheels. [48]

Support for St. George's Day has spread slowly to the political left. The growing sentiment is that St. George, his day, and his flag needs to be reclaimed from radicals. Billy Bragg, a left-leaning musician, actively promotes the celebration of St. George, and desires to turn St. George's Day into a unifying event. In a 2008 editorial in *The Guardian*, he wrote, "We need to find a way to overcome that reticence and repossess the symbols of what it means to be English. St. George's Day can help us do that if we can make it less inward looking and more like St. Patrick's Day where everyone can be Irish for the day, wherever they come from." [49] The sentiment was echoed in another article in *The Guardian* entitled "Saint George is our saint too." The piece questioned the history of St. George and England, but went on to state, "This is the country we've got, and this is the flag we've got, and if we can get better at waving the latter, that's got to be a good thing. Let the bigots and racists go and get their own

[47] English Heritage, http://www.english-heritage.org.uk/server/show/ConWebDoc.13535 (accessed January 4, 2010); English Heritage, "How to Celebrate St. George's Day," http://www.english-heritage.org.uk/upload/pdf/Howto_celebrate_St_Georges_Day_guide.pdf?1262634257 (accessed January 4, 2010).
[48] Jack Malvern, "St. George invades London with a lamb that survived the chop," *The Times*, April 23, 2010, http://www.timesonline.co.uk/tol/news/uk/article7106635.ece (accessed May 26, 2010).
[49] Billy Bragg, "Let's celebrate what it means to be English," *The Guardian*, April 23, 2008, http://www.guardian.co.uk/uk/2008/apr/23/britishidentity (accessed January 4, 2010).

one."[50] The progressive think-tank Ekklesia went further and argued that "St. George and his national Day needs to be 're-branded' (re-thought and re-defined) for the 21st century." An article on Ekklesia's website highlighted that St. George died protesting the abuse of a minority within a large empire. Moreover, St. George was not English, but from the Middle East, and is venerated by Muslims as Al-Khader. The article maintained that the story of St. George positions him as a "defender of the vulnerable." It continues, "We see that he does not truthfully belong to those who seek to dominate or exclude others." St. George's Day, therefore, should become a "Day of Dissent when we mark and celebrate the noble, alternative English tradition of rebellion against the abuse of power." A new public holiday on St. George's Day, they argued, should celebrate movements of rebellion, such as those of the Levellers, abolitionists, suffragettes, peacemakers, anti-racism campaigners, human rights activists, and others.[51]

St. George's Day is on the ascendance once again, aided by its association with the popular activities of sports and drinking. The importance of the holiday is also intertwined with a rise in English nationalism, and celebrations will only increase if April 23 becomes a bank holiday. This revival, however, is not centered on religious devotion to a saint. One telling indication is a press release from Boris Johnson, mayor of London and supporter of St. George's Day. The statement reads, "St. George, a Cappadocian merchant who sold bacon to the Roman army – let's raise a flag, if not a glass for our patron saint."[52] Detractors of St. George for centuries claimed he was a fake

---

[50] Stephen Tomkins, "St. George is our saint too," *The Guardian*, April 8, 2009, http://www.guardian.co.uk/commentisfree/belief/2009/apr/07/religion-christianity-sentamu-st-george (accessed January 4, 2010).

[51] Simon Barrow and Jonathan Bartley, "When the Saints Go Marching Out: Redefining St. George for a new era," Ekklesia, April 2007, http://www.ekklesia.co.uk/node/5083 (accessed January 5, 2010).

[52] Boris Johnson, "London raises a flag for Saint George," April 23, 2009, http://www.london.gov.uk/view_press_release.jsp?releaseid=21797 (accessed January 5, 2010).

saint inspired by the corrupt George of Cappadocia, but ironically, current supporters do not care if he was a dishonest heretic or a heroic martyr, or if he even existed. St. George's Day, presently, is not concerned with St. George, but immigration, football, devolution, European federalism, beer, nationalism, political dissent, and a score of other issues.

Acknowledgements

Without the help of many people, this book would have never come into existence. From its inception, the history department at The Catholic University of America was instrumental in the molding of my ideas into a workable project. I am particularly grateful to Jerry Muller and Owen Stanwood for reading the text and offering thoughtful insights. Yet, no one has left a greater mark on the project than my advisor, Laura Mayhall. She worked through numerous iterations, and crafted my dissertation in countless ways. My cohort of graduate students always reminded me that I was not alone on this journey, and Jay Harrison stands out as a constant companion during this time.

I received great assistance from my current institution, Howard Community College, and Jerry Casway in particular encouraged me to revise my dissertation into a published work. Numerous readers reviewed the text before publication, and I appreciate their thoughtful comments: Sam Bianchi, Joe Langan, George Matysek, Robert Baker, Ortrud Bianchi, and Paul Bianchi.

My family offered great support for this project. I am grateful to my in-laws for many child-free days, to my siblings for constant encouragement, to my brother, Muriel, for countless conversations on calendars and religion, and to my parents for fostering my interests in religious history and supporting my education.

Since I began this endeavor, Jonathan and Damian have entered my life, and their smiles and invitations to play were welcome distractions. Lastly, I owe Tiffany a huge debt of gratitude. I barely knew St. George when we met. While no fan of history, she read more versions of this text than anyone else and endured far too many conversations on St. George's Day. Thank you for your unconditional love and constant support.

Bibliography

Newspapers

The Aberdeen Journal (Aberdeen).
The Albion, A Journal of News, Politics and Literature (New York).
All the year round (London).
The Anglo-American, A Journal of Literature, News, Politics, the Drama (New York).
Atkinson's Saturday Evening Post (Philadelphia).
Baltimore Patriot (Baltimore).
Belle assemblee; or Court and fashionable magazine (London).
Chambers's journal of popular literature, science and arts (Edinburgh).
The Cornhill magazine (London).
Daily Mail (London).
The Daily Telegraph (London).
English Standard (Folkestone).
The Guardian (Manchester).
The New - York Mirror: a Weekly Gazette of Literature and the Fine Arts (New York).
New York Times (New York).
Niles' Weekly Register (Baltimore).
Morning Advertiser (Crawley).
Oswego Daily Times (Oswego).
The Outlook (New York).
The Pall Mall Gazette (London).
The Stage and Television Today (London).

The Sun (London).

The Sydney Morning Herald (Sydney).

The Times (London).

Western Mail (Cardiff).

Printed Primary Sources

Adamnan. *De locis sanctis.* Edited by Denis Meehan. Dublin: Dublin Institute for Advanced Studies: 1958.

Adams, John, and Abigail Adams. *The Letters of John and Abigail Adams.* Edited by Frank Shuffelton. New York: Penguin Books, 2004.

Aelfric. *Lives of Saints.* Edited by Walter Skeat. London: Early English Text Society, 1881.

The Alternative Service Book 1980. Cambridge: Cambridge University Press, 1980.

Ambroise. *The History of the Holy War.* Translated by Marianne Ailes. Woodbridge: Boydell Press, 2003.

Anderson, J. J., ed. *Records of Early English Drama. Newcastle Upon Tyne.* Toronto: University of Toronto Press, 1982.

The Anglo-Saxon Chronicle. Edited by James Ingram. Translated by James H. Ford. Texas: El Paso Norte Press, 2005.

Anstis, John. *The Register of the Most Noble Order of the Garter: Usually Called the Black Book.* London: John Barber, 1724.

Arndt, Wilhelm. "Passio Santi Georgi." *Berichte über die Verhandlungen der Königlich Sächsischen Gesellschaft der Wissenschaften zu Leipzig. Philologisch-Historische* 26 (1874): 43-70.

Ashmole, Elias. *The Institution, Laws and Ceremonies of the Most Noble Order of the Garter.* London: T. Dring, 1693.

Baden-Powell, Robert, and Elleke Boehmer. *Scouting for Boys: A Handbook for Instruction in Good Citizenship.* Oxford: Oxford University Press, 2004.

————. *Rovering to Success; A Book of Life-Sport for Young Men.* London: H. Jenkins, 1922.

Bliss, William Henry, ed. *Calendar of Entries in the Papal Registers Relating to Great Britain and Ireland: Petitions to the Pope, A.D. 1342-1419*. London: Eyre and Spottiswoode, 1896.

The Book of Common Prayer: From the Original Manuscript Attached to the Act of Uniformity of 1662, and Now Preserved in the House of Lords. London: Eyre & Spottiswoode, 1892.

Bray, Gerald Lewis, ed. *Documents of the English Reformation 1526-1701*. Cambridge: James Clarke, 2004.

Browne, Gerald M. *The Old Nubian martyrdom of Saint George*. Lovanii: Peeters, 1998.

Budge, Ernest. A. Wallis. *George of Lydda, the Patron Saint of England: A Study of the Cultus of St. George in Ethiopia*. London: Luzac, 1930.

_____. *The Martyrdom and Miracles of St. George of Cappadocia*. London: D. Nutt, 1888.

Byrom, John. *The Poems of John Byrom*. Edited by Adolphus William Ward. Manchester: Chetham Society, 1894.

Calvin, John. *Institutes of the Christian Religion*. Translated by Henry Beveridge. Edinburgh: Calvin Translation Society, 1845.

La Chanson d'Antioche. Edited by Jan A. Nelson. Tuscaloosa: University of Alabama Press, 2003.

La Chanson d'Aspremont. Translated by Michael A. Newth. New York: Garland Publishing, 1989.

Churchill, Winston. *Never Give in!: The Best of Winston Churchill's Speeches*. New York: Hyperion, 2003.

Clarke, George Herbert. *A Treasury of War Poetry, British and American Poems of the World War, 1914-1919*. Boston: Houghton, Mifflin Co, 1919.

Clay, William Keatinge. *Liturgical Services: Liturgies and Occasional Forms of Prayer Set Forth in the Reign of Queen Elizabeth*. Cambridge: Cambridge University Press, 1847.

Clopper, Lawrence M., ed. *Records of Early English Drama. Chester*. Toronto: University of Toronto Press, 1979.

Common Worship: Services and Prayers for the Church of England. London: Church Publishing House, 2000.

Conway, Moncure Daniel. *Addresses and Reprints, 1850-1907: Published and Unpublished Work Representing the Literary and Philosophical Life of the Author.* Boston: Houghton Mifflin, 1909.

Cranmer, Thomas. *Miscellaneous Writings and Letters of Thomas Cranmer.* Edited by John Edmund Cox. Cambridge: Cambridge University Press, 1846.

Cyril. *Lives of the Monks of Palestine.* Translated by R. M. Price. Kalamazoo: Cistercian Publications, 1991.

Davies, R. T. *Medieval English Lyrics: A Critical Anthology.* London: Faber and Faber, 1987.

Davies, Richard, and Thomas Corser. *Chester's Triumph in Honor of Her Prince, As It Was Performed Upon St. George's Day, 1610, in the Foresaid Citie.* Manchester: Chetham Society, 1844.

The Durham Collectar. Edited by Alicia Correa. Woodbridge: Boydell, 1992.

Ellery, Henrietta. "Diary of the Hon. William Ellery, of Rhode Island, June 28 – July 23, 1778." *The Pennsylvania Magazine of History and Biography*, no. 11 (1877): 476-94.

Erasmus, Desiderius. *The Praise of Folly.* Ann Arbor: University of Michigan Press, 1958.

Eusebius. *The Church History: A New Translation with Commentary.* Translated by Paul L. Maier. Grand Rapids: Kregel, 1999.

The First and Second Prayer Books of Edward Sixth. London: J.M. Dent & Sons, 1910.

Foxe, John. *The Acts and Monuments of John Foxe: A New and Complete Edition.* Edited by Stephen Reed Cattley and George Townsend. London: R.B. Seeley and W. Burnside, 1837.

Frend, W. H. C. "A Fragment of the *Acta Sancti Georgii* from Q'asr Ibrim (Egyptian Nubia)." *Analecta Bollandiana* 100 (1982): 79-86.

_____. "Fragments of a Version of the *Acta Georgii* from Q'asr Ibrim." *Jahrbuch für Antike und Christentum* 32 (1989): 89-104.

Froissart, Jean. *Chronicles*. Translated by Geoffrey Brereton. Harmondsworth: Penguin, 1968.

Gairdner, James, ed. *Letters and papers, foreign and domestic, of the reign of Henry VIII*. London: Eyre and Spottiswoode, 1887.

Galloway, David, ed. *Records of Early English Drama. Norwich, 1540-1642*. Toronto: University of Toronto Press, 1984.

Gee, Henry, and William John Hardy. *Documents Illustrative of English Church History*. London: Macmillan, 1896.

George. *George, Duke of Cambridge; A Memoir of His Private Life Based on the Journals and Correspondence of His Royal Highness*. Edited by Edgar Sheppard. London: Longmans, Green, 1906.

George, David, ed. *Records of Early English Drama. Lancashire*. Toronto: University of Toronto Press, 1991.

Gesta Francorum: The Deeds of the Franks and the Other Pilgrims to Jerusalem, Edited by Rosalind Hill. Oxford medieval texts. Oxford: Oxford University Press, 1972.

Gibson, James M., ed. *Records of Early English Drama. Kent: Diocese of Canterbury*. London: British Library, 2002.

Grace, Mary, ed. *Records of the Gild of St. George in Norwich, 1389-1547*. Norfolk Record Society 9. Norwich: NRS, 1937.

Hamilton, Anthony, Philibert Gramont, and Walter Scott. *Memoirs of the Court of Charles the Second*. London: Henry G. Bohn, 1846.

Henschen, Godefroid, and Daniel Van Papenbroeck. *Acta Sanctorum Aprilis. III : 22-30*. Bruxelles: Culture et civilisation, 1968.

Heylyn, Peter. *The Historie of That Most Famous Saint and Souldier of Christ Jesus, St. George of Cappadocia*. London: Printed for Henry Seyle, 1631.

Ingram, R. W., ed. *Records of Early English Drama. Coventry*. Toronto: University of Toronto Press, 1981.

Jacobus de Voragine. *The Golden Legend: Selections*. Translated by Christopher Stace. London: Penguin Books, 1998.

_____. *The Golden Legend, or, Lives of the Saints as Englished by William Caxton.* Edited by Frederick Startridge Ellis. London: J. M. Dent & Sons, 1900.

Johnson, Richard. *The Seven Champions of Christendom (1596/7).* Edited by Jennifer Fellows. Aldershot: Ashgate, 2003.

Johnston, Alexandra F., and Margaret Rogerson, eds. *Records of Early English Drama. York.* Toronto: University of Toronto Press, 1979.

Kemble, Fanny. *Further Records, 1848-1883; A Series of Letters.* New York: H. Holt and Company, 1891.

Keyes, Roger, and C. Sanford Terry. *Ostend and Zeebrugge, April 23 - May 10, 1918: The Dispatches of Vice-Admiral Sir Roger Keyes, and Other Narratives of the Operations.* London: Oxford University Press, 1919.

Kipling, Rudyard. *A Book of Words.* New York: Charles Scribner's Sons, 1928.

Klausner, David N., ed. *Records of Early English Drama. Herefordshire, Worcestershire.* Toronto: University of Toronto Press, 1990.

Krumbacher, Karl. *Der heilige Georg in der griechischen uberlieferung.* Munchen: J. Roth, 1911.

Louis, Cameron, ed. *Records of Early English Drama. Sussex.* Toronto: University of Toronto Press, 2000.

Malaterra, Geoffrey. *The Deeds of Count Roger of Calabria and Sicily and of His Brother Duke Robert Guiscard.* Translated by Kenneth Baxter Wolf. Ann Arbor: University of Michigan Press, 2005.

Marcellinus, Ammianus. *The Later Roman Empire: A.D. 354-378.* Translated by Walter Hamilton. Harmondsworth: Penguin, 1986.

Mather, Cotton. *Magnalia Christi Americana; Or, The Ecclesiastical History of New-England, from Its First Planting, in the Year 1620, Unto the Year of Our Lord 1698.* Hartford: S. Andrus & Son, 1853.

Mills, Clifford, and John Ramsey. *Where the Rainbow Ends: acting edition.* London: Samuel French Limited, 1951.

Mirk, John, *Mirk's Festial: a collection of homilies.* Edited by Theodor Erbe. Early English Text Society no. 96. London: K. Paul, Trench, Trubner & Co., 1905.

The Missal of the New Minster. Edited by D. H. Turner. London: Henry
　Bradshaw Society, 1962.

National Rose Society. *The Rose Annual.* Croydon: Jesse W. Ward,
　1915.

Newlyn, Evelyn, ed. *Records of Early English Drama. Cornwall and Dorset.*
　Toronto: University of Toronto Press, 1999.

Nichols, John Gough. *Chronicle of the Grey Friars of London.* London:
　Camden Society, 1852.

An Old English Martyrology. Edited by George Herzfeld. London: Eng-
　lish Early Text Society, 1900.

The Old French Crusade Cycle Volume VI: La Chanson De Jérusalem. Edited
　by Nigel Thorp. Tuscaloosa: University of Alabama Press, 1991.

Pegge, Samuel. "Observations on the History of St. George, the Pa-
　tron Saint of England." *Archaeologia* 5 (1779): 1-32.

Pettingal, John. *A Dissertation on the Original of the Equestrian Figure of the
　George and of the Garter.* London: Samuel Paterson, 1753.

Pilkinton, Mark C., ed. *Records of Early English Drama. Bristol.* Toronto:
　University of Toronto Press, 1997.

The Portiforium of Saint Wulstan, Edited by Anselm Hughes. London:
　Henry Bradshaw Society, 1958-1960.

Powicke, F. M. and C. R. Cheney, eds. *Councils and Synods and other
　Documents relating to the English Church II, Part 1 1205-1265.* Oxford:
　Clarendon Press, 1964.

The Roman Calendar: Text and Commentary. Washington D.C.: United
　States Catholic Conference, 1976.

Royal Commission on Ecclesiastical Discipline. *Royal Commission on
　Ecclesiastical Discipline: Minutes of Evidence.* London: Wyman and
　Sons, 1906.

The Royal Society of St. George. *The Royal Society of St. George* [Pam-
　phlet]. London: 1905.

_____. *Annual Report and Year Book 1904.* London: 1904.

_____. *Annual Report and Year Book 1905.* London: 1905.

Sandford, Francis. *The History of the Coronation of King James II*. London: Thomas Newcome, 1687.

Saxe, John Godfrey. *Poems*. Boston: Ticknor and Fields, 1866.

Selden, John. *Titles of Honor*. London: R. Whittakers, 1631.

Shakespeare, William, *King Henry V*. Edited by T. W. Craik. London: Routledge, 1995.

Sharp, Thomas. *A Dissertation on the Pageants or Dramatic Mysteries Anciently Performed at Coventry*. Totowa, N.J.: Rowman and Littlefield, 1973.

The South English Legendary. Edited by Anna J. Mill and Charlotte D'Evelyn. London: Oxford University Press, 1956.

Speculum Sacerdotale. Edited by Edward H. Weatherly. London: Oxford University Press, 1936.

Spenser, Edmund, *The Faerie Queene, Book One*. Boston: Houghton, Mifflin and Company, 1905.

St. George's Society (New York, N.Y.). *Rules of the Society of St. George Established at New-York, for the Purpose of Relieving Their Brethren in Distress*. New York: J. M'Lean, & Co., 1787.

Stephens, Archibald John. *The Statutes Relating to the Ecclesiastical and Eleemosynary Institutions of England, Wales, Ireland, India and the Colonies with the Decisions There*. London: John W. Parker, 1845.

Stephens, William. *The Journal of William Stephens, 1741-1743*. Edited by Ellis Merton Coulter. Athens: University of Georgia Press. 1958.

Stokes, James, and Robert Joseph Alexander, ed. *Records of Early English Drama. Somerset*. Toronto: University of Toronto Press, 1996.

Thompson, Samuel. *Reminiscences of a Canadian Pioneer for the Last Fifty Years*. Toronto: Hunter, Rose, 1884.

Tocqueville, Alexis de. *Democracy in America*. New York: Vintage Books, 1945.

Vitalis, Orderic. *The Ecclesiastical History*. Edited by Marjorie Chibnall. Oxford: Clarendon Press, 1972.

Wasson, John M., ed. *Records of Early English Drama. Devon*. Toronto: University of Toronto Press, 1986.

White, James F. *Documents of Christian Worship: Descriptive and Interpretive Sources.* Louisville: John Knox Press, 1992.

Wormald, Francis, ed. *English Kalendars Before A.D. 1100.* Woodbridge, Suffolk: Boydell Press, 1988.

_____. *English Benedictine Kalendars After A.D. 1100.* London: Harrison and Sons, 1939.

Printed Secondary Sources

Aldridge, Alan. *Religion in the Contemporary World: A Sociological Introduction.* Cambridge: Polity Press, 2000.

Anderson, Benedict R. *Imagined Communities: Reflections on the Origin and Spread of Nationalism.* London: Verso, 1991.

Arnold-Forster, Frances. *Studies in Church Dedications; Or, England's Patron Saints.* London: Skeffington & Son, 1899.

Barberis, Peter, John McHugh, and Mike Tyldesley. *Encyclopedia of British and Irish Political Organizations: Parties, Groups and Movements of the 20th Century.* New York: Continuum, 2001.

Baring-Gould, S. *Curious Myths of the Middle Ages.* London: Longmans, Green, 1914.

Barrow, Julia, and Nicholas Brooks eds. *St. Wulfstan and His World.* Aldershot: Ashgate, 2005.

Batterberry, Michael, and Ariane Ruskin Batterberry. *On the Town in New York, from 1776 to the Present.* New York: Scribner, 1973.

Baumann, Gerd. *Contesting Culture: Discourses of Identity in Multi-Ethnic London.* Cambridge: Cambridge University Press, 1996.

Baxter, Dudley. *The Reformation at St. Martin's, Leicester.* London: Catholic Truth Society, 1898.

Begent, Peter J., and Hubert Chesshyre. *The Most Noble Order of the Garter.* London: Spink, 1999.

Beito, David T. "'This Enormous Army': The Mutual-Aid Tradition of American Fraternal Societies before the Twentieth Century." In *The Voluntary City: Choice, Community, and Civil Society,* edited by

David T. Beito, Peter Gordon, and Alexander Tabarrok, 182–203. Ann Arbor: University of Michigan Press, 2002.

Beltz, George Frederick. *Memorials of the Order of the Garter.* London: William Pickering, 1841,

Bengtson, Jonathan. "Saint George and the formation of English nationalism." *Journal of Medieval and Early Modern Studies* 27 (1997): 317-40.

Berger, Peter L. *The Sacred Canopy; Elements of a Sociological Theory of Religion.* Garden City, N.Y.: Doubleday, 1967.

Bianchi, Hanael P. "The St. George's Society of New York and the Resurgence of England's National Holiday." *New York History* 92 (Winter–Spring 2011): 53-64.

Binns, Alison. *Dedications of Monastic Houses in England and Wales, 1066-1216.* Woodbridge: Boydell Press, 1989.

Blunt, John Henry. *The Annotated Book of Common Prayer: Being an Historical, Ritual, and Theological Commentary on the Devotional System of the Church of England.* London: Longmans, Green and Co., 1907.

Bond, Maurice. *The Saint George's Chapel Quincentenary Handbook: Programme of Events and Catalogue of the Exhibition.* Windsor: Oxley and Son Ltd, 1975.

Boulton, D'Arcy Jonathan Dacre. *The Knights of the Crown: The Monarchical Orders of Knighthood in Later Medieval Europe 1325-1520.* Woodbridge: Boydell, 1987.

Bowling, Benjamin. *Violent Racism: Victimization, Policing, and Social Context.* Oxford: Oxford University Press, 1999.

Bowring, Charles W., Francis Hebard Tabor, Robert Waller, Edward F. Beddall, and H. A. Racker. *A History of St. George's Society of New York from 1770 to 1913.* New York: Federal Printing Company, 1913.

Bradley, Ian. *Believing in Britain: The Spiritual Identity of "Britishness."* London: Tauris, 2007.

Brantlinger, Patrick. *Rule of Darkness: British Literature and Imperialism, 1830-1914.* Ithaca: Cornell University Press, 1988.

Braudel, Fernand. "Histoire et sciences socials: La longue durée." *Annales ESC* 4 (1958): 725-53.

Bridenbaugh, Carl, and Jessica Bridenbaugh. *Rebels and Gentleman; Philadelphia in the Age of Franklin*. New York: Reynal & Hitchcock, 1942.

Brown, Callum G. *The Death of Christian Britain: Understanding Secularisation, 1800-2000*. London: Routledge, 2001.

Bueltmanna, Tanja and Donald M. MacRailda. "Globalizing St George: English associations in the Anglo-world to the 1930s." *Journal of Global History* 7, no. 1 (2013): 79-105.

Bulley, Margaret H. *St. George for Merrie England*. London: G. Allen, 1908.

Burke, Peter. *What Is Cultural History?* Cambridge: Polity Press, 2008.

Burkitt, F. C. "The Decretum Gelasianum." *Journal of Theological Studies* 14 (1913): 469-71.

Butler, Alban, David Hugh Farmer, and Paul Burns. *Butler's Lives of the Saints: April*. Collegeville, Minn.: The Liturgical Press, 1999.

Cahill, Thomas. *How the Irish Saved Civilization*. New York: Nan A. Talese, Doubleday, 1995.

Carrington, Ben, and Ian McDonald. *'Race', Sport and British Society*. London: Routledge, 2002.

Carrington, Hereward. *Psychical Phenomena and the War*. New York: Dodd, Mead and Co, 1918.

Chambers, E. K. *The English Folk-Play*. Oxford: Clarendon Press, 1933.

_____. *The Mediaeval Stage*. Oxford: Clarendon Press, 1903.

Chambers, Robert. *Chambers's Book of Days*. Philadelphia: J.B. Lippincott, 1879.

Cheney, C. R. "Rule for the observance of Feast-Days in Medieval England." *Bulletin of the Institute of Historical Research* 34 (1961): 117-147.

Clapton, Edward. *The Life of St. George*. London: Swan Sonnenschein & Co. Ltd, 1903.

Clark, Peter. *British Clubs and Societies, 1580-1800: The Origins of an Associational World*. Oxford: Oxford University Press, 2002.

Clark, Peter, and Paul Slack. *Crisis and Order in English Towns, 1500-1700; Essays in Urban History*. Toronto: University of Toronto Press, 1972.

Clarke, David. "Rumours of Angels: A Legend of the First World War." *Folklore* 113, no. 2 (October 2002): 151-73.

Clowes, W. Laird, and Clements R. Markham. *The Royal Navy: A History from the Earliest Times to the Present*. London: Chatham Pub, 1996.

Colley, Linda. *Britons: Forging the Nation, 1707-1837*. New Haven: Yale University Press, 1992.

Collier, John Payne. *The History of English Dramatic Poetry*. London: J. Murray, 1831.

Collins, Hugh. *The Order of the Garter 1348-1461: Chivalry and Politics in Late Medieval England*. Oxford: Clarendon, 2000.

Cooney, Anthony. *The Story of Saint George: The Life and Legend of England's Patron Saint*. Cheltenham: This England Books, 1999.

Cooper, Kate, and Julia Hillner. *Religion, Dynasty, and Patronage in Early Christian Rome, 300-900*. Cambridge: Cambridge University Press, 2007.

Corning, Caitlin. *The Celtic and Roman Traditions: Conflict and Consensus in the Early Medieval Church*. New York: Palgrave Macmillan, 2006.

Corrsin, Stephen D. *Sword Dancing in Europe: A History*. Enfield Lock, Middlesex: Hisarlic Press, 1996.

Cressy, David. *Bonfires and Bells: National Memory and the Protestant Calendar in Elizabethan and Stuart England*. Berkeley: University of California Press, 1989.

Cronin, Mike, and Daryl Adair. *The Wearing of the Green: A History of St. Patrick's Day*. London: Routledge, 2002.

Dalmais, Irénée Henri, Pierre Jounel, and Aimé Georges Martimort. *The Liturgy and Time*. Collegeville, Minn.: Liturgical Press, 1986.

Daniels, Roger. *Coming to America: A History of Immigration and Ethnicity in American Life*. New York: HarperCollins, 1990.

Delehaye, Hippolyte. *Les légendes grecques des saints militaires*. Paris: Picard, 1909.

Denis-Boulet, Noele M. *The Christian Calendar*. New York: Hawthorn Books, 1960.

Doughty, Arthur G., and N. E. Dionne. *Quebec Under Two Flags*. Quebec: Quebec News Company, 1903.

Douglas, George William, and Hellen Douglas Compton. *The American Book of Days*. New York: Wilson, 1952.

Duffy, Eamon. *The Stripping of the Altars: Traditional Religion in England, C.1400-C.1580*. New Haven: Yale University Press, 1992.

_____. *The Voices of Morebath: Reformation and Rebellion in an English Village*. New Haven: Yale University Press, 2001.

Durkheim, Émile. *The Elementary Forms of the Religious Life, A Study in Religious Sociology*. New York: Macmillan, 1915.

Dyer, Thomas Henry. *British Popular Customs, Present and Past*. London: G. Bell, 1900.

Egan, Pierce, William Heath, Henry Thomas Alken, Richard Dighton, and Thomas Rowlandson. *Real Life in London, or, The Rambles and Adventures of Bob Tallyho, Esq., and His Cousin, the Hon. Tom Dashall, Through the Metropolis: Exhibiting a Living Picture of Fashionable Characters, Manners, and Amusements in High and Low Life*. Illustrated pocket library of plain and coloured books. London: Methuen & Co, 1905.

Elder, Isabel Hill. *George of Lydda: Soldier, Saint and Martyr*. London: Covenant, 1949.

"The Emperor Sigismund at Windsor." *The Retrospective Review* 2 (1854): 233-49.

Eriksen, Thomas Hylland, and Richard Jenkins. *Flag, Nation and Symbolism in Europe and America*. London: Routledge, 2007.

Etzioni, Amitai, and Jared Bloom, eds. *We Are What We Celebrate: Understanding Holidays and Rituals*. New York: New York University Press, 2004.

Evans, David M. *The Remains of Distant Times: Archaeology and the National Trust.* Woodbridge: Boydell, 1996.

F., H. O. *Saint George for England. The Life, Legends, and Lore, of Our Glorious Patron.* London: Edwards, 1911.

Fleming, William. *The Life of Saint George, Martyr, Patron of England.* London: R. & T. Washbourne, 1901.

Fletcher, Alan J. *Drama, Performance and Polity in Pre-Cromwellian Ireland.* Toronto: University of Toronto Press, 2000.

_____. "Playing and Staying Together: Projecting the Corporate Image in Sixteenth-Century Dublin." In *Civic Ritual and Drama*, edited by A. F. Johnston and W. Hüsken, 15-37. Amsterdam: Rodopi B.V., 1997.

Foot, Sarah. *Monastic Life in Anglo-Saxon England, C. 600-900.* Cambridge: Cambridge University Press, 2006.

Forbes, Bruce David. *Christmas A Candid History.* Berkeley: University of California Press, 2007.

Ford, Judy Ann. *John Mirk's Festial: Orthodoxy, Lollardy, and the Common People in Fourteenth-Century England.* Cambridge: D.S. Brewer, 2006.

Fox, David Scott. *Saint George: The Saint with Three Faces.* Windsor Forest, Berks: Kensal Press, 1983.

Gascoigne, Margaret, *Discovering English Customs and Traditions.* Princes Risborough: Shire, 1980.

Geertz, Clifford. *The Interpretation of Cultures.* New York: Basic Books. 1973.

Geike, Cunningham. *The English Reformation: How It Came About, and Why We Should Uphold It.* New York: D. Appleton and Co, 1879.

Gellner, Ernest. *Nations and Nationalism.* Ithaca: Cornell University Press, 1983.

Gerould, Gordon Hall. *Saints' Legends.* Boston: Houghton, Mifflin, and Company, 1916.

Gibbon, Edward. *The History of the Decline and Fall of the Roman Empire.* New York: Macmillan, 1914.

Gibson, John. *The War on Christmas: How the Liberal Plot to Ban the Sacred Christian Holiday Is Worse Than You Thought*. New York: Sentinel, 2005.

Gillingham, John. *The English in the Twelfth Century: Imperialism, National Identity, and Political Values*. Woodbridge: Boydell Press, 2000.

Girouard, Mark. *The Return to Camelot: Chivalry and the English Gentleman*. New Haven: Yale University Press, 1981.

Good, Jonathan. *The Cult of St. George in Medieval England*. Woodbridge: Boydell Press, 2009.

Gordon, E. O. *Saint George: Champion of Christendom and Patron Saint of England*. London: S. Sonnenschein & Co, 1907.

Griffiths, David N. *The Bibliography of the Book of Common Prayer, 1549-1999*. London: British Library, 2002.

Groves, John Percy, Richard Cannon, and G. H. Waller. *Historical Records of the 7th or Royal Regiment of Fusiliers, Now Known As the Royal Fusiliers (the City of London Regiment), 1685-1903*. Guernsey: F.B. Guerin, 1903.

Haigh, Christopher. *The English Reformation revised*. Cambridge: Cambridge University Press, 1987.

Haile, Martin. *James Francis Edward, the Old Chevalier*. London: J. M. Dent & Co, 1907.

Hampson, Robert T. *Medii Ævi Kalendarium; Or, Dates, Charters, and Customs of the Middle Ages*. London: H. K. Causton, 1841.

Halpern, Paul G. *Naval History of World War I*. Pasadena: Theosophical University Press, 1995.

Hastings, Adrian. *The Construction of Nationhood: Ethnicity, Religion, and Nationalism*. Cambridge: Cambridge University Press, 1997.

Hayden, Ilse. *Symbol and Privilege: The Ritual Context of British Royalty*. Tucson: University of Arizona Press, 1987.

Heale, Elizabeth. *The Faerie Queene: A Reader's Guide*. Cambridge: Cambridge University Press, 1987.

Hearnshaw, F. J. C. "The Empire and The Schools." *The School World* 9 (June 1907): 204-5.

Hill, Joyce. "Saint George before the Conquest," *Society of the Friends of St. George's and the Descendants of the Knights of the Garter* 6 (1986): 284-95.

Hobsbawm, Eric J. *Nations and Nationalism since 1780: Programme, Myth, Reality*. Cambridge: Cambridge University Press, 1990.

Hogg, John "Supplemental Notes on St. George the Martyr, and on George the Arian Bishop." *Transactions of the Royal Society of Literature of the United Kingdom* 2, no. 7 (1863): 106-36.

Holden, Anthony. *William Shakespeare: The Man Behind the Genius: a Biography*. Boston: Little, Brown, 1999.

Homberger, Eric. *The Historical Atlas of New York City: A Visual Celebration of 400 Years of New York City's History*. New York: Henry Holt, 2005.

Horne, Charles F. and Walter F. Austin. *The Great Events of the Great War, A Comprehensive and Readable Source Record of the World's Great War*. New York: J. J. Little & Ives Co, 1920.

Hughes, John. *Liverpool Banks & Bankers, 1760-1837: A History of the Circumstances Which Gave Rise to the Industry, and of the Men Who Founded and Developed It*. Liverpool: H. Young & Sons, 1906.

Hunt, Tamara L. *Defining John Bull: Political Caricature and National Identity in Late Georgian England*. Aldershot: Ashgate, 2003.

Hulst, Cornelia Steketee. *St. George of Cappadocia in Legend and History*. London: D. Nutt, 1909.

Hutchinson, John. *The Dynamics of Cultural Nationalism: The Gaelic Revival and the Creation of the Irish Nation State*. London: Allen & Unwin, 1987.

Hutton, Ronald. *The Rise and Fall of Merry England: The Ritual Year, 1400-1700*. Oxford: Oxford University Press, 1994.

_____. *Stations of the Sun: A History of the Ritual Year in Britain*. Oxford: Oxford University Press, 1996.

James, Lawrence. *The Rise and Fall of the British Empire*. New York: St. Martin's Griffin, 1995.

Jones, Charles Williams, and Wesley M. Stevens. *Bede, the Schools, and the Computus*. Aldershot: Variorum, 1994.

Jones, Howard. *Crucible of Power: A History of American Foreign Relations to 1913*. Lanham, Md.: Rowman & Littlefield Publishers, 2009.

Keene, Derek, Arthur Burns, and Andrew Saint. *St. Paul's: The Cathedral Church of London, 604-2004*. New Haven: Yale University Press, 2004.

Kelly, William. *Notices Illustrative of the Drama, and Other Popular Amusements, Chiefly in the Sixteenth and Seventeenth Centuries, Incidentally Illustrating Shakespeare and His Contemporaries Extracted from the Chamberlains' Accounts and Other Manuscripts of the Borough of Leicester.* London: J. R. Smith, 1865.

Kestner, Joseph. "The Return of St. George 1815-1951." In *King Arthur's Modern Return,* edited by Debra N. Mancoff, 83-98. New York: Garland Pub., 1998.

Kilroe, Edwin P. *Saint Tammany and the Origin of the Society of Tammany, Or Columbian Order in the City of New York.* New York: 1913.

King, John N. *Tudor Royal Iconography: Literature and Art in an Age of Religious Crisis.* Princeton: Princeton University Press, 1989.

Kirby, E. T. "The Origin of the Mummers' Play." *Journal of American Folklore* 84 (1971): 275-88.

Knauff, Theodore Christian. *A History of the Society of the Sons of Saint George, Established at Philadelphia, for the Advice and Assistance of Englishmen in Distress, on Saint George's Day, April 23, 1772.* Philadelphia: 1923.

Knowles, David, and R. Neville Hadcock. *Medieval Religious Houses: England and Wales.* London: Longmans, Green, 1953.

Laborderie, Olivier De. "Richard the Lionheart and the Birth of A National Cult of St. George in England: Origins and Development of a Legend." *Nottingham Medieval Studies* 39 (1995): 37-53.

Lash, Scott, and Celia Lury. *Global Culture Industry.* Cambridge: Polity, 2006.

Luebke, David Martin, ed. *The Counter-Reformation: The Essential Readings.* Malden, Mass: Blackwell, 1999.

Luckmann, Thomas. *The Invisible Religion: The Problem of Religion in Modern Society*. New York: Macmillan, 1967.

MacGregor, James B. "Salue Martir Spes Anglorum: English Devotion to Saint George in the Middle Ages." Ph.D. diss., University of Cincinnati, 2002.

Machen, Arthur. *The Bowmen, and Other Legends of the War*. New York: G.P. Putnam's Sons, 1915.

Mackenzie, John. "The Popular Culture of Empire in Britain." In *The Oxford History of the British Empire*, vol. IV: *The Twentieth Century*, edited by Judith M. Brown and Wm Roger Louis, 212-31. Oxford: Oxford University Press, 2001.

Magocsi, Paul R. *Encyclopedia of Canada's Peoples*. Toronto: University of Toronto Press, 1999.

Marcus, G. J. *Saint George of England*. London: Williams and Norgate limited, 1929.

Martin, David. *A General Theory of Secularization*. Oxford: Blackwell, 1978.

Marvin, Abijah P. *History of Worcester County, Massachusetts, Embracing a Comprehensive History of the County from Its First Settlement to the Present Time, with a History and Description of Its Cities and Towns*. Boston: C.F. Jewett, 1879.

Matson, Sarah Anne. *St. George and the Dragon*. London: T. Fisher Unwin, 1893.

Matthews, Albert. *Brother Jonathan*. Cambridge: J. Wilson and Son, 1902.

Matzke, John E. "Contributions to the History of the Legend of Saint George, with Special Reference to the Sources of the French, German, and Anglo-Saxon Metrical Versions." *Proceedings of the Modern Language Association* 17 (1902): 464-535.

_____. "Contributions to the History of the Legend of Saint George, with Special Reference to the Sources of the French, German, and Anglo-Saxon Metrical Versions." *Proceedings of the Modern Language Association* 18 (1903): 99-171.

_____. "The Legend of Saint George; Its Development into a Roman d'Aventure." *Proceedings of the Modern Language Association* 19 (1904): 449-78.

McClendon, Muriel C. "A Moveable Feast: Saint George's Day Celebrations and Religious Change in Early Modern England." *The Journal of British Studies* 38, no. 1 (January, 1999): 1-27.

_____. "Against God's word: government, religion and the crisis of authority in early Reformation Norwich." *Sixteenth Century Journal* 25 (1994): 353-69.

McConville, Brendan. *The King's Three Faces: The Rise & Fall of Royal America, 1688-1776.* Chapel Hill: University of North Carolina Press, 2006.

McMahon, Timothy G. *Grand Opportunity: The Gaelic Revival and Irish Society, 1893-1910.* Syracuse: Syracuse University Press, 2008.

McRee, Ben R. "Religious Gilds and Civil Order: The Cast of Norwich in the Late Middle Ages." *Speculum* 67 (1992): 69-97.

_____. "Unity or Division? The Social Meaning of Guild Ceremony in Urban Communities." In *City and Spectacle in Medieval Europe* edited by Barbara Hanawalt and Kathryn Reyerson, 189-207. Minneapolis: University of Minnesota Press, 1994.

Meyers, Geoffrey. "The Manuscripts of the Old French Cycle." In *The Old French Crusade Cycle: Volume I,* edited by Emanuel J. Mickel and Jan A. Nelson, xiii-lxxxviii. Tuscaloosa: University of Alabama Press, 1977.

Morgan, D. A. L. "The Banner-bearer of Christ and Our Lady's Knight: How God became an Englishman revisited." In *St George's Chapel, Windsor, in the Fourteenth Century,* edited by Nigel Saul, 51-62. Woodbridge, Suffolk: Boydell Press, 2005.

_____. "The cult of St George c.1500: national and international connotations." *Publications du Centre Européen d'Etudes Bourguignonnes* 35 (1995): 151-62.

Morgan, Giles. *St. George: Knight, Martyr, Patron Saint and Dragonslayer.* Harpenden: Pocket Essentials, 2006.

Mosshammer, Alden A. *The Easter Computus and the Origins of the Christian Era.* Oxford: Oxford University Press, 2008.

Muir, Edward. *Ritual in Early Modern Europe.* Cambridge: Cambridge University Press, 2005.

Nicolas, Nicholas Harris. *History of the Orders of Knighthood of the British Empire.* London: J. Hunter, 1842.

Nissenbaum, Stephen. *The Battle for Christmas.* New York: Vintage, 1997.

Nutt, Charles. *History of Worcester and Its People.* New York: Lewis Historical Pub. Co, 1919.

Pegge, Samuel. "Observation on the History of St. George, the patron of England." *Archaeologia* 5 (1779): 1-32.

Perrin, William Gordon. *British Flags, Their Early History, and Their Development at Sea; With an Account of the Origin of the Flag As a National Device.* Cambridge: Cambridge University Press, 1922.

Powell, Timothy. "The 'Three Orders' of society in Anglo-Saxon England." *Anglo-Saxon England* 23 (2007): 103-32.

Price, Charlotte A. "St. George and the Dragon." *Belgravia: a London magazine* 79 (September 1892): 23-27.

Quentin, Henri. *Les Martyrologes Historiques Du Moyen Age: Étude Sur La Formation Du Martyrologe Romain.* Paris: Librairie Victor Lecoffre, 1908.

Raikes, G. A. *The History of the Honourable Artillery Company.* London: R. Bentley & Son, 1878.

_____. *The Royal Charter of Incorporation Granted to the Honourable Artillery Company* London: C.E. Roberts, 1889.

Rait, Robert S. *Royal Palaces of England.* New York: James Pott & Co, 1911.

Rappaport, George David. *Stability and Change in Revolutionary Pennsylvania: Banking, Politics, and Social Structure.* University Park: Pennsylvania State University Press, 1996.

Raven, James. *London Booksellers and American Customers: Transatlantic Literary Community and the Charleston Library Society, 1748-1811.* Columbia: University of South Carolina Press, 2002.

Reames, Sherry L. *The Legenda Aurea: A Reexamination of Its Paradoxical History*. Madison: University of Wisconsin Press, 1985.

Richards, E. G. *Mapping Time: The Calendar and Its History*. New York: Oxford University Press, 1999.

Riches, Samantha. *St. George: Hero, Martyr, and Myth*. Stroud: Sutton, 2000.

Rubin, Miri. *Corpus Christi: The Eucharist in Late Medieval Culture*. Cambridge: Cambridge University Press, 1991.

Salih, Sarah. *A Companion to Middle English Hagiography*. Cambridge: Brewer, 2006.

Salmon, Thomas. *A New Historical Account of St. George for England and the Original of the Most Noble Order of Garter: Illustrated with Cutts*. London: R. Janeway, 1704.

Santino, Jack. *Halloween and Other Festivals of Death and Life*. Knoxville: University of Tennessee Press, 1994.

Scharf, J. Thomas, and Thompson Westcott. *History of Philadelphia, 1609-1884*. Philadelphia: L. H. Everts & Co, 1884.

―――――. *History of Baltimore City and County, from the Earliest Period to the Present Day: Including Biographical Sketches of Their Representative Men*. Philadelphia: L. H. Everts, 1881.

Schoenbaum, S. *William Shakespeare: A Compact Documentary Life*. New York: Oxford University Press, 1987.

Segni, Leah di. "Horvath Hesheq: The Inscription." In *Christian Archaeology in the Holy Land New Discoveries: Essays in Honour of Virgilio C. Corbo, OFM*. Collectio maior, no. 36., edited by G.C. Bottini, 379-87. Jerusalem: Franciscan Print Press, 1990.

Selby-Lowndes, Joan. *The Conti Story*. London: Collins, 1954.

Shagan, Ethan H. *Popular Politics and the English Reformation*. Cambridge: Cambridge University Press, 2003.

Sharpe, J. A. *Remember, Remember: A Cultural History of Guy Fawkes Day*. Cambridge: Harvard University Press, 2005.

Sherington, Geoffrey. "Fairbridge Child Migrants." In *Child Welfare and Social Action in the Nineteenth and Twentieth Centuries: International*

Perspectives, edited by Jon Lawrence, 53-81. Liverpool: Liverpool University Press, 2001.

Shoberl, Frederic. *Horse-Racing: Its History and Early Records of the Principal and Other Race Meetings: with Anecdotes, Etc.* London: Saunders, Otley, and Co., 1863.

A Short Narrative of the Fifth Regiment of Foot: or Northumberland Fusiliers, with a Chronological Table and Succession List of the Officers, from 1st January, 1754, to 1st May, 1873. London: Howard, Jones and Parkes, 1873.

Skal, David J. *Death Makes a Holiday: A Cultural History of Halloween.* New York: Bloomsbury, 2002.

Smith, Bruce R. *The Acoustic World of Early Modern England: Attending to the O-Factor.* Chicago: University of Chicago Press, 1999.

Smith, E. A. *George IV.* New Haven: Yale University Press, 1999.

Smith, Georgina. "Chapbooks and Traditional Plays: Communication and Performance." *Folklore* 92, no. 2 (1981): 208-17.

Smith, Hannah. *Georgian Monarchy: Politics and Culture, 1714-1760.* Cambridge: Cambridge University Press, 2006.

Smith, Joshua Toulmin. *English gilds.* London: N. Trubner & Co, 1870.

Smith, William George, and Henry Wace. *A Dictionary of Christian Biography, Literature, Sects and Doctrines.* London: J. Murray, 1877.

Snodgrass, Mary Ellen. *Coins and Currency: An Historical Encyclopedia.* Jefferson, N.C.: McFarland, 2003.

Somerset, Alan. "Mysteries End: Edam, Reed, and the Midlands." *Medieval and Renaissance Drama in England* 16 (2003): 17-31.

Sommerville, C. John. *The Secularization of Early Modern England: From Religious Culture to Religious Faith.* New York: Oxford University Press, 1992.

"St. George and the Guild of Play," *Practical Teacher* 30, no. 12 (June 1910): 712-14.

St. George's Society of Quebec. *St. George's Society, Quebec, Founded 1835, Officers and Members, with the Reports, Ending 5th January, 1847.* Quebec: J. C. Fisher: 1847.

Stace, Christopher. *St. George: Patron Saint of England.* London: Triangle, 2002.

Staley, Vernon. *Liturgical Studies.* London: Longmans, Green, and Co., 1907.

Stanley, Arthur Penrhyn. *Historical Memorials of Westminster Abbey.* London: Murray, 1886.

Stevens, Albert Clark. *The Cyclopedia of Fraternities.* New York: E.B. Treat and Co., 1907.

Stevens, Wesley M. *Cycles of Time and Scientific Learning in Medieval Europe.* Aldershot, Hampshire: Variorum, 1995.

Storey, Anne. *The St. George's Society of Toronto: A History and List of Members, 1834-1967.* Agincourt, Ontario: Generation Press, 1987.

Thompson, Anne B. *Everyday Saints and the Art of Narrative in the South English Legendary.* Aldershot: Ashgate, 2003.

Thompson, James. *The History of Leicester.* Leicester: J. S. Crossley, 1849.

Thompson, Peter. *Rum Punch and Revolution: Taverngoing & Public Life in Eighteenth-Century Philadelphia.* Philadelphia: University of Pennsylvania Press, 1999.

Tiddy, Reginald John Elliott. *The Mummers' Play: With a Memoir.* Edited by Rupert Spens Thompson. Oxford: Clarendon Press, 1923.

Toland, John. *No Man's Land: 1918, the Last Year of the Great War.* Lincoln: University of Nebraska Press, 2002.

Trombley, Frank R. *Hellenic Religion and Christianization C. 370-529.* Leiden: E.J. Brill, 1995.

Twycross, Honora. "St. George for England." *The English Illustrated Magazine* 33 (April 1905): 3-22.

Underdown, David. *Revel, Riot, and Rebellion: Popular Politics and Culture in England 1603-1660.* Oxford: Oxford University Press, 1987.

_____, Susan Dwyer Amussen, and Mark A. Kishlansky. *Political Culture and Cultural Politics in Early Modern England: Essays Presented to David Underdown.* Manchester: Manchester University Press, 1995.

Vale, Juliet. *Edward III and Chivalry: Chivalric Society and Its Context, 1270-1350*. Woodbridge, Suffolk: Boydell Press, 1982.

Wager, Daniel E. *Our County and Its People, Oneida County*. Boston: Boston History Co, 1896.

Walter, Christopher. "The Origins of the Cult of St. George." *Revue des Études Byzantines* 53 (1995): 295-326.

_____. *The Warrior Saints in Byzantine Art and Tradition*. Aldershot: Ashgate, 2003.

Wasson, John. "The St. George and Robin Hood Plays in Devon." *Medieval English Theatre* 2, no. 2 (1980): 66-69.

Weber, Max. *The Protestant Ethic and the Spirit of Capitalism*. New York: Scribner, 1930.

_____. *Economy and Society: An Outline of Interpretive Sociology*. New York: Bedminster Press, 1968.

Weintraub, Stanley. *General Washington's Christmas Farewell: A Mount Vernon Homecoming, 1783*. New York: Free Press, 2003.

Westlake, H. F. *The Parish Gilds of Mediæval England*. London: Society for Promoting Christian Knowledge, 1919.

Wilson, Bryan R. *Religion in Secular Society: A Sociological Comment*. London: Watts, 1966.

Wheeler, Michael. *Ruskin's God*. Cambridge: Cambridge University Press, 1999.

White, Eileen. "Bryngyng forth of Saynt George: The St. George Celebrations in York." *Medieval English Theatre* 3, no. 2 (1981): 114-21.

_____. *The St. Christopher and St. George Guild of York*. York: Borthwick Institute, 1987.

Whiting, Robert. *The Blind Devotion of the People: Popular Religion and the English Reformation*. Cambridge studies in early modern British history. Cambridge: Cambridge University Press, 1989.

Wilkinson, John. *Jerusalem Pilgrims Before the Crusades*. Warminster: Aris & Phillips, 1977.

Willis-Bund, W., and William Page. *The Victoria History of the County of Worcester*. London: James Street Haymarket, 1906.

Winthrop, William. *Military Law*. Washington, D.C.: W. H. Morrison, 1886.

Withington, Robert. *English Pageantry: An Historical Outline*. Cambridge: Harvard University Press, 1918.

Wood, Walter. *The Northumberland Fusiliers*. London: G. Richards, 1901.

Wrigley, E. A., and Roger Schofield. *The Population History of England, 1541-1871: A Reconstruction*. Cambridge: Cambridge University Press, 1989.

Index

8332395R00169

Printed in Great Britain
by Amazon.co.uk, Ltd.,
Marston Gate.